Jonathan Clements is the author of many books on China and Japan, including *A Brief History of the Samurai*, *An Armchair Traveller's History of the Silk Road*, *Christ's Samurai: The True Story of the Shimabara Rebellion*, profiles of Khubilai Khan and Chairman Mao, *The Art of War: A New Translation*, and both *Modern China* and *Modern Japan* in the All That Matters series. His biographies of the First Emperor of China and Empress Wu have both been translated into Chinese, and his *Anime: A History* was a 2014 *CHOICE* selection as one of the year's outstanding academic titles. In 2016, he was the presenter of *Route Awakening*, National Geographic Asia's TV serial on the historical underpinnings of Chinese culture.

A Brief History of the Martial Arts

EAST ASIAN FIGHTING STYLES FROM KUNG FU TO NINJUTSU

JONATHAN CLEMENTS

ROBINSON

ROBINSON

First published in Great Britain in 2016 by Robinson

Copyright © Jonathan Clements, 2016

3 5 7 9 10 8 6 4 2

A CIP catalogue record for this book
is available from the British Library.

ISBN: 978-1-47213-646-6

Typeset in Scala by Hewer Text UK Ltd, Edinburgh

Printed and bound by Clays Ltd, Elcograf S.p.A.

Papers used by Robinson are from well-managed
forests and other responsible sources.

MIX
Paper from
responsible sources
FSC® C104740

Robinson
An imprint of
Little, Brown Book Group
Carmelite House
50 Victoria Embankment
London EC4Y 0DZ

An Hachette UK Company
www.hachette.co.uk

www.littlebrown.co.uk

For Kari and Timo

Contents

CONTENTS

CONTENTS

Acknowledgements

....

The seed for this book was sown in 1990, when I met Samuel Jacobs on the first day of our Chinese and Japanese studies at the University of Leeds, and he began to tell me about the world of the martial arts. Three years on, it was his frustrations when writing his bachelor's thesis on the history of a particular martial art that led me to wonder how many of them had similarly precarious pasts. A decade later, my marriage to Kati Mäki-Kuutti, now a third-degree black belt, exposed me to the inner workings of a martial arts organisation, and formed my first encounter with many of the daily logistical issues that turn out to concern most schools of unarmed combat.

Many others have offered vital help and food for thought, in a variety of unexpected ways. Lisa Lau was an invaluable, illuminating guide at the Shaolin Temple in Henan, China; David Lei helped me break in to a San Francisco Wing Chun hall; my teacher in Taiwan at National Cheng Chi University, Shu Wen-wu, first pointed out the political uses of Buddhism; the Morikawa family were generous and informative hosts at the Rakutō Dōin in Kyoto; Ellis Tinios, honorary lecturer in history at the University of Leeds, has offered much help and advice on matters oriental. Any martial artist I have met may have involuntarily said things that informed my research, regardless of whether they were neophytes or black belts – thanks are due at very least to Melanie Feeney, Justin Jennings, Simon Jowett, Kirsi Mäki-Kuutti, Gilbert Mackay, Adrienne Roche, Adrian Starr, Alexander Tilly, Stephen Turnbull and the two fifth-*dans*, Kari and Timo, to whom this book is dedicated. I have probably forgotten many others. None of them knew

I was writing a book, because at the time we talked, I wasn't; conclusions herein are all my own.

Mike DeMarco at Via Media offered valuable tech support in accessing archived articles from his *Journal of Asian Martial Arts*. The library of the London School of Oriental and African Studies provided the modern equivalent of a mountaintop retreat. In the process of bringing this manuscript to fruition, my agent Chelsey Fox and my editor Duncan Proudfoot were instrumental in championing the proposal. My friend Andrew Deacon was my first reader and proofer. Tony Kehoe read through the manuscript and offered comments, but refused on ethical grounds to take any money for labour involving the martial arts. His editorial fee was instead donated to the charity of his choice. Emily Kearns rode shotgun on the final edit, diligently arguing many fine points of interpretation and nomenclature.

My appointment from 2013–16 as a visiting professor at Xi'an Jiaotong University (I much prefer an English translation of *tepin yanjiu-yuan* as 'visiting research fellow', but cannot fight the bureaucracy) exposed me to much more of the martial arts and all-important access to massive Chinese bookshops. This came courtesy of Professor Li Qi, whose brother Li Shaohao in Chongqing turned out to be *the* Li Shaohao, master of the 66 forms of Dragon Style *taiji*.

The Invention of Tradition

It was supposedly a translation of an ancient Japanese text, revealing important underground connections with the world of the martial arts. But even in the opening lines, I could see it for what it was: a shoddy pastiche of Sun Tzu's *The Art of War*, knocked up by a retired samurai and forgotten in an attic for a couple of hundred years. Opening a facsimile of the original seventeenth-century document, I could see where the over-eager translator had rushed to fill in spaces and added invasive annotations, dragging the meaning far away from the original author's intent. Already cited as a modern proof of esoteric connections in the Japanese martial arts, the English-language text was corrupted beyond all meaningful use, drawing just as heavily on twentieth-century movies as on the ruined original.

This happens more than you might think. East Asian organisations are rooted in a respect for elders and authority; they cling to a guild-like secrecy of learning materials and jealously guard their inner knowledge from outsiders. No martial art tests its upper grades by giving them a fake 'secret scroll' and waiting to see if they doubt its authenticity. Instead, initiates advance through access to new manuscripts and techniques, taught by elites that appeal to ancient authorities, bogus or otherwise. By the time one knows enough about a martial art to truly understand it, one has usually sworn never to reveal its secrets. Questioning authority runs counter to Confucian culture; as a result, rumours and Apocrypha abound and multiply.

What are the martial arts? A lot depends not on whom you ask, but on when. 'Studying the "traditional" martial arts,' observe the authors of a recent book, 'is actually a quintessentially *modern* activity.' Wing Chun, for example, a form of kung fu with worldwide name recognition today, had barely a thousand practitioners when its most famous student, Bruce Lee, studied in Hong Kong in the 1950s. And when Lee's own teacher, Ip Man, was himself a student in Foshan, Guangdong province, fifty years earlier, he was one of only two dozen.[1] How many other forms have been refined, perfected and then forgotten over the centuries, for want of a film-star poster boy?

Brian Kennedy and Elizabeth Guo, the authors of *Jingwu: The School that Transformed Kung Fu*, stress that:

> Up until about 1900, Chinese martial arts training was conducted either in the military by active duty soldiers or in villages, where martial arts were practiced as either a recreation for children or by adults who were involved in village defence as part of militias . . . Learning martial arts was not an adult hobby, recreation or pastime; it was a practical skill, a manual trade.[2]

A soldier, now just as much as then, will regard martial arts as a vital skillset for combat – fighting, grappling and weapons training. But our term 'martial arts', only recently translated by the Chinese themselves as *wushu*, sits at the midpoint of several unrelated fields. Various practitioners have sought to downgrade its aggressive stance, into a non-violent form of self-defence. Others have emphasised the martial arts as an exercise regime or a competitive sport. Some emphasise a philosophy, not merely of combat techniques, but of a way of life. Others take this even further, demanding a code of conduct that goes beyond philosophy into actual religion. I hope that this book will inform and entertain many disparate readers, from the pensioner serenely rehearsing slow-motion taiji moves, to the kung fu film buff, to the newly minted black belt.

Many times in the research for this book, I have uncovered claims in official histories that require a religious suspension of disbelief – the master who is led to his practice by a divine vision, or tall tales of run-ins with brigands and thugs. As Kennedy and Guo observe: '. . . discussions of martial arts in both Asian and Western publications too often tend to slip off into the realm of fantasy. It seems that when discussing . . . martial arts, common sense is quickly left behind. Things are often written, and thereafter generally accepted as fact, that a four-year-old child would not, and should not, believe.'[3]

As befits a history of the martial arts, I approach the materials here not as a believer or practitioner, but as a historian. This has often led me into frustrating dead ends and quagmires as paper trails go cold or evaporate into hearsay. Many times, I have had to force myself to bear in mind a comment made by Stephen Turnbull, who has similarly struggled with the contradictions of martial arts history: 'All invented traditions have a basis in fact, no matter how tenuously the links may be made between the developed tradition and recorded history.'[4]

In other words, there is no smoke without fire. But it does not matter what I believe, or want to believe, it only matters what I can *prove*, and what I can prove with historical documentation does not go back past the 1560s.[5] Nor am I alone in this: even in China, a healthy scepticism about the historical provenance of the martial arts has been part of public debate since the 1920s.[6] Meanwhile, in 1998, Stephen Vlastos' landmark work *Mirror of Modernity* applied the concept of 'invented tradition' to a number of Japanese sacred cows, including sumo and judo, suggesting that much of their contemporary form is indeed a contemporary creation.

Modern trends, favouring overheard 'conversations' and allusions in the historical record, allow us to push back our sense of the origins of martial arts a few years earlier than that, but only by citing legends and assumptions. There was a strong temptation to draw a line through everything before the Ming dynasty, and begin with what is now my third chapter, with the martial arts already fully formed in Qi Jiguang's *New Manual on Military Efficiency*, but I realised that doing so would merely leave too much empty space, both in my narrative and in the critical knowledge that my readers would be able to bring to their own subsequent arguments. It is not that you need to know these details in order to understand the real-world existence of the martial arts, but you will require them to hold off the debates of others who are less informed. As a result, this book begins with two chapters of Apocrypha and tall tales, matters of religious belief rather than historical fact, muddled half-truths and extrapolations derived from archaeology.

I maintain this attitude in the chapters that follow, in the understanding that it is possible for a martial art to exist – to have a materiality and a physical presence – even if its true origins are shrouded in doubt. As noted by the historian Sugie Masatoshi, our contemporary sense of the martial arts is often *created* by 'the conflict between tradition and modernisation'.[7] The phenomenon is all around us, in television, in books, in sports halls, but its means of formation is worthy of investigation. Nobody is disputing the right of Hatsumi Masaaki, holder of multiple black belts, to set himself up as the teacher of a martial art that he calls *ninjutsu*. But we might question whether he really learned his skills from the last survivor of a secret army of wizards.

Not every martial art scrambles for old-world connections and divine portents. Bruce Lee's Jeet Kune Do openly borrows from two thousand years of Chinese tradition, drawing on the established practices of Wing Chun kung fu and several previous years of Lee's teaching of his own derivative, alluding with mottoes such as 'Be Like Water' to the ancient writings of Laozi. But it is also proudly modernist, founded in 1967 and priding itself on its 'non-classical' techniques and its openness to experimentation. Many other martial arts are similarly recent retellings of older traditions, such as judo, a nine-teenth-century reworking of the old samurai grappling of jujutsu.

Jeet Kune Do also demonstrates all too well the fragility of so many systems that have surely been created and lost in the past, leaving no record of their existence. The security of transmission of certain styles and forms has often been tantalisingly flimsy, relying on a set of conditions for training, pupillage and access that are rarely all in alignment. The American classes that Bruce Lee taught in his invented Jeet Kune Do lasted for barely four years before he shut them down himself, having decided that the very notion of separate styles was an unnecessarily confrontational and exclusive notion, as pointless as trying to learn to swim on dry land.[8] After his death two years later, his students revived his work, but split into two contending factions based on matters of interpretation and form, and how they thought the martial art *would* have evolved if Lee had lived. Now there are two kinds of Jeet Kune Do, but there could have very easily been none.

Even well-established martial arts are often rooted in unsure pasts. Patrick McCarthy's *Bubishi: The Classic Manual of Combat* has achieved a status as something of a karate bible, and contains infor-mation from many documents that link Japanese karate to the martial arts styles of mainland China. McCarthy himself cautions his reader that his book, cogent and sensible, with numbered pages and rationalised spelling, is the result of an extensive editorial process, imposing meaning and narrative on piles of jumbled papers. 'I am sure it may come as a surprise,' he wrote, 'to learn that the original document I received from the Konishi family was unbound and in a random order . . . As such I found it necessary to reorganise the articles in which I received them for the sake of producing a coherent publication.'[9]

Even by attempting to sort things into some sort of order, we run the risk of imposing what historians call a mode of emplotment: an unjustified fallacy of order and progression. It would be convenient if martial arts had a single narrative arc, in which one development led to another like a well-told story, but sometimes we must present things out of order, or leap between unconnected locations, in order to present a fuller picture.

Much of the history of the martial arts is in the hands of writers who want to place their own memory in the centre. They want to commemorate the achievements of their own practitioners, often within a narrative that suggests the superiority of a particular tradition. As noted by the historian Matsuda Ryūichi: 'ninety per cent of books about martial arts history are inaccurate because authors tend to make their teacher and their school sound better than they are. These authors exaggerate things or make up stories entirely. Oftentimes they create stories that establish a well-known figure as the founder of their school. They then go on to conjure up stories about that fictional founder.'[10]

They want to tell a story that is aesthetically pleasing, with a suitably Hollywood storyline that would make a good movie. And they are often ignorant, wilfully or otherwise, of any information that would bring any of the above errors into question.[11] For Stanley Henning, most accounts of martial arts are ruined by the assumption of:

> ... two widely accepted, deeply ingrained and hard to quash myths: one attributing the origins of Chinese boxing to the Indian monk, Bodhidharma, who, according to tradition is said to have resided in the famous Shaolin Monastery around 525 AD; and the other attributing the origins of *taiji-quan*, or Chinese shadow boxing as it is sometimes called in the West, to the mythical Taoist hermit, Zhang Sanfeng, whose dates have never been confirmed . . .[12]

Henning stresses that martial arts have their origin in the brutal and sadly universal matter of killing people. It is only later that they

6

become ingrained in political or moral philosophies, as the tactical realities of a fight to the death are subsumed beneath the strategic ideals of running a state or becoming a better person. Archaeology alone makes it abundantly clear that the Chinese, like everyone else, were busily murdering each other in battles long before the alleged arrival of Indian mystics or sorcerous hermits. It is hence merely common sense to begin an account of martial arts with actual fighting. What makes 'the martial arts' different from a list of simple twists and holds is the incorporation of these many other ideas – particularly the clash of rival philosophies and beliefs.

However, I am also interested in the 'stories they tell themselves about themselves' – the legends and lore of the martial arts tradition.[13] The historian Thomas A. Green agrees that: 'Clearly, some of the claims made about martial arts systems are fraudulent, and a few stories are simply bad fiction composed by self-serving instructors.'[14] But he argues for a more forgiving stance that recognises the formation and uses of 'folk history' as being radically different from the concerns of the 'scientific' history that picks at sources and attributions. Green suggests that the folk history of the martial arts performs the same functions as literal 'legends' in other communities: establishing credibility, telling stories of resistance against an oppressive enemy, and presenting parables about the lives of the founders, designed to teach lessons to their inheritors. This perspective on the martial arts sees them as a culture all of their own, with customs and legends, etiquette and taboos. Many of these are, indeed, very modern creations, as evolving, unclassified styles of fighting are suddenly forced to systematise, to develop credentials for progress and achievement, and to develop terminology and forms that can be transmitted and taught far beyond their original, localised places of origin.

One certainly gets a sense, in the 1940s and afterwards, of innumerable local trainers all over the world suddenly deciding to give a name and a history to what was previously simply 'what they did' when someone tried to punch them. We also see nationalist agendas, as governments seek to impose a unified identity – such as in Indonesia where the Javan fighting style of *pencak* and the Borneo/ Sumatra style of *silat*, both with multiple origins and contentious histories, links and crossovers, not the least with Indian and Chinese influences, were suddenly combined in 1948 to create the 'new' fighting art of Pencak Silat. Pencak Silat is undeniably a symbol of Indonesian-ness, with a history that reaches back into the colonial past of secret resistance to the Dutch colonial powers, back into unclear origins of secret societies and simple village brawls. What is simply a name for 'fighting' on many islands of the archipelago is now capitalised and branded, as a specific artefact, even though seventy years earlier, locals could not even agree on its name.

Stanley Henning has decried what he calls 'the appalling state of ignorance' among the very people we might expect to preserve historical memory, ever ready to present myths as facts.[15] But fiction has become an immensely influential element within the community of martial artists, sometimes accepted as a form of shared delusion. 'While almost all of these stories are late inventions, dating to the end of the nineteenth century or the start of the twentieth,' note the Wing Chun historians Benjamin Judkins and Jon Nielson, 'the fact remains that they are meaningful to the communities that transmit them.'[16] Modern visitors to the Shaolin Temple are told of all its folklore and legends, superstitious ways of gaining merit by walking on particular flagstones, and tall tales about the dents supposedly punched in the ancient 'bachelor' tree, but always prefaced with the caveat 'some people say . . .' as if leaving due diligence in the hands of others. Fictional influences can be seen not merely among modern children who emulate things they have seen in kung fu films, but ever since the Red Turban rebels of 1850s Foshan, who marched into battle dressed in the costumes of characters from Cantonese opera. We might even say that, somewhat fittingly for something that in

English is called the 'martial arts', matters of theatricality, performance and fiction often seem second only to the martial element.

At a certain level, it doesn't matter if you doubt that Kanō Jigorō, founder of judo, once fought a disguised Buddhist saint in his practice hall; that Ueshiba Morihei, founder of aikido, claimed to be able to dodge bullets; or that Bodhidharma, alleged founder of kung fu, meditated with such intensity that his shadow was burned into the wall of his cave. It matters that these are stories that their followers tell each other, only half in jest.[17] This is not merely a book about the facts of martial arts; it is also a book about fictions – legends of great warriors and noble rebels, doubtful lineages of transmission from ancient immortals to the teacher standing before you in a draughty church hall, and the kung fu stories that often form the public's first contact with Asian fighting styles.

Fictional influences become increasingly relevant in modern times, as cinema and television gain an ever-greater influence on how the public sees the martial arts. This is not merely a case of the privileging of certain styles above others, but can also lead to concrete developments. The 1982 movie *Shaolin Temple* not only multiplied tourist attendance at the temple itself by a factor of ten, but also led to the lifting of a Chinese government ban on monks wearing robes. As noted by the abbot, Shi Yongxin, this 'signalled the thawing of the country's policy on religion'. His own chronology of the temple's development and renewal is consequently divided into periods before and after the movie's release.[18]

Whose martial arts? Fashions come and go. In Edwardian England, the best-known Asian fighting style was jujutsu, famously adopted by the suffragettes in order to demonstrate the possibility of equality for the 'weaker sex'. In 1980s New York: it was karate, adopted by many a fitness instructor as a means of self-defence. In 2016, walk into a bookstore in the People's Republic of China and go to the sports section, where the martial arts books are usually shelved, and the most common sight is *taiji quan*, a fighting technique that has acquired an immense second life through its transformation into slow-motion callisthenics for pensioners.

This book lacks the space to deal with the minutiae of every single splinter and sub-group. If you are actively involved in a martial art, I doubt I will have anything new to tell you about your personal style, although hopefully there will be much new information on everyone else's. There are sure to be readers who are disappointed that their individual school does not receive an entire chapter to itself. In painting the development and history of the phenomenon in necessarily broad strokes, there will inevitably be omissions and edits – no space for Muay Thai; no time for Choy Li Fut. Instead, I have concentrated on important points of transformation in the nature of the martial arts, in what often amounts to a cultural history of East Asia told from the point of view of the unarmed and marginalised. Although there is some mention of armed combat, my interest is largely in the field of martial arts that do not involve weapons.

Chapter One includes the fundamentals of Chinese military manuals, and the origins of key concepts in early philosophy. We know almost nothing about unarmed combat in the China of two millennia ago, but the philosophers of that time form the bedrock of much East Asian discourse, and often form touchstones in later debates and materials. Rare indeed is the military work of the last two thousand years that does not at least mention Sun Tzu and *The Art of War*, for example. The Daoist thought of Laozi is deeply ingrained in all the 'internal' martial arts. The ideas of Confucius are nothing to do with combat, but usually form the basic organisational structure of any East Asian institution, including a school of martial arts.

Chapter Two deals with the rich intercultural contacts of China's medieval period, the height of the Silk Road, and the impact made by Indian ideas on Chinese religion and military practice. Particular weight here is accorded to stories of the Shaolin Temple, cited with varying degrees of credulity by many later martial arts as the root of their traditions.

After a preamble through the Song dynasty and the century-long Mongol interregnum, Chapter Three deals with the first real documentary evidence of martial arts from the Ming dynasty (1368–1644), when particular strategic conditions on the northern border caused the authorities to cast around in search of paramilitary assistance for defending the rest of the country from pirates and bandits. The requirements for sourcing and training soldiers, and for providing the common man with the means to defend himself in a time of increasing outlawry, created the first true materials from which so many martial arts are likely to have sprung.

Chapter Four examines China's all-important Qing dynasty (1644–1912), a period of stern and censorious domination by what was then regarded as a foreign elite, in which internal and external threats to the regime both nurtured and occasionally culled underground organisations that may have studied certain martial arts. It explores the martial arts in both fact and fiction, as a sporting or exercise activity, or as a ritual of rebellion, at first in the face of two centuries of Manchu rule, then against invaders from Europe and America, and sometimes both.

Chapter Five moves to Japan to approach a similar diversification in the Tokugawa and Meiji periods (1603–1912) as the practical *bujutsu* crafts of the samurai battlefield evolved into the *budō* of sporting or ritual events, and an immense publishing industry of military manuals for the armchair samurai.

Later chapters must, by necessity, overlap in terms of their geographical and chronological compass, as the martial arts become a multinuclear, contending series of topics. The true origins of many modern martial arts arise in the ferment of the twentieth century in Chapter Six, with a rich hybridity of contacts between Japan, China and Korea.

Chapter Seven deals with the migration of martial arts to the English-speaking world. This chapter also deals with the sad truth of the mass extinction of much Chinese martial arts knowledge as the result of a century of unrest and war, and the awful purges of the Cultural Revolution. This is a vital element in understanding the development of the culture of the martial arts, not the least because it reverses the earlier northern bias of the Jingwu school from the 1910s and 1920s, creating a massive, irreparable gap which has largely been filled with the legends and lore, rituals and forms of southern Chinese martial arts traditions, as preserved by overseas communities and film producers. Fictional influences come to the fore as mainstream culture comes to understand martial arts solely through its depiction in unreal cinematic forms, thick with wire-work and digital effects.

Chapter Eight deals with the problems facing the martial arts in a global environment, as evolving disciplines face new issues of diversification, diversity, succession, recruitment and competition, legal status and doctrinal disputes over sportification and marketing. The chapter includes the last martial art to be covered in this narrative – *ninjutsu*, which sprang into being in the latter half of the twentieth century and yet which claims a tradition far older for itself.

A closing Chronology allows for an overview of key events in the timeline of the martial arts, including verifiable destructions of the Shaolin Temple, revolutions and rebellions, and the first introductions of many elements that are now widespread, such as belts and ranks. I lack the space to include every single media appearance of the martial arts, and, indeed, every split and spat that sees prominent schools dividing and subdividing into rival disciplines, but I have done my best to hit the high points here, even when there was no space for them in my main text.

Note on Translation and Spelling

....

For an English-language author attempting a clear and readable account of the martial arts, editorial consistency is a problem. Romanisation of Asian languages often requires an anachronistic application of acceptable spellings. In the case of *jūjutsu*, for example, general use in the English-speaking world usually drops the macron accent that denotes a long 'u'. Even as I type it here, Microsoft Word insists on correcting it to *jujutsu* before we can even start discussing variant spellings over the last hundred years, which have often rendered it as *jyujutsu* or even *jiujitsu*. In the interests of preserving editorial sanity, I have generally given the correct romanisation in the first instance, and thereafter used the most popular version in my text – for popular, assume that **if the word appears without diacritic marks in a standard English dictionary, it will usually appear so here as well.** Hence, *jūjutsu* is normally rendered as jujutsu; a *dōjō* (training hall) as dojo; *gongfu* ('diligent practice' – not applied specifically to the martial arts until the twentieth century) as kung fu; Sunzi as Sun Tzu. However, when it comes to quotes from the writings of others, I have preserved the authors' variants, hence there are references in the quotes of others to Taoism, although in my own text it is called Daoism.

A single letter can make all the difference. Here is John Stevens in his excellent book *The Way of Judo*, offering a human glimpse of the colourful language of Kanō Jigorō:

It may come as a surprise that the favourite saying of the dignified grand master of Kōdōkan judo and principal of the Tokyo Teacher Training College was literally 'What is this shit!' (*Nani kuso*). By this, Kanō was saying to his students, 'Shit happens. Deal with it!'[1]

This may even be true. But surely a simpler explanation would be that Kanō's most common utterance was the far less exciting 'What's this?' (*Nani koso*)? Kanō the cussing educator makes for an interesting anecdote, and has been spun here into a doubtful extrapolation of a deeper intended meaning. Stevens' ability in Japanese is certainly not in question, but I wonder whether his informants were bending the truth for aesthetic purposes, in order to make a funny story to tell over a bottle of *sake*.

We must remain wary, even of native sources and even of 'authorities'. In Japanese, the term 'karate' is usually used to describe fighting forms that reached Japan, supposedly from China, up through the Ryūkyū Islands. The term *kenpō* (a calque of the Chinese *quanfa*) is used to denote fighting forms thought to have migrated directly from China. This fact, however, seems to have eluded Ed Parker in 1954, when he decided to call his new martial art American Kenpo Karate. The term is legitimate because it is what Parker decided to call the thing he did, but to a Japanese speaker it sounds somewhat tin-eared.

Even the terminology used to describe the subject of this book is a matter of some debate, and has been ever since Sun Tzu's *Bingfa* was first translated from Chinese as *The Art of War*, rather than the more accurate *Military Models* or *Army Methods*.[2] The Japanese language, too, contains multiple terms translatable as 'martial arts', each of them with a slightly different nuance. *Bujutsu* is the basic samurai craft of killing people; *budō* is its Tokugawa-era refinement for a warrior aristocracy with nobody left to fight, adding a degree of ritualisation and ethics; *kakutogi* is the modern word for combat as a sport, occasionally incorporating elements of the previous two, as well as foreign imports like boxing. But Japanese also distinguishes *bugei*, which is a performance with martial elements, such as spear-bending or brick-smashing, intended for entertainment and usually for money; and there is also *bukyō*, a term for heroic fiction concentrating on martial artists, exported in the twentieth century into Chinese, where it is pronounced *wuxia*.[3]

Since the text requires a large number of foreign words, I have done my best to use the minimum number possible in the chapters that follow, which often requires me to avoid specific jargon like *jūdōka* (a practitioner of judo) or *kareteka* (a practitioner of karate). In order to prevent many proper nouns from arriving with an entire entourage of alternative readings, I have also tried to simplify certain names. I use, for example, anachronistic Pinyin romanisation when referring to the Pure Martial Athletic Association founded in Shanghai in 1909 as the *Jingwu* Callisthenics School, not the *Jing Mo* by which it is known in *Fist of Fury*, or the *Chin Woo* one often hears in South East Asia and among overseas Chinese.[4] I refer to Bodhidharma's most famous pupil as Huike, his later honorary title as a monk, rather than his original given name of Shengguang, the old Wade-Giles transliteration of Hui-k'o, or the commonly seen Japanese pronunciation of Eka. Bruce Lee's famous teacher Ip Man is referred to by the spelling employed by his modern biographers, not the Yip Man variant sometimes used previously. Itosu Ankō, leading light of karate, is known by his honorific name, and not by the more everyday pronunciation that would be Itosu Yasutsune. Li Shimin, eldest son of the first emperor of the Tang dynasty, is referred to by his reign title of Taizong, even before he was crowned as emperor. Similarly, I refer to China's western regions as Xinjiang, even though that name, meaning 'the New Frontier', dates only from the Qing dynasty, and is an anachronism in my first three chapters. All of these fudges are deliberately undertaken to make the text smoother and more readable for the lay reader, in the style of previous books in the *Brief History* series. For the reader who wishes to wallow in the pickier debates about the underlying terms and terminology, the notes and bibliography offer many further directions.

I have also wrestled with thorny issues in capitalisation, where some martial arts prefer a capital initial letter, and others do not. There is, in fact, no such thing as a 'capital letter' in Chinese, Korean or Japanese, but they often creep in during translation into English. Sometimes, this is a matter of trademarks and brands; sometimes, it has more to do with original meaning. Strictly speaking, *Kara-te* was originally the 'China-hand' in Japanese, altered for political reasons in 1936 to *karate*, the 'empty-hand'.[5] Wing Chun is a particular martial art, but it supposedly derives its name from the component parts of a person's name, which I would transliterate with only one capital, as Yim Wing-chun. Consequently, while capitalisation in this book might occasionally appear random or contrary to the style guides used by specific organisations, it reflects the original meaning – proper nouns such as Shaolin are capitalised; simple nouns such as boxing or wrestling are not, until they are incorporated within a proper noun. Hence: 'Shōtōkan karate'. Transliterations for Asian languages follow popular usage, so that the Japanese *kenpō* uses standard Hepburn romanisation, but the name Shorinji Kempo spells the same word with an 'm', as per the World Shorinji Kempo Organization's own branding.

Certain politicised debates in the martial arts world can manifest in quibbles over terminology. Some of these are rooted in translation or carry over disputes from the Chinese language. There are readers whose hackles will rise at the use of 'kung fu' rather than '*wushu*'; others who regard '*wushu*' as an invasive modern sportification; still others who prefer 'boxing'; and an equally large community who do not like the implications of the word for its echoes of the Boxer Uprising...and so on.[6] I also deliberately say 'Boxer Uprising' rather than the more popular 'Boxer Rebellion', in keeping with a trend since 1987 in modern scholarship, discussed in greater detail in Chapter Four.

Taking such matters to extremes, I would be treading on *someone's* toes if I dared to translate *taiji* accurately as 'supreme ultimate', since some might surely say I was making claims for it that were undeserved. I have no personal bias in my presentation of the martial arts. I am not a secret supporter of something I believe to be the one true kung fu, and if I inadvertently say something that offends the tender sensibilities of trained fighters, I apologise in advance. I shall never tell you: 'My style is the best, and so I challenge you, that my style should stand alone.' Others may object even to my focus on China and Japan, particularly since 'Chinese' ethnic identity and Mandarin pronunciation has often been imposed retroactively on peoples once written off as 'barbarians' in the chronicles of early dynasties. This is certainly an issue – were there more space, extra chapters could entirely reposition the narrative of this book considered entirely from the perspective of Korea or Mongolia, for example. But that is an argument better made in more specialised books.[7]

In some cases, I have had to break my own rules in order to avoid confusion in the text, capitalising the game of Go in order to make it stand out from the simple verb in English. I have also deliberately adhered to interpretations of certain titles and concepts that have been used in earlier books I have published through Constable & Robinson – for example, I refer to the *Daode Jing* as *The Book of the Path and the Power*, retaining the translation I used in my 2010 *Brief History of Khubilai Khan*, and when translating from Sun Tzu's *The Art of War*, use my own text published by Constable in 2012.

To those who would complain about any of these decisions, I recall a phrase attributed to the swordsman Miyamoto Musashi: 'It takes one thousand days of sweat to forge the spirit, and ten thousand days to polish it. But a bout is decided in less than a second.'[8]

CHAPTER ONE

The Arts of War

···············

I am a world away from the Tang dynasty. If I had travelled a thousand years in time from medieval China to this hall in modern Japan, there would be very little about contemporary Osaka that would feel familiar to me. The Chinese characters are still the same in all the signs, although in this sports hall they are oddly bloated and squashed, fat words that have eaten too many pies, gamely trying to squeeze themselves into a box that is too small. I happen to know that many of the Japanese pronunciations of Chinese words struggle to replicate the forms used a thousand years ago, although it is not obvious to the layman. But a visitor from the Tang dynasty would be able to read the word for 'wrestling' plastered on the billboards, and he would certainly recognise the layout of the ring, its floor scattered with sacred sand, albeit not the edges delineated by chunky lumps of rope.

I, too, must squeeze myself into a space that is too small, edging myself over an ankle-high rail to perch, already uncomfortable, on a thin red cushion. The entire section near the front is subdivided in this way, with a grid forcing people into intimate little boxes of four. The real hard-core fans in the crowd have been here all day, arriving early in the morning for the novice matches. The less devoted don't turn up until a few hours later, when the intermediate matches begin. A real dilettante like me would just show up in the afternoon, for the big-name smackdowns.

I am the youngest person in my row. My neighbour is an old man in a brown suit that probably fitted him at his daughter's wedding, but into which he has now somewhat shrunken. His teeth are stained by a lifetime of tobacco, and his face has a ruddy, boozy shine. We clink cups in mutual appreciation. Sumo as a spectator sport attracts remarkably few audience members under fifty, although I spot a scattering of fangirls and sulking teenage tag-alongs. Much of the audience are grazing on lunch boxes bought from the kiosks outside; overpriced, over-designed confections of chicken pieces and decorated rice, often with a small beer and a commemorative trinket.

The referee is dressed like a Shinto priest, imparting a relict religious air to what was once a holy ceremony. He announces the name of the two competitors, and there are 'oohs' of approval.

Even if they weren't built like trucks, sumo wrestlers would be easy to spot. Their guild insists that they dress the part whenever they go out in public, attired in traditional robes and with a lacquered, high topknot – fancy dress for a samurai bath time. They must wear the *geta*, clip-clopping wooden clogs, whenever they are out and about. But the wrestlers here have only their loincloths, displaying powerful bodies shielded by rolls of blubber. Our modern admiration of lithe, limber bodies is a relatively recent fetish. Even Roman gladiators favoured a little natural padding to ward off the softer blows.

They squat, lifting their legs and slapping them down like bulls pawing at the ground, their gazes locking. This is supposed to be intimidating, but they both seem faintly bored. Each takes a pinch of salt to scatter on the ring. One does so in a desultory fashion, as if he is already impatient. The other flings his salt high in the air, causing a ripple of excitement from the audience. He's a feisty one, it seems.

They squat again, clapping their hands to dispel evil spirits, their fleshy arms shuddering in echo, returning to the edges of the ring while minions whip out banners that proclaim the bout's prize money. Then they advance on each other, the priestly arbiter backing off with a raised fan.

I'm expecting them to grapple, but the first couple of attempts end with avoidance and recoils. Snatches turn into slaps, but the referee does nothing – slapping is okay, apparently. Then a hand grabs the right bit of flabby shoulder, someone finds purchase, and they ram into each other like stags. Two unstoppable forces contend over the same space, shunting and heaving. A charge is deflected by an artful repositioning of the feet, but the charger has the upper hand. His momentum is pushing his opponent, back . . . back . . . tantalisingly close to the edge of the ring. The defender's foot inches ever nearer, until with a heave of his own, he twists, deflecting the attacker's momentum past him.

They twist and fall, the defender's foot touching the outside of the ring, but doing so mere milliseconds after the attacker's elbow has touched the ground. They are both down, but who came down first?

And the crowd goes wild. It sounds for a moment like they are bellowing poetry at the ceiling about cardinal directions, times of year, weather features . . . but then I realise they are yelling the name of the wrestler they favour, assaulting rival fandom with a wall of sound.

Can we shrug and say best of three? Apparently not. The referee must rule, and there is real money at stake, not to mention prestige. With prestige comes rank, with rank comes further opportunity – sponsorship deals and the chance to open one's own training studio. Although fate very rarely hinges on a single match, there is an accumulation of points and merit, and every point counts. Those fleeting seconds in the ring might make all the difference for one of them, between fortune and failure.

The referee's eyes shift to the side of the stage, and back to the breathless competitors. Then he announces the winner. Neither competitor betrays much emotion, but their thoughts are writ large

21

in the voices of the crowd, precisely half of whom are as angry as hell.

My companion in the brown suit is definitely unhappy. He fulminates about injustice and scandal, climbing with impressive speed to his feet and hurling his cushion at the stage. It sails lazily through the air, spinning like a four-sided Frisbee, before coming down in quiet, unremarked failure a few feet short. But it is one of many, and soon the hall is full of flying cushions, pattering down on the ring in harmless but demonstrative ire.

The losing wrestler tries not to smile, but fails.

CONFUCIUS AND THE WAR DANCES

We begin with bones and stones. Before there was a written record, before there was a history to speak of, humans have always fought. Bamboo and wood swiftly decay in geological terms, but flint spear-heads and arrowheads endure. The earliest flint arrowhead in China is 28,000 years old – perhaps the first skill that required mastery beyond the most basic of struggles was archery, initially designed to give hunters the edge over their prey.[1]

Archaeologists have uncovered human remains with broken bones, missing fingers, staved-in skulls. Other skeletons have been found scattered with arrowheads that would have once lodged in the flesh before it decayed – the last ghastly evidence of some kind of ritual killing by multiple archers, or some forgotten, grisly death as a human target.[2]

The bow and arrow was surely the most influential development in ancient weaponry. It extended the reach of a hunter beyond that of a human throwing spear, without the indirect trajectory of a sling. It presented the opportunity to bring down large game or threatening pred-ators from a position of relative safety. It brought the hunter or warrior the chance to carry not one or two projectiles, but an entire quiver.

It should come as no coincidence that as prehistory was subsumed into written history, the skills of those deemed to be 'the aristocracy' should focus upon the ability to wage war. Whatever the egalitarian proclamations of one's nation and government, there was a time when someone fought for the land you stand on. Someone claimed ownership of it, and lordship over others. They did this by fighting, although ever since ancient times, technology has played an important part in victories. Although historical elites are often apt to celebrate pure strength, one of the benefits accruing to a military aristocracy is access to better tools than mere bare hands. David would never have bested Goliath if he could not have hurled a rock from a distance at a vulnerable spot. Similarly, the ancient nobility of China valued material objects that required the dual privilege of wealth and training. Archery and charioteering were particularly good examples of this, since both required more than physical inheritance, and both significantly increased the martial prowess of their user.

By the time Confucius (551–479 BC) codified and confirmed many traditions and practices of the aristocracy of his era, archery and charioteering were considered to be two of the great skills required of a gentleman. In *The Book of Rites*, said to have been used by Confucius as a teaching aid, there are references to archery contests in which the brutal realities of hunting or war have been tamed, ritualised and transformed into a contest that seems more like a sporting event.

> Therefore, anciently, according to the royal institutes, the feudal princes annually presented the officers who had charge of their tribute to the son of Heaven, who made trial of them in the archery-hall. Those of them whose bodily carriage was in conformity with the rules, and whose shooting was in agreement with the music, and who hit the mark most frequently, were allowed to take part at the sacrifices.[3]

Much has been said about Confucius's obsessions with rites and ritual – the correct number of officials required for certain sacrifices or the correct number of bearers for a sedan chair. His insistence on correctness has often been cited in the philosophies of martial arts, as the basis from which all will to fight should stem – Confucianism required men to know what was worth fighting for, by teaching them first the nature of right and wrong.[4]

But reading between the lines, certain comments of his seem to have been garbled by drifts in the meaning of Chinese over the ensuing millennia. He alludes on several occasions, for example, to the importance of something that he calls 'dances', pointing out to his disciples that it is often possible to observe someone's nationality by the posture they have acquired through such exercises. His talk of 'bodily carriage' and keeping 'in agreement with the music' at an archery competition suggest a performative quality that we rarely associate with archery today, although elements of posture and performance still lurk in the Japanese practice of *kyūdō*. Although the comment derives from much later in Chinese history, one chronicler noticed that the rise of archery tournaments was part of a deliberate transformation of what had once been martial skills into something more befitting peacetime. Following a period of warfare in ancient China, a unifying ruler committed a series of public statements about an end to conflict – locking away much military hardware in arsenals, appointing generals to peace-time ministerial positions and effectively decommissioning formerly necessary skills of harming others. It led to the inauguration of archery competitions in which the objective was to hit an allotted target with precision, rather than to pierce its hide, as had presumably once been the case.[5] In this regard it is the first, but by no means last, incidence of formerly practical martial arts being de-fanged and repurposed in a period of supposed peace – in later chapters, we will see its echoes in the Ming dynasty and Qing dynasty, on samurai-era Okinawa and in Japan under the US Occupation.

Confucius wrote during a period when what we call China was still a patchwork of contending kingdoms. During the subsequent wars that eventually led to the unification of China under its First Emperor, the increased use of massed ranks of spearmen, as well as the escalation in army size from raiding parties to battalions, probably led to an emphasis on the importance of coordinated movement by masses of warriors. We know that soldiers were expected to march in formation and turn on command or drum signal. But it seems that there were also stylised performances of martial movements, given as court entertainments or shows of military strength, and seemingly developed out of these military drills, with musical accompaniment. We have no visual or written record of what these performances might have been, only occasional references in ancient chronicles to 'war dances' (*wǔwǔ*).[6]

'Dance' may be a false friend, as it may have been in the writings of Confucius. The word *wǔ* has had centuries to twist and transform, and even in modern Chinese, one of its many definitions is 'to flourish or wield'.[7] The term comes up again around the time of the founding of the Han dynasty (206 BC–195 AD), when a plot to murder the future Han emperor manifested as a 'sword dance' at a banquet. The would-be assassin Xiang Zhuang proclaims that there is no entertainment in the camp, and instead offers to 'dance a sword dance'. He does so perilously close to his target, until a loyal retainer of the future Han emperor leaps to his feet and joins in, somehow placing himself in between them.

It is unclear what the rules or performance of a 'sword dance' would entail – there is no mention in the Xiang Zhuang story of any actual music, although it is implied that a second 'sword dancer' is not permitted to actually clash swords with the first. However, the existence of a sword dance implies the existence of steps and forms that can be learned and choreographed.

A Han dynasty dictionary directly equates belligerence with coordinated movement, commenting: 'The movements of an assault are like the drumming out of a dance.'[8] There are descriptions in ancient texts of such 'war dances' performed at court, with the performers bearing weapons in their hands – were these ritualised shows of strength, or perhaps re-enactments of famous battles from the past? But if the moves of such dances were stylised forms of combat, they would form the distant ancestors of the many *kata* or positions of modern martial arts. It seems only natural, considering the serried masses of contemporary martial artists, that we might describe the coordinated performance of a series of forms to be a kind of 'dance', and that until such time as a fighter squares off against an opponent to put his skills to practical use, 'dance' is as good a word as any.

Another passage in the Confucian *Book of Rites* lists 'wrestling' among the skills expected of a gentleman, as part of the quasi-military festivities that accompany a harvest festival: 'The son of Heaven orders his leaders and commanders to give instruction on military operations, and to exercise in archery and chariot-driving, and in *jiaoli*.'[9]

I have left *jiaoli* in the original Chinese because later scholars have quarrelled over its precise meaning. James Legge's translation renders it as 'trials of strength', a term that conjures images of weightlifting. We know that such activities went on in ancient China, the great grand-uncle of the First Emperor actually died after such a game, when he dropped a heavy bronze cauldron on his foot.[10] Statues of weightlifters have been uncovered among the burials of the Terracotta Army, unsurprisingly suggesting that the rulers of its military aristocracy placed value on brute strength.

Others, particularly Chinese wrestling associations in search of an ancient provenance, have chosen to translate *jiaoli* as 'wrestling', suggesting that there was an ancient school of unarmed grappling that was on display at these events. It is logical to believe that soldiers' training involved some consideration of how they would fight if they lost their weapons, but there is no proof of this school's existence. Another term in use was *jiaodi*, or 'horn-butting', said to be an ancient ceremonial game in which fighters charged each other wearing horned helmets, in imitation of rutting cattle. The problem for the translator here is deciding what the *jiao* of *jiaoli* is supposed to refer to. If it is a horn, then the term is simply 'horn-strength' and it is presumably a variant name for the head-butting game. But *jiao* can also mean 'corner' or 'angle', which would make *jiaoli* a likely contender for the first reference to wrestling.[11]

By the third century AD, ritualised wrestling practices had acquired a new term: *xiangpu* or 'paired shoving'.[12] The combatants stripped to the waist and leaned in, grasping each other's shoulders. They would wrestle within a marked area, beginning by stepping into it and bowing in the four cardinal directions. Although the rules of such wrestling are unclear, it seems likely that the combatants would be faulted on either touching the ground with any part of the body except their feet, or being pushed out of the ring. As in most forms of wrestling, the nature of *xiangpu* favoured not merely strength but also bulk, and medieval images of wrestlers show them with pronounced bellies and spare flesh, their hair tied in Tang-dynasty topknots.

The transformation of wrestlers from occasional warriors having a little physical fun, into literal 'heavies' performing ritualised combats, caused, or perhaps reflected, their co-option into an entire underworld of sideshows, travelling players and similar performers. We read, particularly in the medieval period, of 'wrestlers' in the company of acrobats and jugglers, conjurors and illusionists, evoking Chinese elements of what we might call a circus or carnival. The wrestlers, it seems, were often the strongmen of such itinerant groups, performers in their own right who could also be counted on as bouncers and bodyguards. One telling incident in 822 AD features a courtier who wished to clear three hundred tax-evading residents off a patch of land in the Chinese capital of Chang'an. In order to do so, he ordered 'fifty wrestlers' to carry out the eviction, leading to a mass brawl in the streets.[13]

Medieval China, particularly the Tang dynasty, was also the period that saw the first prolonged cultural contacts with Japan, leading to many elements of medieval Chinese life enduring in Japan as a form of living fossil. These include the dresses and hairstyles of Tang court ladies, visibly preserved in the fashions of the geisha, architecture and temple designs, and even in ergonomic principles, like the aversion of traditional Japanese home designers to including anywhere to sit – the chair being a Song dynasty fad that came after the Tang. Medieval Chinese wrestling similarly survives, with *xiangpu* being transliterated straight across into Japanese as *sumō* – the characters are the same, it is merely the pronunciation that has changed. One such wrestling match is described in *The Chronicle of Japan* (*Nihongi*) – written in the 8th century:

> Thereupon Nomi no Sukune came from Idzumo, and straightway he and Taima no Kuyehaya were made to wrestle together. The two men stood opposite to one another. Each raised his foot and kicked at the other, when Nomi no Sukune broke with a kick the ribs of Kuyehaya and also kicked and broke his loins and thus killed him.[14]

Although Japanese tradition soon claimed a legendary, local provenance for it (the match reported above supposedly took place around the time of Christ!), sumo wrestling seems only to have flourished in Japan from the time of the Tang contacts, although it did swiftly evolve in the wake of an edict from an emperor in the mid-ninth century, who noted that '[sumo] is not just an entertainment; it is an ideal means for cultivating real martial skills'.[15] By 868 AD, it had bifurcated in Japan from its common, ritual status, under the jurisdiction of the Ministry of Ceremonies, into a more practical form of combat training under the jurisdiction of the Ministry of Martial Affairs. Its evolution thereafter continues in Chapter Five.

LAOZI AND THE CULTIVATION OF QI

Confucius was a practical man, much of whose work was an attempt to create a workable response to old-fashioned ways that were more suitable for running a village rather than a country. His senior, Laozi, was a semi-legendary figure thought to have flourished in the sixth century BC – as an old man, he is alleged to have had a conversation with a young Confucius in the national archives at Luoyang. In his old age, Laozi is supposed to have set down his thoughts in *The Book of the Path and the Power (Daode Jing)*, now regarded as the point of origin and most sacred scripture of Chinese animism, or Daoism. Daoism, or more archaically Taoism, is a particularly 'Chinese' ethical system, which would come to be distinguished in the medieval period, when Chinese traditions were perceived as under attack from foreign philosophies like Buddhism. It values formlessness and harmony, and acknowledges that much is unknowable and subject to attrition over prolonged time periods. Unlike Confucius, who concerns himself with the comportment of a gentleman or ideal subject, Laozi aims far higher, at the ideal behaviours of a 'sage', a venerable being so at one with the universe that he might even aspire to drift into immortality.[16]

Classical Chinese is a tough language to translate. So much of it seems to exist less as complete texts than as lecture notes or mind-maps to prompt a speaker – to 'read' a classical Chinese text under ideal conditions, we might say that one is best served by handing the book to its original author and asking him to perform it.[17] Texts can be compromised even further by the decay of manuscripts, all the more so in Chinese before the invention of paper, when bamboo 'books' were liable to collapse over the centuries into bundles of single-sentence slivers. *The Book of the Path and the Power* is even more compromised because it was rather vague from the very beginning, starting with the word *Dao* itself, variously translated as the Way, the Path, a method, or even simply 'conduct'.[18] Laozi's work has been much misinterpreted over the centuries, not the least by innumerable Chinese emperors who regarded it as a coded manual for achieving immortality by somehow achieving a perfect balance of the negative forces of *yin* and the positive essence of *yang*. The twinned, orbiting black-and-white paramecia of *yin* and *yang*, each bearing a dot of the other in its head, often forms a recognisable component in the symbols and logos of modern martial arts.

Daoism led many a ruler, including the First Emperor himself, on a wild goose chase in search of magical potions and elixirs, whereas even the most cursory reading of what it actually says seems, to me at least, to be a clear instruction to let it all go and accept that death, too, is part of life.

Laozi's philosophy has become a quintessential part of Chinese tradition, not the least in its faith in the path of least resistance, and in the likelihood that the 'soft' can overcome the 'hard' given time – much as weathering will eventually crack rocks. One of his most-quoted aphorisms is that 'the highest goodness resembles water . . . it does not struggle for any form or position, but puts itself in the lowest places that no one wants.'[19]

Laozi has rather a lot to say about military matters, starting with his aversion to all weapons: 'The best weapons are ill-omened instruments that all beings hold in fear. Therefore, those who conform to the Principle [Dao] do not use them.'[20]

30

Deeply opposed to military action, Laozi regarded 'the only place really fitting for a conquering general is that of chief mourner,' that a condition of the creation of an ideal state would be the prohibition of all weapons, and that 'it is the charitable aggressor who wins the battle; it is the charitable defender who is impregnable'. *Charitable* here is a false friend: we might equally consider it to be empathy, or understanding, or mastery of a bigger picture. For Laozi, the idealised sage should consider the possibility of using an aggressor's strength against them, of seeming to yield to pressure in order to deflect it. 'The man who wants to kill may end up like those who play with carpenter's tools, and often lose a finger in their play.'[21]

Laozi was not merely opposed to conflict, he was also something of an anti-intellectual, suggesting that the inhabitants of his ideal state should be deprived of books, and made so fearful of accidents that they would not dare to travel far from the place of their birth: 'My subjects would hear the noise of the cocks and dogs of the neighbouring state, but die from old age without having crossed the border and [having] relationships with the people there.'[22]

Laozi's ideal Chinese state lives in blissful ignorance, happy with the simple things because the people are unaware of anything else, unheeding of the prospect of adventure or exploration, but also of conflict or conquest. When one reads *The Book of the Path and the Power* in its entirety, it swiftly reveals the circumstances of its ancient creation, in a 'China' that was little more than a village, with a small mindset and rural concerns. It is a hidebound, incredibly localised concept, which has echoes in Confucianism's focus on familial relationships and obligations, but is also at odds with Confucian aspirations to higher culture and self-improvement.

Laozi is the baseline of Chinese philosophy; he is often the unseen authority with which many later philosophers are really arguing. Later philosophers would build on his thoughts, contending with them or offering new solutions more appropriate to a more populous age. We can see his shadow even in the draconian state of the First Emperor, who implemented some of Laozi's small-town injunctions on a countrywide scale. In later centuries, the Daoist thought that Laozi represents was often regarded as a retreat from the real world – the pensioned contentment of old men and retired politicians, but also an assertion of a uniquely Chinese pattern of thoughts and attitudes. In his urge for the cultivation of positive life force, and his injunctions to preserve harmony in all things, he formed the origins of an entire sector of Chinese spirituality, to do with unseen energy.

Ancient Chinese belief included much discussion of *qi* – the life force or vital ethers of living things. The concept of *qi* is likely to have begun with its initial meaning of 'breath', as being that ineffable thing, the absence of which distinguishes a living body from a dead one.[23] However, as with so many other parts of ancient Chinese thought, our sense of what *qi* may have meant is compromised by the number of elements that have been co-opted by the rational sciences. *Feng shui*, which contained some sensible ideas about, for example, ergonomics and architecture, is no longer associated with common-sense rules about, say, south-facing houses, but now solely with the mysticism and folklore that is left when science has taken the rest. Similarly, the concept of *qi* may have been intended in classical Chinese to refer to simple, sensible matters of biomechanics, posture and physical health. It may even have been thrown into debates as a default shrug – as the answer given by teachers for a concept that they were themselves unable to explain.[24] Although *qi* is usually associated with Chinese mysticism, it was as much as part of ancient Chinese thought as moods or emotions today, and was alluded to without any supernatural intent even in the writings of some Confucians.[25]

The term was also used to refer to 'anger' in some texts, making it a common term in any discussion of combat. *Qi* was associated with martial ability at least as early as the third century BC, when it was mentioned in the Chapter 'Assuring Victory' of *The Annals of Lü Buwei*, intended as the ultimate encyclopaedia of the First Emperor: 'People are neither consistently courageous nor consistently cowardly. If they possess *qi* vital energy, they are full; if full, they have courage. If they lack *qi* vital energy, they are empty; if empty, they are cowardly.'[26]

Although there is no specific mention of *qi* within the 'inner' martial arts until the first extant discussions of them in the Ming dynasty some 1,500 years later, belief in some kind of life force, and its circulation through and around all living things, is a fundamental part of the traditional Chinese world view. Its fluid, continuous flow, its existence and cultivation are central to the development of Daoism and a number of related Chinese beliefs, including parts of *feng shui*, the meridians and humours treated in acupuncture, and the expectations, methods and outcomes of traditional Chinese medicine. Daoists, observed one ancient sceptic: '. . . suppose that if you do not shake, bend and stretch the arteries in your body they will block up and not circulate, and if they do not circulate the accumulation will cause illness and death.'[27]

There is no direct evidence that *qi* was part of ancient Chinese military training, although a desire for good health, when expressed in classical Chinese, would naturally require a diagnosis of 'good *qi*'. A series of wall paintings in the second century BC tombs at Mawangdui, near Changsha, only unearthed in the early 1970s, clearly depict forty-four figures going through a series of callisthenic exercises, some noted with the name of a particular animal, and the nature of the ailment that might be cured or eased by holding certain positions. These have since been co-opted by the modern *taiji quan* movement as the earliest extant examples of supposed taiji exercises, although their explicit relationship to the martial arts is tenuous.[28]

Later in the Han dynasty, in the second century AD, similar exercises formed the basis of the physician Hua Tuo's 'Five Animal Frolics' (*Wu Qin Xi*), an exercise regime patterned on the movements of certain animals – initially the tiger, deer, bear, monkey and bird. Since the bear, monkey and crane all appear in the Mawangdui illustrations that predate Hua Tuo by a couple of centuries, we may reasonably conclude that he was summarising medical lore that was already in existence in the early Han dynasty, rather than creating it from scratch – this is an important assertion, not only for avoiding the fallacy of crediting Hua Tuo with their invention, but also the common error of suggesting that the Five Animal forms of kung fu were invented at the Shaolin Temple, which was not even founded until two centuries later. In particular, such stretching forms were used by Charles Luk as the basis for a 1970 book that coined the term 'Taoist yoga' (sic), joining two very different traditions that were often on opposite sides of conflicts in Chinese history.[29]

Although we may reasonably suppose that discussion of someone's *qi* – attempts to increase it and manage it through diets and exercise; its focus in physical attacks; its likely subversion through ganglia and pressure points – would have formed part of almost every conversation about the martial arts over the past two thousand years, its absence from any specifically martial manual before the Ming dynasty causes me to remain silent on it for the next couple of chapters. The association of exercises with the patterns of movement of certain animals would return to the kung fu tradition in later periods, not just in the styles of certain temples – tiger, crane, snake, monkey and mantis, or the southern styles of tiger, leopard, snake, crane and dragon – but also in many forms invented to add spice to modern martial arts movies.

SUN TZU AND THE MAIDEN OF YUE

For someone whose name has been trotted out by generation upon generation of soldiers, Sun Tzu (c.544–496 BC) was surprisingly pacifist. Believed to have been a contemporary of Confucius, his *Art of War* spends much of its time detailing the awful logistics of a military campaign, the hidden costs, collateral damage, clean up and aftercare. Sun Tzu went to war only with the deepest of reluctance and as the very last resort, and he was prepared to do literally anything to prevent it. His first chapter is less a collection of epigrams than a box-ticking form, asking would-be generals to tally up the variables of their current situation, in order to decide whether they should fight at all. Another chapter is a detailed account of espionage, since Sun Tzu would rather send in agents to steer an enemy away than confront them directly.

Despite being the father of Chinese martial philosophy, Sun Tzu has nothing to say about unarmed combat. We know that he put his men (and in one famous incident, his women) through a series of drills, but there is no surviving evidence of what those drills might have been, or if they extended to any consideration of how to fight without swords or spears. What survives of Sun Tzu's work is limited to operations, tactics and strategy. There is nothing in his work about how his sergeants may have trained his men, but his chapter on 'Momentum' has obvious applications in hand-to-hand combat:

And so, for the skilled warrior, momentum should be focused, and timing swift. Momentum is like a drawn crossbow; timing like the released trigger.

In the tumult and confusion, in the chaos of battle, he is not confused. In the mud and clamour, his formations wheel, but they cannot be defeated. Chaos begets order. Fear begets courage. Weakness begets strength.

Between order and chaos, there is calculation. Between courage and fear there is momentum. And so, he who is skilled at manipulating the enemy creates formations that draw the enemy in. He gives what the enemy will certainly take, and so lures him onward, his own soldiers lying in wait.[30]

Although Sun Tzu's philosophy is resolutely strategic, something very similar to it was plainly already being applied at a practical, tactical level of individual fighters. The *Spring and Autumn Annals* of the kingdoms of Wu and Yue, recounting events in the generation immediately following that of Sun Tzu, records a meeting between King Goujian of Yue and an anonymous woman later known as the Maiden of Yue. According to legend, she had grown up in the wilderness and was entirely self-taught, but already enjoyed a reputation as the greatest sword fighter in his kingdom. Goujian hired the Maiden of Yue to train his own soldiers after she talked him through some of her ideas.

The theory is very subtle yet easy to understand. Its true significance is hidden and deep. The theory includes both large [double/offence] and small [single defence] doors, and *yin* [passive/yielding] and *yang* [active/attacking] aspects. Open the large door and close the small one [move from the defence to the offence], passivity recedes and activity rises. The following precepts are applicable to all forms of hand-to-hand combat: strengthen the spirit within, appear calm without, **give the appearance of a proper woman** and fight like an aroused tiger; generate throughout your body and move with your spirit; remain distant and obscure as the sun, **and quick and agile as a bounding hare**; now your opponent sees you, now he doesn't and the sword blade flashes similarly; breathe with movement and do not break the rules;

36

side-to-side, back-and-forth, direct attack or reverse blow, the opponent does not hear these. This body of theory will allow one person to resist one hundred and a hundred to resist ten thousand.[31] (My emphasis in bold.)

The translation above by Stanley Henning makes several sallies into breaking down the obscure, quasi-Daoist allusions of the text, with its comments on 'big and small doors' and the more familiar references to *yin* and *yang*. But he seems to have missed direct allusions to *The Art of War*, the author of which had been a celebrity guest of one of Yue's enemies. Here, for example, is Sun Tzu on strategic thinking: 'When your enemy leaves an opening, be sure to go straight through it. First see what he loves and conceal your timing. Bumble along as if blind, until the crucial moment of battle. And so, at first, **you should seem coy like a woman**, so that the enemy opens the door. **But then dart like a hare**, and the enemy cannot hold you back.'[32] (My emphasis in bold.)

The story of the Maiden of Yue is notable for two reasons. Firstly, even though it was not set down until several centuries after the events it describes, it still dates from, at the latest, the Han dynasty (around the second century AD), making it one of the earliest extant discussions of physical martial arts. It also matter-of-factly recounts the hiring of a female martial arts instructor, at a time when most soldiery was usually assessed in terms of brute strength, and when chauvinism was so ingrained into Chinese culture that nobody seems to even blink at an instruction to 'give the appearance of a proper woman'.

MOZI AND SELF-DEFENCE

Another philosopher with an indirect but palpable influence on the history of martial arts was Mozi (c.470–391 BC), whose 'Mohist' school briefly flourished in the warring chaos of the two centuries after Confucius.

Mozi was an uncharacteristically catty philosopher, scornful of many of his predecessors, and hectoring towards his students – many of his sayings begin with the angry, defensive rebuke: 'You have not examined the class of words I have used nor have you understood the reasoning behind them.' It is likely that his antipathy towards Confucius in particular was instrumental in his fall from favour by the time of the Han dynasty, when Confucianism was adopted as a state ideology. Mozi regarded Confucius as a buffoon and a hypocrite, wittering about propriety and etiquette when it suited him, even though he reportedly lived off the spoils of criminal activity when times were hard.[33] It is in the works of Mozi that we find many quotes attributed to Confucius's rivals – exasperated ministers complaining to their kings that Confucius's airy ideas and idle theories have led them into political disasters.

Mozi does not specifically attack Sun Tzu by name, but takes the time in his writings to criticise the activities of the states where Sun Tzu was believed to be working as a general. That said, much of Mozi's thought mirrors the logistic concerns of Sun Tzu, taking great pains to instruct rulers in the terrible human cost of actually fighting. Instead, the controversial Mohist line was to plan military action only in self-defence.

From beyond the grave, Sun Tzu might well have cited himself in counter-argument: 'Do not trust that they will not come. Trust that you will be ready when they do.'[34]

Even during his own lifetime, Mozi's philosophy seems to have been regarded as somewhat naïve, even by those clients who were prepared to cherry-pick his ideas. Where, the ghost of Sun Tzu might ask, does 'self-defence' begin? Is it when the enemy army arrives at your gates? When he crosses your border? When he is visibly preparing for war? A pro-active, sensible strategy of self-defence would surely amount to the entire contents of Sun Tzu's *The Art of War*, and Mozi must have realised this. As a result, he made himself invaluable by becoming truly expert at siege defence and fortification – the latter part of his *Book of Master Mo* is an incredibly detailed manual of city defence, even down to the required length of ladles and placement of battlements. Legendarily, he once turned back an invading army by demonstrating with a hastily constructed model that a Mohist strategy could effectively repel any assault, and by revealing that three hundred of his disciples were waiting on the walls of the target city to do just that.

Mozi, too, had nothing to say about unarmed combat, but his idea that an entire philosophical structure should derive from the idea of fighting only in self-defence would have repercussions two millennia after his death. In modern times, the repurposing or rebranding of many martial arts as 'methods of self-defence' would put Mohist attitudes to new uses at the level of an individual. Now, as then, there are those who find such claims to be doubtful, but we can see the ghost of Mozi, and of Sun Tzu, in those contemporary martial arts that argue for fighting only as the very last resort. But as Peter Lorge writes: 'Only by excluding soldiers and militiamen, who constitute the vast majority of martial artists in all time periods including the present, and focusing on the relatively tiny number of civilian martial artists can we make self-defence the main goal of martial arts training.'[35] In doing so, modern martial artists invoke the ghost of Mozi, even if they have never heard of him.

CHAPTER TWO

The Shaolin Temple
....

Luoyang is a grubby town. Throughout my stay there, the grey smog does not let up, often so thick that it is difficult seeing the other side of the road. Mr Yuan's taxi nudges and hoots its way through the multi-directional traffic, and out on to the trunk road that leads into the mountains. Fog lights appear in the haze before us, often mere seconds before they herald the arrival of overloaded coal trucks, looming out of the mist on the tight, winding road.

The climb into the mountains takes an hour, on a road rarely fenced between us and the long plummet back towards town. Before long, there are patches of grey snow on the ground . . . and then suddenly we are above the mists, beneath a sky that is almost blue.

The Shaolin Temple is here, above the pollution, in a time warp where it could still be the Ming dynasty. Its location was chosen because it was circled by other mountains, which appear to the indulgent eye to form a silhouette of a reclining Buddha. Thanks to the fame of Shaolin kung fu, and also of Zen Buddhism, which began here with the monk Bodhidharma, it has a lot of money to spend, and is a massive hilltop complex, ringed by kung fu high schools, halls of residence for the two hundred remaining monks, and temples and pagodas in memory of great Shaolin achievements. It is not the most richly appointed temple I have seen in China, but it is possibly in the top ten, its coffers swelled by religious and martial tourism.

Although the precincts are not devoid of gift shops, the temple remains pleasantly unspoilt by many of the excesses of modern Chinese tourism. A controversial figure who has excited praise and damnation in equal measure, the current abbot Shi Yongxin famously cleared out many of the old chancers and hangers-on and fiercely protected the temple's brand identity. Other elements are discreet – the hotel is tucked away in a corner, and the theatre is walled away from passers-by. If you want to eat something, you need to head back outside the gates, past the giant statue of a meditating monk, and down into the little vale near the petrol station in search of a restaurant to serve you Shaolin herbs.

Walking beneath a searing blue sky, I find myself in a place described by a 1,200-year-old proclamation: 'To the west [the monastery was built] by the side of a mountain torrent, lined with lonely woods of pine and cypress and to the north, over against a lofty bluff, covered in dense thickets of bamboo. Smoke patterned the dense clouds and darkness brought down heavenly incense. The mountain spring bubbled a clear note as dawn carried the Buddhist chant.'[1]

Although the grounds are impressive and the mountain vistas are sweeping, the entrance to the temple itself is somewhat low-key. It looks like little more than a red-walled hut atop a small staircase. The words 'Shaolin Temple' are engraved on a sign above the door, a gift from the Kangxi Emperor in 1704.[2]

Lisa Lau works in marketing for the temple, and doubles up as a tour guide. Hands in the pockets of her orange anorak, her breath fogging in the January cold, she shepherds me through the temple precincts, and the Forest of Pagodas where the remains of past monks are enshrined. The courtyards are packed with stone tablets, giving the names of prominent donors and important events. The most famous, the Shaolin Temple Stele, has been glued back together after being smashed up in 1928 – one of many occasions when the physical buildings of the temple were razed to the ground, only to spring up once more.

Here is the place where centuries of stamping feet have worn hollows into the flagstones; here is the tree trunk that bears the marks of monks' stabbing fingers. Or does it? Please make up your own mind, because the temple has no policy on superstition, for or against. Here is a medicine centre where you can buy Shaolin cough drops, Shaolin wound salve, and a giant sachet of herbs and berries that will make 'Shaolin medicine wine' when you mix it with four litres of vodka. Here is a statue of a mythical creature without an anus, which can only accumulate and never divest. It is a symbol of wealth and you may want to touch it for luck. Some people like to walk on the lotus flagstones to gain merit – you may want to do so. Or you may not.

Where does the Shaolin Temple come in the history of Chinese martial arts? Tales of its warring monks form the opening paragraphs of many a martial art's history. Shaolin is cited as the spiritual ancestor of most East Asian styles, particularly, of course, Shaolin kung fu, the Wing Chun school and the karate that carried it to Japan. But if we tell the story of the Shaolin Temple using actual historical documents, in the order those documents were produced, it takes literally centuries for the best-known and most-cited tales to appear. Shaolin is world-famous, but as noted in *The Princeton Dictionary of Buddhism*, this is only 'according to later traditions'.[3]

The Shaolin Temple was founded on the outskirts of Luoyang, then the capital of the Northern Wei dynasty, when the Tuoba tribe ruled much of north China. The Tuoba had enthusiastically adopted Buddhism, not the least because it was a foreign import like them, leading both Luoyang and the former capital at Datong to gain extensive grottoes depicting the images of saints.[4]

Foreign missionaries were also welcome. The Indian monk Buddhabhadra arrived in the 460s and served in the Wei capital for three decades before an emperor granted him a hillside near the city as the site for a temple complex in 495. His temple was sited on the Shao slope of Mount Song, one of China's sacred mountains, and derived its name from the surrounding forests of green saplings – *Shaolin*, the young groves.⁵ But Buddhabhadra was not the most famous resident at Shaolin; he was overshadowed by another figure that arrived three decades later.

LEGENDS OF BODHIDHARMA

The first historical mention of Bodhidharma comes in *A Record of Buddhist Monasteries in Luoyang*, a sixth-century account of what was then the capital of the Northern Wei dynasty, written by an imperial secretary in the days of the Tuoba's decline, when many of the religious buildings described were already in ruins. After singing the praises of the Yongning Monastery, the one-time pride of the capital, the book includes the name Bodhidharma among the people who come to wonder at it.

> The monk Bodhidharma of the Western Regions was a native of Persia [sic – other accounts specify India]. He came from the desolate frontier to visit China . . . Bodhidharma claimed at that time to be one hundred [and] fifty years old. But during his extensive travels, which had taken him to every corner of many countries, nowhere in the sullied world had he seen a monastery as elegant and beautiful as this one.⁶

The *Record* does not have anything else to say about Bodhidharma – it reserves its comments solely to his praise for the Yongning Monastery. Only later books make it sound as if he were something more of a celebrity, engaging a local ruler in a surreal debate, and moving to Mount Song to become a fixture at the Shaolin Temple. The stories of Bodhidharma gradually take on an oddly passive-aggressive nature, as the Buddhism he espoused seemed to drift away from previously accepted traditions. The first sign of it, unmentioned for centuries but retrospectively dated to around 527, was when he was permitted into an audience with Emperor Wu, founder of a successor dynasty to the Northern Wei.

Doubtless fancying himself as a wise ruler deserving of a walk-on part in a scripture or two, Emperor Wu asked Bodhidharma how much merit would accrue to him on account of all the monasteries he had founded and scriptures he had ordered copied.

'No merit at all,' said Bodhidharma.

Presumably thinking he had misunderstood or misinterpreted, the Emperor instead asked his visitor about the greatest of the 'noble truths.'

'Emptiness,' said Bodhidharma. 'No nobility whatsoever.'

Exasperated, the Emperor demanded to know who the hell Bodhidharma thought he was.

'I do not know,' came the reply.[7]

The Emperor was deeply unimpressed, although he had a change of heart soon after he had dismissed Bodhidharma from his presence. It was, however, too late. Bodhidharma left Emperor Wu's relatively new capital and made his way back to the old religious centre, Luoyang, where he made just as many enemies at the Shaolin Temple. That, at least, is the claim made in eighth-century chronicles, which are the first to associate Bodhidharma with the Shaolin Temple at all.[8]

There have been suggestions that Bodhidharma had trouble making himself understood, but whether that was his unexpected doctrines or a straightforward language barrier, it is difficult to say. Much early Buddhism was lost in translation, and the first few centuries of Buddhism in China are attended by multiple waves of charity-funded translation mills. The Shaolin Temple was one of them, but it was established so early in the history of Chinese Buddhism that it initially represented the elitist Hinayana tradition. Later arrivals like Bodhidharma were often representatives of

Mahayana Buddhism, a newer sect that offered the prospect of enlightenment to all comers, not merely a select few. That, at least, is what many locals must have assumed when Bodhidharma stated that his personal version of Buddhism was:

A special transmission outside the scriptures;
No dependence upon words or letters;
Direct pointing at the soul of man;
Seeing into one's nature.[9]

Bodhidharma was an unwelcome gatecrasher in the credential-obsessed world of the translator-monks. He could claim to represent a Buddhism that was both more modern and more closely Indian than whatever scriptures the Shaolin experts were currently pushing. Moreover, his preaching seemed to reject much of the documentary support of earlier Buddhist traditions: 'Long ago, the monk Good Star was able to recite the entire Canon. But he didn't escape the Wheel [of reincarnation] because he didn't see his nature. If this was the case with Good Star, then people today who recite a few sutras or shastras and think it's the Dharma are fools. Unless you see your mind, reciting so much prose is useless.'[10]

Bodhidharma came for an entirely new school of Buddhism, which he called *Dhyana* – 'meditative absorption'. This would eventually be translated into Chinese as *Chan*, but is best known to foreign readers by its Japanese pronunciation: *Zen*. Spurned by the monks of the Shaolin Temple, he then supposedly spent the next nine years practising what he preached, staring at the wall of a cave on a nearby mountainside. Supposedly, his shadow was burned into the rock – like many other miraculous elements of Shaolin, convincing evidence of this was supposedly destroyed in 1928 during a tussle between warlords.[11] It was during this period of intense concentration, according to another highly unlikely story, that

Bodhidharma became so frustrated with drowsiness that he tore off his own eyelids and cast them on to the ground, where they miraculously flowered into the first tea bushes. It is for this reason that extant portraiture of him often has a certain bug-eyed look.[12]

At some point during Bodhidharma's meditative seclusion, he was approached by Huike, a would-be disciple determined to learn from him. Bodhidharma, however, ignored his visitor, leaving Huike outside shivering in the cold as the snowflakes drifted around his knees. With Bodhidharma still refusing to teach him 'until the snows turned red', Huike supposedly cut (or according to the most sensational of accounts, cut *off*) his arm, spattering the ground with blood. The earliest extant source to mention the historical Huike, *The Continued Biographies of Eminent Monks* written a century after his death, does mention that he only had one arm, but accredits the loss of the limb to an encounter with 'scoundrels'.[13]

This is another dubious story of the Shaolin tradition, receiving lip service in the temple's contemporary layout, which includes a 'Standing in Snow' Pavilion. But Huike, so the story goes, was also a former military man, trained in elements of armed and unarmed combat. When Bodhidharma did eventually take him on, was it Huike who introduced elements of martial arts training to the religious life? And if so, why?

There is no answer in any manuscript from the first few centuries of Shaolin. But by the medieval period, when Zen Buddhism had grown from an obscure splinter group into a popular form of belief, new claims were made about Bodhidharma's contribution to the Shaolin Temple. His anti-intellectual approach to enlightenment, focusing on individual concentration and contemplation, was no easy road, since it demanded a great degree of physical fitness from his acolytes. According to the Shaolin Temple's own oral tradition, this led Bodhidharma to instruct the monks in a workout regime that included yogic breathing and callisthenics. Exercises anachronistically credited to Bodhidharma include the 'horse-riding stance', in which a student maintains a semi-squatting posture for up to an hour, ignoring the pain of their straining muscles by concentrating on a single thought. These exercises, it was said, included fighting moves.[14]

If this is true, then Bodhidharma was going against the injunctions of one of Buddhism's best-known scriptures. Buddha did not associate with boxers. That, at least, is the tone of the famous *Lotus Sutra*, the fourteenth chapter of which has a long list of inappropriate companions for an enlightened saint, including, but not limited to actors, dancers, nihilists, butchers and fishermen: 'A bodhisattva . . . is not intimate with kings, princes, ministers, and rulers; nor intimate with heretics . . . nor does he resort to brutal sports, boxing, and wrestling . . .'[15]

The placing of boxers and wrestlers in the admonitions of the *Lotus Sutra*, amid what other translations have called 'pranksters and jugglers', suggests that a class of professional fighters already existed in ancient India in addition to the military men one might expect, and that they were associated with what we might call sideshow spectacles.[16]

The *Lotus Sutra* was one of the first to be translated into Chinese; in fact, by the time Bodhidharma died, it existed in three different Chinese versions, so it was well known and highly valued among China's Buddhist community. However, we should also bear in mind that, if Bodhidharma transmitted any knowledge of fighting at all, it is more likely that he did so not from the perspective of a circus strongman, but from the *Kshatriya* warrior class from which he was purportedly descended. Nor should we immediately discount something merely because the *Lotus Sutra* warns against it – there are plenty of examples in later literature of 'Buddhist monks', even from the Shaolin Temple itself, seen to have been eating meat and drinking alcohol, also proscribed in the *Lotus Sutra*. Explanations have varied, from simple acceptance of the consequent bad karma, to a waiver granted them in order to increase their strength, to the more believable excuse that the 'monks' seen behaving in such a manner were merely toughs or refugees who had adopted monk status in order to evade capture and persecution, and hence were not monks at all.

An unarmed martial art, *kalaripayit*, is recorded as having been practised in India since at least the sixth century AD.[17] The yoga sutras date even earlier, first partially known in Chinese in ancient Chang'an in 148 AD, when the Parthian monk An Shigao translated the *Anapanasati Sutra*, introducing a Buddhist sense of 'mindfulness of breathing' that would have been familiar or attractive to any Daoist. 'On whatever occasion,' it says, 'the monk remains focused on the body in and of itself – ardent, alert, and mindful – putting aside greed and distress with reference to the world, on that occasion his mindfulness is steady and without lapse. When his mindfulness is steady and without lapse, then mindfulness as a factor for awakening becomes aroused.'[18]

Here, unlike many other critical junctures of the martial arts, there is at least circumstantial evidence of two elements existing at the same point in time, with further evidence of travellers who might have carried them from one point to the other.

But we are already getting ahead of ourselves, because there is no mention of such skill or training in the Chinese writings of the time, the most famous of which is still preserved, pieced back together, on the grounds of the Shaolin Temple.

THE SHAOLIN TEMPLE STELE

The Shaolin Stele is a four-metre high stone tablet, carved with important texts for conveying the history of the monastery. One dates from 621, and is the first mention of the temple in what we might call military dispatches. Another recounts an official snafu in 635, when the temple was accidentally included in a shutdown order issued against all Buddhist monasteries in former rebel territory. Still another dates from 728 and belatedly fills in some of the gaps in the temple's history, at a historically shaky distance of some two centuries from actual events.

Although it is only one of many stone tablets on the temple grounds, it is often referred to as *the* Stele, since it is the biggest and most influential. Topped with a dragon apex that denotes imperial approval, it is a vital document for understanding the history of the temple and the special place it occupies in history.

Part of the Stele records the service rendered by the monks of the Shaolin Temple to a prince in China's seventh-century civil wars – a prince who was eventually crowned as an emperor. In the unrest that attended the collapse of the short-lived Sui dynasty, one conniving nobleman forced his father's hand in choosing sides by smuggling some palace ladies out of the imperial capital, presenting them to his father as a *fait accompli*, and thereby incriminating him in a human-trafficking scandal that would force him to take a stand against the incumbent emperor.[19] Loyalists to the Sui dynasty put down rebellions with increasing wariness, as each became painfully aware of the machinations that were sure to lead at least some of them to proclaim their own dynasties. The Tang dynasty would eventually win the upper hand, but in 621 its founders were deeply grateful for any support they received from the temples and estates that surrounded the beleaguered capital.

The first emperor of the Tang, Gaozu, 'sent' his belligerent son to clean up a revolt by a Sui loyalist – the verb is questionable, because the son, the future Taizong Emperor, was so proactive and pushy that he had been manipulating his father like a puppet ever since the smuggled-concubine scandal. Regardless, the future Taizong Emperor got bogged down in the hills outside Luoyang, and would eventually order the carving of a monument on the grounds of Shaolin Temple, making it clear how much he valued the support of the monks in his time of need.

> You, Venerable Sirs, all possessing the ability to comprehend fully the principle of change and long ago having reached an understanding of karma, were able to make wondrous plans and restore the happy land to its rightful ruler, seizing that murderous bastard [Wang Shichong] and opening up that pure plot [the monastery and its estate]. The result of your obedience and loyal service has now come to the attention of the royal court, and your proven enlightenment and cultivation of Buddha nature have brought greater glory to the Buddhist persuasion.[20]

The nature of the Shaolin Temple's service is not all that clear. Unsupported Internet supposition suggests that Taizong was *captured* by Wang Shichong's agents, and only rescued by a heroic mission led by a dozen fighting monks. Similarly speculative historians suggest that Taizong was grateful for the arrival of a platoon of warrior monks in the final battle against Wang, although how a couple of dozen soldiers, no matter how well-trained, would help turn the tide against an enemy force of 300,000 men, nobody can say. Considering that the Stele records that the 'murderous bastard' Wang Shichong 'trespassed within the sacred Buddhist confines in perverse pursuit of his treasonable course', the monks may have merely done something so simple as detaining an unwelcome guest, taking a prominent strategic hostage and thereby allowing Taizong to win without fighting. Other parts of the Stele specify that the monks adjudged Taizong to be the subject of prophecies concerning the future ruler of China, captured his enemy's nephew and sent Taizong a statement of loyalty.[21]

There may even be meaning attached to the comment about their 'understanding of karma', in the sense that the monks of Shaolin saw which way the wind was blowing, and made a smart decision to back the eventual winner in China's internal struggles. The proclamation is dated five years before Taizong was crowned, and goes some way towards explaining how Shaolin, relatively close to the sometime Tang capital and famous for backing the winner before victory was clear, could be so highly regarded by the ruling house of the Tang dynasty.

A later proclamation, from 632, chronicles an about-face by civil servants, who had issued a closure order against all temples on former rebel territory, including the Shaolin Temple itself. The monks swiftly protested, reminding the throne of the Temple's previous service to Taizong, and leading to a hasty reversion of the order. This second document makes it abundantly clear why stone steles were required in medieval China – nothing would cut through red tape faster than a rubbing from an imperial decree, after all. Such tablets were carved and erected, literally set in stone, as safety measures in case of unrest and religious purges. Buddhism remained a foreign religion to the Chinese, and subject to occasional putsches and fluctuations in fortune. A lynch mob of rebels, bandits or religious fanatics from a rival order would be expected to think twice after seeing such an artefact, carved with the proclamations of two emperors, and topped by the emperor's own branding – twin dragons snapping at a giant pearl.

There may be other issues at work, as indicated by the fact that it is the Taizong Emperor, not his father, who so prominently supports these particular Buddhists. If – and it is a big if – Taizong had a particular love for the Shaolin Temple that went beyond a dashed-off thank-you note, it may have been related to the early stirrings of Zen that he found there.

THE NIRVANA SUTRA AND THE ICCHANTIKAS

Taizong was no mere princeling; it is better to think of him as the kingmaker of the Tang dynasty. Although it was his father who became the first emperor of the Tang, Taizong soon supplanted the official founder after a skirmish within the imperial palace itself, in which he killed two of his brothers. Taizong was an incredibly martial ruler, a general and soldier before he was ever an emperor. Establishing a new dynasty was only one of his achievements; soon after ascending the throne, he would plunge China into a war on foreign soil by embarking on an ill-fated invasion of the Korean peninsula.

Arguably, Taizong did not merely count on the Buddhists for their temporal support, but for the religious loopholes they offered that allowed him to continue a trend in his era for what has been called 'the nationalisation of warfare', taking war from a ritualised series of skirmishes between rival elites to a more generalised, all-inclusive, national campaign of conscription and conflict.[22] This involved not merely recruiting and training soldiers, but in persuading them to march and fight far from home. Traditional Chinese religion, mired in the considerations of Daoist sages like Laozi, preferred a gentle, inactive home life – the perfect death was achieved in one's home village, surrounded by one's family, not on a distant battlefield. Buddhism offered a new, remote alternative to such a parochial outlook, allowing Taizong to encourage his soldiers to march with him far away from home. He would eventually establish the Beijing area's first Buddhist temple as a repository for the souls of those soldiers who did not make it back alive from Korea.

The Buddhism of the Shaolin Temple may have held another kind of appeal for Taizong, in the form of its approach to killing. Among the religious texts translated by Buddhabhadra and his team in the temple's early days was the *Nirvana Sutra* (*Mahayana*

Mahaparinirvana Sutra), a first-century Indian document also known as *The Discourse on the Great Decease*, recounting the last six years of Buddha's earthly existence, and the agonies of his final days.[23] It is regarded in the wider Buddhist tradition as Buddha's last will and testament, and includes some defining elements of later Buddhist practice, including a direct admonition for true Buddhist believers to abstain from eating meat.[24] More controversially, among its many clauses and anecdotes there is a sudden mention of *icchantikas* – souls who have no chance of achieving enlightenment.

An obscure part of the *Nirvana Sutra* recounts the adventures of Buddha in a previous life, in which he felt completely within his rights to order the execution of priests who were slandering the true teaching, since he judged them to be incapable of achieving enlightenment. By the karmic reasoning of Buddhism, killing them would be a service of sorts, as it prevented them from generating even more adverse karma for themselves in this life, and might even be doing them a favour.[25] The reader can, perhaps, see how this facet of religious thought might meet with the approval of a ruler seeking to draft religious believers into his army. The concept, which in the wrong hands could be used as a justification for violence against non-Buddhists and even against fellow Buddhists decreed to be 'lost', is widely discredited in modern Buddhist thought, not the least because fuller translations of the *Nirvana Sutra*, including verses missing from the early Chinese versions, make it clear that even an *icchantika*, given the right re-education, might clamber his way out of a cycle of bad karma and towards enlightenment. Although the *Nirvana Sutra*, better translated, speaks of *icchantikas* as being on the brink of death and imprisoned within a negative cycle of karma, it merely recommends that Buddha's disciples 'drive away, reproach or impeach such a person'.[26] However, in the early days of the Shaolin Temple, its monks were seemingly armed with something more powerful than weapons: a scripture that, they believed, gave them permission to take up arms against their enemies.

A century later, another inscription was added to the Shaolin Stele, recounting the entire history of the temple and its fluctuating fortunes. It's only here, in 728 AD, that the monks' service is mentioned in any great detail, set within the context of the fall of the Sui dynasty: 'Rebel hordes attacked and pillaged, making no distinction between clergy and laity. The monastery was attacked by mountain brigands. When the monks and their disciples fended them off, the brigands set fire to the monastery and put the pagoda and cloisters to the torch. All the buildings along the cloisters suddenly went up in flames. The famous sacred pagoda alone remained, standing in solitary splendour.'[27]

Notably, the monks and disciples of the Shaolin Temple are powerful enough to hold off, at least temporarily, an attack by armed bandits. Clearly we are not dealing with archetypal pacifists. With the temple in ruins, the rebel general Wang Shichong seizes the nearby heights and begins recruiting soldiers for his bid for the throne, only to be opposed by the glorious soldiers of the Tang, led by Taizong who 'leapt forth as a dragon' from the central plains. 'The monks, Zhicao, Huiyang, Tanzong and the rest . . . led the monastic community in opposition to the rebel general and memorialised to show their supreme loyalty. They captured [Wang Shi]chong's nephew, Renze, and came over to the court.'[28]

No wonder Taizong seemed forgetful. The capture of an important hostage was certainly of valuable strategic use, but it probably amounted to a single skirmish in his long lifetime of warfare. The monks in question had turned down almost all tokens of imperial gratitude, grudgingly accepting a small grant of farmland to be added to the temple precincts, but refusing to take up several official government titles offered to them, including military sinecures.[29]

But while the Stele contains much about the mutual admiration of the temple and the early Tang emperors, there is nothing about military prowess. There is plenty about the pleasant views and the peaceful grounds, incense and sunlight, wise abbots and devout worshippers, and a long chronicle of celebrity visitors and donors during the seventh century, but no direct mention of the martial arts skills that would supposedly make Shaolin famous. In fact, apart from the cryptic reference to the temple's support for Taizong, the implication that the monks can hold their own in a fight, and a single line about the kidnapping of a prominent enemy, there is no mention at all of Shaolin's martial prowess or training anywhere in Chinese writing for another nine hundred years.[30]

THE EIGHTEEN HANDS OF THE LUOHAN

The intervening centuries did see several new stories arising about the later life of Bodhidharma, but only in terms of his philosophical achievements. One tradition stated that he somehow made his way to Japan, appearing as a starving beggar before the early Japanese Buddhist Shōtoku Taishi, and encouraging him to propagate the Buddhist faith.[31] Another suggests that he was spotted by a traveller in the distant western regions, walking back towards his native India, carrying a single sandal. When this sighting was reported back in Shaolin, his tomb was opened, and found to contain nothing but the other shoe.

In both cases, however, Bodhidharma's departure from this world came after a legendary conference with his greatest disciples, in which he asked them to express their understanding of Zen. Each pupil attempted to sum up his teachings. The first suggested that understanding Zen required an avoidance of scripture, but not entire detachment from it. Bodhidharma announced that the pupil had attained his skin. The second equated Zen with a flash of insight, like a fleeting glimpse of paradise. Bodhidharma said that the pupil had attained his flesh. The third stated that there was nothing to aspire to, because everything was meaningless. Bodhidharma said that the pupil had attained his bones. Then it was Huike's turn. But Huike simply stood, bowed, and sat down again. Bodhidharma said that Huike had attained his marrow, thereby suggesting that he had somehow understood the deepest and innermost nature of his teachings. It was as a result of this council that Huike, the former military man, was conferred with the leadership of the Shaolin sect after Bodhidharma's departure, entangling the monastery's subsequent fortunes with both Zen and martial arts.

Bodhidharma's fame grew along with that of Zen Buddhism itself, turning him into a sagely character in several popular Buddhist case histories and parables. But any involvement in the martial arts went entirely unmentioned until 1624, when a Daoist priest at Mount Tiantai wrote a manuscript on exercises, and falsely attributed it to Bodhidharma. Forged prefaces, purporting to be the work of Tang dynasty officials, claimed that renovations on Bodhidharma's tomb had uncovered an iron box containing two precious scriptures. The first was *The Muscle Change Classic* (*Yijin Jing*), an exercise manual divided into both 'inner' and 'outer' techniques for improving the physique – callisthenic regimes and breathing exercises. The Shaolin student was expected to master all the techniques of *The Muscle Change Classic* before moving on to the inner knowledge of *The Marrow Washing Classic* (*Xisui Jing*), which was later alleged to have been squirrelled away by the monks of Shaolin, and retained as a secret teaching.[32]

Devoted to the refinement of body and mind, and the strengthening of inner energies to bolster the immune system and fire up the brain, those fragments of *The Marrow Washing Classic* that have made their way into the public domain are almost incomprehensible, and if there were once any explanatory images, they have long since been lost. The monks of Shaolin themselves were said to have had trouble understanding its original Sanskrit annotations, and consequently to have only put some of its more esoteric elements successfully into practice.

The Muscle Change Classic, however, has been cited as the point at which the Indian tradition of yoga crossed over into the Chinese world. The timing is persuasive – yoga exercises flourished in India in the second century AD, and could easily have migrated into China with the same speed, and at the same points, as Buddhist scriptures.[33] But while the transmission seems plausible, there is no actual evidence of it, and certainly no directly visible connection to Bodhidharma. What little scholarly reaction there was to *The Muscle Change Classic* centred on the two prefaces, which were riddled with historiographical errors, including claims by the authors to have visited temples that were not yet founded at the time the text was supposedly written, and an intense confusion over reign dates and titles. The second, attributed to the famous general Niu Gao, claimed that its author was illiterate, despite the real Niu Gao's high-class education.[34]

But mere facts do not necessarily get in the way of a good story. Suitably dusty, *The Muscle Change Classic* was republished in 1827 – it is this edition, at least, less than two hundred years old, which is the oldest extant version of the work. The prefaces remained in place, despite their counterfeit origins, and have consequently confused all discussion of Bodhidharma's influence on martial arts ever since. He is, for example, cited as the author of both books in a recent American translation, despite the absence of any evidence associating him with them.[35]

A stripped-down version of *The Muscle Change Classic* was published under a different title, in a form that, if not representative of the martial arts of the Tang dynasty, is far more likely to reflect the training regime of at least one institution in the later Song or Yuan dynasties. Also attributed to Bodhidharma, and also with no real link to him, this is *The Eighteen Hands of the Luohan* (*Shiba Luohan Shou*). If it really did date from the sixth century AD, and Bodhidharma's interest in improving the physical condition of his disciples, then *The Eighteen Hands* would be the first extant manual of martial arts *kata*, a series of positions that can be combined into fighting movements. Unfortunately, the concept of eighteen *luohan*, which is the translation for an *arhat* or enlightened disciple of Buddha, does not appear to have even existed in Chinese until three hundred years after the time of Bodhidharma – in this case, it is the words of the title that let the forgers down.[36]

As with other stories, there is no actual evidence to connect him with either the topic or the time, but it is understandable why a narrator searching for an appropriate celebrity would latch on to him. Bodhidharma did, after all, arrive in China mere decades after the creation of the *Yoga Sutras of Patanjali*, a series of positions and poses incorporated into both Indian meditation and martial arts, and lived at a time when it is reasonable to assume he had access to Indian texts relating to the *silambam* staff-fighting technique, and the dance-like *Nara* fighting art alluded to in the *Lotus Sutra*. The eighteen hands include such stances as 'Lifting the Sky', 'Shooting Arrows' and 'Plucking Stars', and more demonstrative fighting moves such as 'Thrust Punch', 'Big Windmill' and 'Presenting Claws'. However, there is no way to accurately place the eighteen hands within the context of a development of martial arts skills before the seventeenth century.

SWORD DANCES OF THE SILK ROAD

There is little firm evidence of how the Shaolin Temple developed over the years immediately following Bodhidharma's departure. The published history of the Order of Shaolin Ch'an claims that martial arts and Zen Buddhism were firmly integrated at the Shaolin Temple within a century, and that the peculiar aspects of the Shaolin sect kept it relatively localised and obscure. Among such unique elements, it is claimed, was the number of reformed or escaped convicts who flocked to the temple, forming a lower echelon of novices who stood no chance of becoming fully fledged priests, but swelled the temple ranks.[37] Buddhist institutions certainly faced fluctuating fortunes during the Tang dynasty – often honoured by imperial decrees and donations, but occasionally swept up in putsches against religious organisations and tax evaders.

The Tang dynasty also presided over the height of the Silk Road, a time of great cross-pollination of contacts and the origins of a civil examination system that remained in place, more or less, until the early years of the twentieth century. However, when it came to testing an official's ability at 'the martial arts', the civil examination system required him to demonstrate a mastery of strategy, based on the military classics such as Sun Tzu, and archery, that old holdover from ancient times. Tests of brute strength were also often part of the examinations, but there is no mention of specific skills required in unarmed combat, nor would we necessarily expect them for soldiers who were expected to be either armed and armoured in the thick of the fighting, or issuing orders from a distant position of safety. The medieval examinations did not change much until 1898, when marksmanship with a rifle was belatedly added to the list of requirements. The exams themselves were suspended in 1902, since they were plainly woefully out of date.[38]

The Tang dynasty exposed the people of China to numerous influences from along the Silk Road – not merely the continued expansion of Buddhism from India, but new foods, luxuries and materials. Dances, too, migrated along the Silk Road from points further west, including the scandalous Sogdian Swirl, references to the 'bare-shouldered' finale of which seem to imply a topless big finish. Possibly in an effort to hold off such stripper pursuits with something more wholesome, the Tang court began to favour 'sword dances' performed by women, which appear to have duplicated many of the forms of combat-ready soldiers, but in a format now divorced from their original purpose. Once again, there is little clear information on the form that these 'sword dances' took, or their fellow 'spear dances', 'lion dances' and 'great face dances', although they are celebrated in poetry and chronicles from the eighth century, including cryptic references to one performed 'with empty hands' (*kong shou*). However, it is not clear whether this is the first reference to a series of forms and poses for unarmed combat, or an adaptation of a male sword dance by unarmed female dancers.[39] By the end of the medieval period, such a performance style had made it all the way to Japan, where the increasingly samurai-dominated ruling class developed a penchant for *shirabyōshi* – female singers in male drag who would dance with swords and scabbards.[40]

The Tang dynasty is justifiably remembered as China's golden age, and it certainly saw a massive and multi-directional number of intercultural contacts. The borders of China expanded to a high watermark that was not matched for many centuries, incorporating many foreign ideas, crops and cultural items into China, where their alien origins were swiftly obscured. At a time when the emperors would even demand a musical tribute – a command to incorporate foreign songs and metres into the local Chinese traditions, we should not be surprised that foreign ideas, exercises and perhaps even 'war' dances were not also imported.[41] What we lack is proof.

CHAPTER THREE

The Fist Canon

....

Night is falling and the smog shrouds the Beijing streets. I bypass the queue of locals lining up for the cheap seats and walk in through the door that brassily proclaims I am a VIP. Everyone is a VIP these days. Anyone with a loyalty card is a VIP, at Starbucks and the dry cleaners. Chinese signage has had to invent a new term, VVIP, for those people who are *very*, very important, whose cars get to drive up to the entrance porch instead of being marooned out in the car park, and who get to wait in a private lobby with plush armchairs and antimacassars.

Inside, there are glass cases containing weapons and costumes, posters of tours around the world. The theatre is promising a 'Shaolin performance: incredible feats of martial prowess'. That will do nicely.

I take my seat at the front row and an acolyte in orange comes out with a long spouted teapot. He launches into a spinning high kick, the splits and a twirl, and then bends his arms far back so that the spout protrudes over his head, pouring tea from a great height into my cup. It's impressive, but it's not what I would call martial. But the show has yet to begin.

There is a multiple clash of cymbals and the clatter of wood-blocks, and Chinese music grinds into life in a pentatonic wail.

Immediately, a troupe of dancing schoolgirls skips on to the stage, their hair tied in bunches, their rictus smiles freezing their faces underneath heavy make-up. They throw large hoops at each other, juggle with skittles and squeeze themselves into tubes. They spin plates on sticks and stack chairs upon the stage and upon each other. Soon they are joined by other performers, who begin by standing on each other before hurling each other through the air. The skills involved are an impressive roster of timing and technique, clearly impossible without years of back-breaking labour at a theatre school.

This is not what I came in for.

Neither is the bluff, striding Face Changer, a masked man with the goose-stepping stride of a Sichuan opera singer, who luxuriates in his own theme song. As the music swells and clangs, he bellows in Chinese about his multiple talents. *He is the man of a thousand faces. You never know who he will become,* and as he sings, his hands occasionally dart up to somehow switch the mask on his face. It changes colour. It is smiling. It is scowling. He stands right in front of me and reaches out his hand to shake mine. As I take his hand, his mask suddenly changes again – lightning-fast, his hands nowhere near it. The audience applauds and he exits with a grin and a flourish.

Finally, the 'monks' arrive. I know they are supposed to be monks because they are in the default orange of Buddhist novices, and with shaven heads. I squint at the programme, trying to identify likely weasel words in Chinese. Have these monks come *from* Shaolin, or did they study there, or near there . . . or are they monks at all? Shaolin is thick with martial arts schools . . . or maybe I am missing a character somewhere on the blurb that merely suggests Shaolin-*style*.

They pose and flail in the forms and positions of Shaolin kung fu, all perfectly in time, all clearly highly experienced in the forms. The music probably helps me consider this to be a modern interpretation of the mysterious 'war dance'. And then the weapons come out. They strut and fight with spears and swords, axes and staffs. A couple of the swords seem laughably flimsy, flexing in all directions as the fighter twists and bends – it is clearly merely for show, as indeed is the pole-arm with a business end that might as well have been made of tin foil.

The panoply of the 'eighteen weapons' has always seemed far-fetched to me. It's not the sort of list I expect to hear from a military man, but rather a second unit director on a movie set, casting around for some sort of original fight scene that hasn't yet been done, like Jackie Chan hitting people with a stepladder. I understand that a different skill is required to use a dagger from a spear, but far too much of the kung fu repertoire seems to be grasping at straws. One performer whirls a pair of incense burners on a chain. Is it really that necessary? Who raises his hand in kung fu class and says: 'What I'd really like to be a master of is the twirly incense burners'?

The performance takes on aspects of a conjuring show. There is some dramatic smashing of breeze blocks with human fists, and a man bending a metal rod over his head. There is some hokey nonsense about the power of human *qi* being able to drive the pointed essence of a steel needle through a pane of glass, to pop a balloon on the other side. Did Bodhidharma say anything about balloons? I don't think he did.

Of course, I am not watching real martial artists. I am watching a performance of martial arts. I am watching a theatrical troupe with a martial theme, designed to be the big finish after the plate-spinners and the chair-throwers. I am definitely seeing forms and performances that have been rehearsed and honed over many years, perhaps even centuries. But is it the martial arts *tradition*, or is it some sort of agglomeration of circus skills? Or are the two more linked than they may first appear?

THE LONG FIST AND THE EIGHTEEN WEAPONS

A generation after the fall of the Tang, China was reunited by the Song dynasty (960–1279), itself born from a coup conducted by a general of a short-lived successor regime. The founder of the Song dynasty, Zhao Kuangyin, the Taizu Emperor, was an experienced soldier, who exercised a powerfully military influence over the early years of his new state. It was the Song dynasty that saw the wider dissemination of the 'seven military classics' – ancient strategy manuals that had previously been far harder to acquire.[1] None of them, however, had anything to say about unarmed combat – that was the emperor's special thing.

He became associated with a martial art known as the Long Fist of the Taizu Emperor (*Taizu zhang quan*), which derived its name from his reign title and largely dealt with a number of unarmed fighting positions. In terms of modern fighting styles, it is oddly sparse – there are no blocks, for example, but a series of kicks and extended punches, seemingly designed to keep an opponent at bay without offering any opportunity for him to grapple. Some have suggested that the terminology used to name it implies the existence of at least one other form, a 'Short' Fist involving closer combat techniques, lost at the time, but possibly reinvented in modern close-fighting techniques of martial arts such as Wing Chun. Supposedly, the thirty-two positions of the Long Fist were invented by Zhao himself, and loosely adapted from forms practised at the famous Shaolin Temple. However, we have no record of them from his era; most of what is written about the Long Fist dates from at least five centuries later, and much of its modern aspect dates only from 1956.[2] Popular accounts of it drop aphorisms like: 'Hold your body like a cat, tense like a tiger, slide like a dragon, but strike like lightning.'[3] However, they neglect to mention that none of these phrases date from the Song dynasty at all, but from much later fictional accounts.

Despite such shaky evidence, the story of the origins of Long Fist seems more credible than most, mainly because of the likely need for such a story during the Taizu Emperor's own reign. Coming to power by overthrowing his own father and betraying the predecessor regime to which they had both previously been loyal, the first Song emperor pursued a policy influenced by Central Asian cultures that held a leader should have direct, demonstrable and superior skills in combat, which he might even be expected to employ in the ousting of other family members. His younger brother, who succeeded him under suspicious circumstances, had nowhere near his battlefield experience, and tried to make up for it instead by being accompanied at all times by a whirling, prancing entourage of flashy sword-dancers.[4]

This highly demonstrative military was often on full show at the Song capital, Kaifeng, with regular wrestling contests and drills designed to impress the populace and train the soldiers. There is evidence from the historical record that the early Song emperors were not above putting on an aggressive series of drills in order to demonstrate to visiting dignitaries just how disciplined and belligerent Chinese soldiers were. Witness this display from the late tenth century, when an ambassador from the Kitan tribes of the north got a real treat at dinner: 'Several hundred men in a great clamour with bare arms entered holding blades, leaping, catching and throwing, the performance complete in wonder. The Kitan envoy dare not look at it directly.'[5]

The performativity of the Song court was echoed in the Song capital, where an increasing urban population led to the rise of a merchant class. Brothels were nothing new in Chinese cities, but the Song saw the diversification of such delights into more general 'entertainment quarters', with palatial wine restaurants, tea houses, theatres and other sideshows. Among such diversions, contemporary diarists list performances of martial arts intended purely as entertainment, including 'boxing, wrestling, archery (with bow and crossbow), fencing, sword dances and so on'.[6]

It is in this period, both during the Song's early flowering, and in its latter-day decline in the south, that we first see references to

65

'the eighteen weapons'. Precisely what the eighteen weapons were is not a subject that Chinese sources can agree on, but the contending lists variously agree on swords, axes and spears – the basic building blocks of the Chinese army.[7] It is the remaining dozen or so that animate so many chroniclers of martial arts history, particularly since they seem so odd. Just as Roman gladiators in search of something new and flashy moved away from simple swords and spears to more complex costumes, themes and weaponry, the martial artists of Song-era China bean to specialise in ever more elaborate skills. Some, admittedly, are simple matters of scale – a two-handed axe versus a single hatchet; a trident instead of a spear. Others seem improvised, such as the various weaponised rice flails that crop up in martial arts accounts from this point on – the ancestors of the infamous *nunchaku*. Still others seem faintly ridiculous, like the twirling 'meteor hammer' or the distinctive tiger-claws.

One can easily imagine the relevance of, say, the so-called 'Shaolin staff'. A stick is a simple tool, after all, and any broom can be repurposed into such a weapon. One can also see the value of certain nuisance weapons that might be used to disarm and apprehend criminals. But in other cases, like the various chain weapons and over-sized blades to be found in many a kung fu performance, the emphasis seems to be merely on variety for its own sake, to give a roster of acrobats and jugglers something new and interesting to wave around on stage. Find me a general who has put in a request for a legion of meteor-hammer twirlers and I shall reconsider.

THE MONGOL CONQUEST

Northern China fell to the Mongols in 1234. The rest of the country was not conquered until the time of Genghis Khan's grandson, Khubilai, who proclaimed himself as the emperor of all China and the founder of the Yuan dynasty (1271–1368).

The Mongol regime marked a century-long gap in Chinese martial arts, in the sense that the Mongols themselves supposedly had no requirement for them. Depending on how one wanted to define it, the Mongol military either had no military training worth speaking of, or existed in a permanent state of military readiness, with each fighting man supplying his own horses and weapons, trained up through a lifetime of hunting and steppe life, with a number of skills that could be readily repurposed on the battlefield. Such a situation left the Mongols wary of their Chinese subjects, whom they much preferred to be gentle farmers, and whom they discouraged from training. That, at least, is the common story, although some modern scholars such as Christopher Beckwith have taken umbrage at the implicit racism – that all Mongols are blood-thirsty horsemen on a permanent war footing, and all Chinese are pacifist peasants.[8]

The Mongols had their own, long-standing tradition of wrestling, seemingly regarded as a relatively harmless pastime and test of manly strength, divorced from the realities of the battlefield – particularly considering the Mongol preference for horseback archery. But China under Mongol rule was an occupied, conquered territory, where the new ruling class imposed restrictions on the ownership of real weapons. 'Han [Chinese] people,' proclaimed a Mongol edict of 1322, 'are prohibited from holding weapons, going out to hunt, and practising martial arts.'[9]

The Mongol state prohibited the access of the general public to the 'eighteen weapons', creating something of a gap in personal protection, constabulary and home defence that is liable to have been filled by training in wrestling, grappling, unarmed combat and staff fighting – staffs, found in the hands of any traveller or monk, did not count as weapons and unarmed combat did not, apparently, count as a martial art.[10] As such, it may well be that the 'eighteen weapons' began as a proscriptive list, with a Yuan dynasty enforcer writing down a list of anything that he thought *could* be used as a weapon, rather than anything that previously had been.

According to the Shaolin Temple's own records – which are not necessarily to be trusted any more than anyone else's – this inadvertently led to the temple's greatest period of influence under the abbot Xueting Fuyu (1203–75), who somehow ingratiated himself with Khubilai Khan. Even before his conquest of south China, Khubilai is known to have surrounded himself with a coterie of religious advisers and wise men, pitting them against each other in a series of debates, with the implication (never quite honoured) that the intellectual victor would win Khubilai's own conversion to his religion.[11] The most famous of the debates was in 1258, when the Buddhist delegation trounced a group of blustering Daoists, whose claims to be able to perform miracles were found to be wanting. Although Xueting Fuyu was only one of three hundred Buddhist delegates, he was high ranking enough to take much of the credit for the debate, and was rewarded with the abbotship of the Wanshou Temple in what is now Beijing in 1260. He served in this position for fourteen years until shortly before his own death, placing the Shaolin sect high in the estimations of the Mongol authorities, and presiding over several conferences of sister-temples and affiliated monasteries.[12] Some Shaolin organisations claim that three of Fuyu's conferences were established with the intention of refining and rationalising disparate martial arts skills. Thus, the Shaolin Temple was not necessarily the *home* of certain forms of kung fu, but was the location where a widespread and diverse number of forms from all over China were debated, swapped, refined and then exported back out to the rest of the country. If this story were true, Shaolin would have been a point of origin in some sense for Chinese martial arts, but as a centre of discussion and dissemination rather than invention.[13]

The idea is beautifully even-handed, but, as ever, there are historical problems with this story. Firstly, today's Wanshou Temple in

Beijing was not established until more than a hundred years after these events supposedly took place, and since its name translates as the commonplace 'Longevity', it is difficult to work out which Wanshou Temple might be intended. Perhaps more importantly, there is no mention in contemporary sources of 'martial arts' being part of the skills and knowledge being discussed, although repeated comments regarding illusions, crowd-pleasing show-offs and impossible feats does suggest that some of the 'debates' between religions at Khubilai's court took a form more like a standoff between magicians.

Xueting Fuyu may well have been a prominent Buddhist in the entourage of Khubilai Khan, and he may well have come from Shaolin. If so, that certainly explains why the Shaolin Temple should suffer so grievously at the hands of the rebels who would eventually toppled the Mongols, as it would have been associated with the outgoing regime. It should, then, come as no surprise that in the 'Red Turban' uprisings that heralded the end of the century of Mongol rule, that the Shaolin Temple was attacked and burned by Chinese rebels in 1356.[14]

The Shaolin Temple would soon be rebuilt again, as it was on multiple occasions throughout history. It would return to the historical record in the Ming dynasty that followed that of the Mongols, when its monks were finally mentioned in reports of military action, rather than vague legend.

WHITE LOTUS AND RED TURBAN

The Ming dynasty (1368–1644) was founded out of nothing. After a century of Mongol rule, a series of natural disasters and a growing anti-foreign movement propelled the bandit leader Zhu Yuanzhang out of poverty and an early life as a minor monk, on to the battle-field, and subsequently to his crowning as the founder of a new dynasty. Zhu had been associated with the White Lotus (*Bai Lian*) cult, which believed in the imminent return of an 'Unborn Mother' who would gather her children to her at the end of the world. He may have even derived the name of his dynasty from the 'Great King of Light' (*Ming Wang*), prophesied by White Lotus believers to arise during the end times and associated with some of his early allies.[15] One of several anti-Mongol organisations, the White Lotus held seditious meetings under the cover of 'incense-burning' ceremonies, and would eventually become instrumental in several uprisings in which rebels wore red headbands and carried red flags. 'White Lotus teachings', in the Mongol period and for centuries afterwards, would become a catch-all title by the authorities for an entire basket of anti-establishment beliefs, and not necessarily the name of a specific secret society.[16] Zhu was one of several leaders in the 'Red Turban' organisations that grew out of the White Lotus meetings, and had slowly risen to the top amid thirty years of constant warring, targeting officials of the Mongol order, and quarrelling with other rebels about the direction of their new idealised society. Unlike the founders of the Tang dynasty, who were keen to associate themselves with Buddhism, the founders of the Ming dynasty were resolutely Daoist, largely in order to push themselves as home-grown, traditional, *Chinese* alternatives to a century of foreign influence, but also as payback for a number of Daoist institutions that had supported them with prophecies of their ultimate victory.

Military reforms were a crucial part of the first Ming emperor's policy. Fearful of a return by the Mongols from their Central Asian heartland, he maintained several standing legions of soldiers, who were settled in marchlands with hereditary positions – it was hoped, at least initially, that their children and their children's children would replace them. Most conspicuous among the military enterprises of the Ming period was the re-establishment of the famous Great Wall – the photogenic spans of it that survive today largely date from this period, and not any other, earlier wall-building regimes. The establishment of Ming dynasty control led to many years of purges and persecutions of anyone associated with the Mongols or with potential imperial rivals. Neither was it over after the first Ming emperor's death, when a conflict broke out among his sons over the succession. The victor, the Yongle Emperor, would move the capital of China from Nanjing in the south to Beijing in the north in order to keep administration close to his own personal fief, which itself had been established in permanent military readiness against Mongol resurgence.

Ming China maintained a huge standing army by historical comparison with other dynasties, not merely to defend against its old enemies, but to police internal unrest. Although the hereditary nature of many of these army postings soon dragged them into mere sinecures and honorary positions, there were still plenty of military men in circulation, some of whom were put to work conquering new territories. It was not that the Ming empire was necessarily expansionist, but rather that its early emperors decided to hang on to Yuan dynasty conquests like Xinjiang and Yunnan that might have fallen away again from the Chinese sphere. The Ming empire would also push into the north-west, settling the forested hills of Manchuria, provocatively to the north of the famous Great Wall, and leading to close and ultimately disastrous encounters with the Jurchen people of Manchuria.

Ming China also faced a new and unexpected problem, in the form of constant attacks from 'Japanese' pirates. Although popular legend often claimed these sea-borne raids originated in Japan, the Ming dynasty's own chronicles would eventually admit that up to 70 per cent of them were Chinese locals. The pirates were sometimes branded as 'Japanese' by local law enforcement, who stood to get higher rewards for a Japanese kill, but also by the Chinese authorities, who did not want to admit that so much internal unrest had local origins. In fact, the pirate problem included Chinese, Koreans and Japanese, an entire underclass of outlaws from the margins of society, whose predations reached a peak in the mid-sixteenth century. Despite early successes and voyages of exploration, the Ming dynasty had largely given up on maritime expansion by this point, leaving the remnants of its navy relatively defenceless against pirates with nothing to lose. As pirate confidence grew, raids became progressively longer and more invasive, until such a time as chronicles offered suspicious accounts of 'pirate' attacks many miles inland, comprising assaults by armoured cavalry. The Ming dynasty, bogged down in the defence of the north from the Mongols and their successor regimes, was forced to recruit its anti-pirate forces from increasingly diverse sources, including pardoned criminals, aboriginal tribesmen, ex-pirates and even monks.[17]

A similar situation appears to have arisen around the same time in Japan, where the spiritual sanctuaries of the temples and monasteries were crowded with less-than-devout acolytes, forming the early ranks of what came to be known in Japanese as sōhei, 'warrior monks'. Becoming an aspirant required three years' study at an accredited institution, the rote memorisation of entire sutras and a demonstrable understanding of complex issues in Buddhist philosophy. It was another three years to become a fully fledged monk, with a job description that came with two hundred new rules, including a ban on meat and violence.

By the ninth century, such strictures were sufficient to put most serious applicants off, although the poor and needy still regarded a monastic life as a step up from the misery of their own existence. Standards predictably fell over the next two hundred years, until temple recruits were largely drawn from vagrants, refugees and low-ranking samurai who had given up on the prospect of promotion.[18]

Usually I shy away from cross-cultural comparisons, but the China–Japan warrior–monk parallels seem both timely and apt. Just as hungry mouths and refugees were flocking to Japanese temples and forming a belligerent underclass of unlikely acolytes, it is reasonable to suspect like-minded figures in China seeking a similar escape. Those who failed to find sanctuary at temples, of course, would instead swell the ranks of the 'pirates' preying upon the Chinese coast, suggesting that much of the development in both piracy and 'warrior–monk' rivalry in the period was a matter of simple demographics. In both China and Japan, temple lands were often used for tax evasion, with powerful local interests 'donating' lands to a temple in order to continue to profit from them, while reaping a holy exemption. These temple tracts could become so large, and so powerful that they would eventually take on aspects of small communities or nations, requiring their own administrations and paramilitary forces. In that regard, we might even *expect* the increasing fame and fortune of the Shaolin Temple to lead inexorably to the development of a paramilitary wing.[19]

The Ming dynasty, for much of its reign, was not troubled by large armies massing on its border; or rather, devoted much of its standing army and wall-building to pre-empting any potential attacks by such foes in the north. Whether it was Mongol raiding parties or pirate strikes, the main and immediate danger to the people of Ming China lay in opportunist banditry. This could be said to have transformed the state of mind of the Chinese in the period, into a constant, watchful state of readiness. Military activities, including training in the martial arts, returned to conditions they may have had in the ancient past, as one of localised, constabulary training.[20]

Popular myth holds that monks from the Shaolin Temple distinguished themselves on the field of battle in the 1500s by participating in the Chinese efforts to thwart attacks by these 'Japanese' pirates. However, although fighting monks are known to have taken part in four battles in the 1550s, these were relatively small-scale affairs. Their most famous victory, at Wengjiagang in 1553, saw a force of 120 monks from several temples, not exclusively Shaolin, fighting a series of skirmishes over ten days, mercilessly pursuing a hundred-strong pirate band even as it retreated, massacring every last one of them, including a fleeing wife, clubbed to death with an iron staff – the fact that roving pirate bands included women and children should be clue enough that these 'raids' were not quite as described in the government accounts.

The degree to which the 'monks' were former soldiers recalled from contemplative retirement is not discussed in the reports of Zheng Ruoceng's report *The Strategic Defence of the Jiangnan Region* (1568). However, it does specifically mention that this 120-strong group of fighting monks was led by Tianyuan, a man from Shaolin who had somehow earned his position by defeating eighteen other local candidates. By chance, the number of opponents suggests that eighteen rival skillsets, like the famous 'eighteen weapons', have been bested by an unknown *nineteenth* technique. It does not take much to imagine old-time storytellers suggesting that this was, in fact, the absence of any weapons – the superiority of the unarmed man who is pure of heart.

'I am *real* Shaolin,' Tianyuan is reported as saying. 'Is there any martial art in which you are good enough to justify your claim for superiority over me?'[21]

The account of Tianyuan's trials is interesting for the specific emphasis placed upon the Shaolin Temple and his mastery of unarmed combat. He is reported as taking on eight further champions selected by his challengers, and defeating them at a gateway outside a temple.

His eight assailants tried to climb the stairs leading to it from the courtyard underneath. However, he saw them coming and struck with his fists, blocking them from climbing.

The eight monks ran around to the hall's back entrance. Then, armed with swords, they charged through the hall to the terrace in front. They slashed their weapons at Tianyuan, who, hurriedly grabbing the long bar that fashioned the hall's gate, struck horizontally.[22]

The breathless, physical account reads like a synopsis from a kung fu movie, but is all the more exciting to the historian because it was written only a decade after the events it is supposed to describe, by an author without a vested interest in promoting Shaolin or kung fu. In fact, Zheng Ruoceng's account is one of the earliest to seriously consider Shaolin kung fu synchronically, which is to say, as it happened. It is a real point in time, discussing real people and verifiable events – the first to not only associate Shaolin monks with the fighting arts, but specifically with unarmed combat skills. Zheng went on to note that Shaolin was the greatest institution for contemporary martial arts, crediting it not only with the skills of its own monks, but with educating the monks at Funiu, the second-best martial monastery. A third, at Mount Wutai, was also credited with fighting skills, but specifically with spears. Zheng finished his report by recommending that the Ming authorities actively conscript monks to fight in bandit suppression.

THE NEW MANUAL ON MILITARY EFFICIENCY

The Ming general Qi Jiguang (1528–87) was instrumental in the suppression of the Japanese raids, and in many attempted reforms of the Ming military. Inheriting a family military position in Dengzhou, he proved himself to be an able commander during the Ming dynasty's troubles against would-be Mongol returners and sea-borne Japanese raiders. In a time when many hereditary sinecures were filled by the idle and feckless, Qi's genuine military acumen swiftly attracted the notice of superiors, who effectively shielded him from jealous rivals, fearful ministers and obfuscating bureaucrats, allowing him to flourish and succeed.[23]

Already an experienced veteran of wars against the Mongols and years of campaigning against pirate infestations in Zhejiang and Fujian, Qi was still in his thirties when he wrote the first edition of his *New Manual on Military Efficiency* (1560), a detailed account of military matters, going far beyond the basics of Sun Tzu's *The Art of War*, into areas of morale, management, drills, specific weapon guides, signals and guerrilla warfare. As one scholar notes in amazement: 'He even handed out a recipe for making field rations!'[24]

Qi's book is captivatingly concerned with the day-to-day management of a military force, complete with formations and tricks designed to take down standard groups of Japanese pirates. Some of these tactics were admirably flexible – small 'Mandarin duck' formations of pikemen protecting a core of more traditional soldiers, designed to take out the maximum number of Japanese attackers before the enemy could get within sword range. Others were more ruthless and questionable – such as his ready acceptance of heavy initial losses, on the grounds that the Japanese would soon tire of the sheer effort involved in flinging them against his defences. In order to maintain such foolhardy loyalty among his men, he was a strict disciplinarian ready to execute any deserters.[25]

Qi Jiguang was no stranger to the use of monks – he was ready to recruit his soldiers anywhere possible, and with an eye always on the longer term, was reluctant to use the farmers on whom he would also have to rely for supplies. His *New Manual on Military Efficiency* openly praises the 'Shaolin staff', not the least for the relative ease with which a mere stick can be sourced for conscripts, as opposed to a technically intricate bow or sword.[26] However, the *New Manual* is most notable for its fourteenth chapter, 'The Fist Canon and the

Essentials of Nimbleness', in which Qi offered a critical assessment of all the unarmed martial arts then in use.

Qi openly states that he does not regard unarmed combat as a practical skill of much use on the battlefield. However, he concedes that it offers a vital edge in physical training and in postures and forms liable to aid any soldier, almost as if going through the attack forms of the Maiden of Yue, but without a sword in hand – perhaps there have been allusions to this in earlier texts, such as the 'empty-handed' sword dancers of the Tang dynasty. Such knowledge, Qi observes, is 'equivalent to an oblique lightning bolt'.[27]

> Among the past and present fist specialists, the Song Great Founder had the Long Fist system with 32 positions, Moreover there are six pace and fist techniques, the Monkey Fist and Feinting Fist. The famous positions each have their own names, but in reality they are quite similar and scarcely differ from one another.
>
> Looking at Master Wen in the present day, we have the 72 moving fist methods, the 36 combining and locking techniques, the 24 counter-spy techniques, the 8 flash flips and the 12 short strikes. They are the best of the lot.[28]

Note that it is here, more than five hundred years after the time of the foundation of the Song dynasty, that the Long Fist system is first mentioned. 'The gentleman well versed in these arts has quick hands and legs like the wind,' Qi writes. 'I myself have the ability to whip my legs and smash things as well as split heavy objects with my hands.'[29]

General Qi's assessment, however, notes that whatever these traditions may have been, many elements of them have already been lost, such that 'some are missing the upper part, some the lower'. He himself attests to having trained in the 'striking fists school of a master called Liu Caotang, but he makes it clear that his assessment of twenty-seven styles is not exhaustive. Other manuals, published around the same time, allude to several other styles in existence, taught by masters not mentioned by Qi, particularly in the south where Qi's researches were less thorough.[30]

This is frustrating for the historian. We go almost overnight from a situation where there is no real evidence, to a situation that plainly points to a multiplicity of schools in existence at the time that Qi undertook his research. Moreover, his accounts of martial techniques repeat what appear to be poetic, mnemonic devices; they lean on stances that are not pictured. Some may be guessed at by association with, for example, the 'Five Animal Frolics' of Daoist exercises, although others are entirely mysterious. 'In the Crouched Tiger posture, angle the body off the centre line and work the leg; whenever the opponent engages me, I stretch out to the front. When I see my opponent poised, his stance is not stable; then I sweep his single supporting leg – the result is clear and decisive.'[31]

General Qi refined the forms he had picked up into thirty-two basic postures, which he taught his men as part of their training. In a difficult chicken-and-egg situation, a good half of Qi's forms survive today in modern *taiji quan* – it is impossible to say whether he learned them from forgotten taiji masters, or if early modern taiji practitioners lifted them from Qi's book. Taiji apologists are ready to believe the former; historians tend to side with Stanley Hemming, who regards modern taiji as an invention of the 1870s that struggles to assign roots to itself before that date.[32]

Qi Jiguang is one of several writers whose works on contemporary martial arts forms have been preserved from the time of the late Ming. Many of them are preoccupied with a similar problem – the separation of a practical system of combat from a number of highly stylised demonstrations. The term *hua quan*, literally 'flowery fists' crops up in a number of works from the period, and seems to refer to an overly flashy series of forms designed more for display than combat.[33] The precise nature of 'flowery fists' has kept scholars busy ever since. Some have suggested that the debate over 'flowery fists' is simply a matter of theatricality and practicality – a split between the performance of what Confucius might have called a 'war dance' in ancient times, and the actual skills required to dispatch a hostile opponent. Others have argued that the most ostentatious moves of what we might call 'shadow boxing', at least in some martial arts, are merely a showcase of distractions designed to fool an observer or opponent, and do not necessarily reflect the true nature of the techniques they conceal.[34] Others have taken it even further, pondering whether it could be the earliest indicator of a debate in the martial arts world between the more obvious 'external' physical forms and a subtler 'internal' spiritual cultivation.[35]

It is likely that certain techniques in the martial arts have been discovered, forgotten and rediscovered on multiple occasions in Chinese history. But the *New Manual on Military Efficiency* and its availability in significantly larger numbers allowed for Qi's discoveries and ideas to survive thereafter, and not merely in China. In 1593, the Japanese warlord Hideyoshi ordered an invasion of Korea, designed in part to shift the passions of thousands of spare samurai from his recently completed civil war, and to make them a foreign country's problem. Chinese troops entered the conflict to shore up the Korean regime and shoo the Japanese off the mainland. In doing so, they carried knowledge of the *New Manual on Military Efficiency* to Korean soldiers. Ordered to produce a local version by the Korean king, the author Han Gyo responded with *The Compendium of Several Martial Arts* (Muyejebo). Unfinished at the time of its patron's death, it was completed in 1610 with the addition of materials lifted from four Japanese manuals to make the *Sequel Compendium of Martial Arts* (Muyejebo Sokjip).

These works remained at the core of the Korean martial arts tradition. They were revised as the *Muye Shinbo* (*The New Compendium of Martial Arts*) in 1759 and eventually into the *Muye Dobo Tongji* (*The Comprehensive Illustrated Manual of Martial Arts*) in 1795. Much of the additions, however, involved the use of certain weapons on horseback and extensive additional comments on cavalry skills. By this point in the evolution of the book, it had firmly included a chapter on boxing (*gwonbeop*) deriving from Qi's own work. With any native Korean material destroyed in various fires and earlier wars, it is this that is likely to have formed the 'traditional' underpinnings of subsequent Korean martial arts.[36] The book was similarly influential in Japan, when the Chinese edition proved to be a major source for the writings of the eighteenth-century author Hirayama Gyōzō, who attempted to adapt what he called the 'eighteen martial arts' (sic – not eighteen weapons!) of Qi Jiguang into an updated, localised version.[37] Ironically, however, the chapter on unarmed combat was dropped from a later edition of General Qi's original book. In 1584, disenchanted with the Ming regime and relieved of his command, he revised his manual, oddly choosing to delete the 'Fist Canon' chapter from it, possibly because he wished his legacy to avoid imitable violence that was outside the purview of the true soldier.[38]

By the 1590s, the Long Fist and several other forms of martial art had become incorporated into household compendia, designed to instruct the ideal homemaker on the essentials of life. Amid chapters on family health, etiquette, animal husbandry and crop management, there also appear brief guides to unarmed combat, complete with rhyming mnemonic devices for memorising the positions of such arts as the 'Wen Family Moving Fist' and the 'Spear-Seizing Fists'. The martial arts, in a form that would be familiar to us today, had entered Chinese popular culture to stay.[39]

THE FIST CANON

THE WATER MARGIN — EVIDENCE FROM FICTION

Qi Jiguang's research pointed to a world of martial arts lore that was taken for granted by his contemporaries and hence not adequately documented. Factually, he represents a Year Zero of verifiable accounts of martial arts, but we can also look to other sources for hints of what may have gone on before.

One of the reasons that the Ming dynasty is such a watershed moment in the history of the martial arts is a matter of volume. Woodblock printing technology allowed for a wider dissemination of texts in larger print-runs, and the relative closeness of the Ming era to our own – separated by a mere handful of centuries – increases the chances of paper artefacts surviving in a legible condition. Ming dynasty printing has preserved, albeit in altered form, many of the stories and plays of previous centuries, such as *Journey to the West*, a heavily fiction-alised account of the monk Tripitaka's quest to bring back sacred Buddhist scrolls from India, in which his pugnacious assistant the Monkey King became a perennial children's favourite. Famously, the Monkey King usually fights with a magical iron staff that only he can lift, but there are occasions in the novel where he must fight unarmed. When he does so, the text throws in a number of forms clearly derived either from the martial arts, or from the theatrical depiction of them:

> They started with a foursquare stance,
> Kicked with pairs of flying feet . . .
> The Immortal Pointing the Way;
> Laozi Riding His Crane . . .
> When the demon used a Guanyin Hand
> Monkey countered with an Arhat's Foot.[40]

The same period also saw the publication of *The Water Margin*, which is likely to have begun as a song cycle in the early days of the Mongol period, before transforming over time to a series of plays, and ulti-mately being set down in novel form in the Ming dynasty. *The Water Margin*, which underwent several revisions and variant editions in the subsequent centuries, lends itself well to diverse storylines, with a general narrative arc of *hao han*, 'good fellows', who are transformed into outlaws by a corrupt regime, and hiding out in the rivers and lakes of the Liangshan marshes in Shandong, north-east China, from which they occasionally ride forth to dispense justice and right wrongs. Coincidentally, the Robin Hood-like tales of the 108 heroes of *The Water Margin* are set in the same era as those of Robin Hood himself, albeit on the far side of the planet.

We must be careful with fictional sources. The martial arts world accretes many more of them from this point on, but the researcher should be wary of according too much credence to some of the claims made within them. Fictional sources, by their very nature, seek to redact and sensationalise, even when purporting to tell a true story they are liable to leave out the boring bits and spice up the encounters. From the earliest days of Chinese theatre, when puppeteers capital-ised on their puppets' abilities to make superhuman leaps, fly and otherwise perform supernatural feats, fictional accounts of the martial arts have been ever subject to the easy temptation of special effects.

Instead, we should look in fiction for inadvertent glimpses of everyday life, of sights and sounds of forgotten eras, and for mundane details that might evade an earnest chronicler. *The Water Margin*, for example, offers an alternative angle on the long tradition of temples as schools of the martial arts, instead suggesting that certain monasteries, remote and protected by imperial fiat, could often function as meeting points for would-be rebels who were already martially skilled, rather than trained on-site.[41] It frequently alludes to the physical benefits of a diet of meat and alcohol, both proscribed to genuine Buddhists, but somehow acceptable to fight-ing monks with a fanatical mission.[42]

More pertinently, it also bestows a glimpse of daily life in the Song dynasty, or at least the Song dynasty as it was imagined by a Ming author. When it comes to the martial arts, one of the most telling things about the dozens of fighters profiled in the book is the way that they have learned their skills.

> The majority of the heroes learned their martial arts while in the military. Many of the bandits picked up their remarkable skills as part of their lawless lifestyle. There are even allusions to a few members of the gentry who collected talented martial artists and taught some of their skills to their own retainers. But of the 108 heroes profiled in the book, *not one* of them learns their martial arts in a formal school with a Sifu [Master] and fellow students.[43]

It is an absence, not a presence, but it is a powerful one. Despite all the claims that would be made from the Qing dynasty (see the next chapter) for martial arts schools and traditions, despite all the depictions of such institutions in a thousand kung fu movies from the twentieth century, exactly none of them appear in China's biggest martial novel. Even if it seems like common sense, it bears repeating here – the bulk of all martial arts training and martial arts knowledge until the Ming dynasty was in the hands of the military, and remained simple and practical.

There is, however, an exception in *The Water Margin*, which itself offers an intriguing window into more performative and theatrical displays. *The Water Margin* does in fact contain scenes in which the martial arts are employed, not in the defeat of an opponent, but as a demonstration routine used to advertise artisanal potions.[44] What better way to demonstrate the efficacy of a medicine man's cure-all, wonder-elixir, health tonic or similar snake oil than to commission a strongman or showman to put on a demonstration of incredible feats of strength or martial prowess? We know that this practice would continue into the modern era – in fact, the son of Ip Man, famous Wing Chun practitioner, would recall similar street performers shilling for medicine salesmen in the twentieth century.[45] But the first evidence of it in olden times comes in fictional form, from *The Water Margin*.

An association with medicine, of course, would also connect practitioners of the martial arts directly to acupuncture, massage and other such physician's arts. As noted by Peter Lorge, if anything is going to distinguish between 'external' martial practice and 'internal' physical well-being, it would be the direct correlation of certain spheres of martial arts knowledge with human health and street showmanship.

CHAPTER FOUR

Secrets and Shadows

············

It only takes our fellow diners a single bottle of Western Phoenix before they are jolly and amenable. Master Li is wearing a little beige hat and a sports shirt that makes him look like a Japanese tourist – a far cry from the cover of his martial arts manual, where he is shown in blazing white, traditional kung fu pyjamas.[1] There is little clue as to his profession, except perhaps the fact that he looks oddly spry for his seventy-two years. He knows his way around acupuncture and Chinese medicine, having practised for many years as a herbalist. This, it seems, in both his native Foshan and his adopted home of Chongqing, is sure to go hand in hand with martial arts knowledge. Master Li has been studying the 'Diamond Fist' style of Shaolin boxing for fifty years, starting under the tutelage of a now-departed twentieth generation grand master, which makes him the twenty-first. He knows his way around the 'Eight Immortals Turn' and the 'Iron Fan', and a bunch of other moves I have never even heard of. He knows the Long and Short Fists, the spear, the sword and the pole, and despite the ideological anguish that it would cause many of his forebears with their legendary Buddhist–Daoist rivalry, has no qualms about learning and teaching taiji as well.

'I hear you are third-rank in Shaolin fists,' he says to my wife. 'Let's see what you've got.'

Mrs Clements is also deep enough in her cups not to feel shy, and leaps to her feet. She immediately launches into a series of punching, grappling forms. They are surprisingly brutish and rough. This is no 'flowery' kung fu – her fighting technique is resolutely practical. Punches come almost two handed, a second hand following fast behind the first, ready to block an anticipated counter-strike. Kicks are low and close – this is a brawler's martial art, undertaken with the expectation of hard knocks and genuine danger. Although her style claims to be descended from Shaolin, it has none of the wide, sweeping gestures that southern Chinese popular culture, and particularly the film industry, associates with Shaolin. Shaolin, if you listen to the armchair pundits and movie buffs, is all about big sweeps, which is why Wing Chun gets in close as soon as possible with little punches, to duck under the radar of so many Shaolin tactics.

She finishes and the Chinese applaud at the novelty of it all.

'Now you,' she says, bowing to Master Li.

He steps back from the table and looks around the banqueting suite with an impish smile.

'You are very practical,' he chuckles. 'What I do is more like an art. This is Dragon style. It is a form derived from the Supreme Ultimate, the body at one with the flows and patterns of the universe. It is fluid, and soft . . .' As he speaks, he begins the familiar slow-motion weaves of taiji, his palms outstretched as if receiving energy from the air next to him, he swirls and bends and twists in the eye of an imaginary storm, every motion following seamlessly from the next, seemingly without stress or strain.

Master Li speeds up. His movements no longer echo the snail's crawl of old people's taiji, but the athletic, blurred motion of a real martial art. He loops and spins, churning unseen forces in the air with his hands . . . and then he comes to a stop.

I suspect that if Mrs Clements could land a single one of her piledriver punches on him, he would go down like a sack of potatoes. But I also seriously wonder if she would be fast enough, or if she would ever be able to hit him square enough that any of the force of her attacks would actually reach him. There is a lot of the 'flowery' martial art in Master Li's display, but it demonstrates all too well how a defensive posture can defeat an offensive one, simply by tiring an attacker out with endless failed punches.

'You are doing very well,' he says to Mrs Clements when the second round of applause dies down. 'I look forward to seeing your next steps.'

He is seventh-*dan* in *wushu*, the Chinese state's sports version of the martial arts. Several decades of experience ahead of Mrs Clements, there is no shame in him out-performing her for the crowd.

There are still plenty of bottles of Western Phoenix to get through, and many more dishes to come. Mrs Clements goes back to talking about handbags with her neighbour. The assembled dignitaries and hangers-on go back to their food. Master Li sneaks outside for a cigarette, and I follow him.

We stand on the riverside balcony in the balmy, wet heat and stare across the Yangtze at the skyscrapers of Chongqing, looming in the haze like a super-sized Manhattan.

'I hear you're writing a book about martial arts,' he smiles. 'How is that going?'

I confess that I am having incredible difficulty nailing down any actual facts. Everything evaporates into bluster. Nothing seems possible to confirm at any point before the Ming dynasty. And the homogenous, unified face of modern China conceals a vibrant, multi-centred world with huge divisions between north and south – cultural, linguistic, aspirational. Maybe some of the legends are true, but even if they are, they were the cant of rebel organisations that have been purged and executed on multiple occasions. Sometimes I am repeating the echo of an echo of an echo, of something that someone may have misheard anyway.

'Someone taught my teacher,' he says. 'Someone taught my teacher's teacher. And back, and back . . .'

Yes, I want to say. But somewhere in that line of transmission, someone was lying.

'My martial art goes back twenty generations,' he continues. 'Or at least, that's what the master told me when he taught me. I can't tell you, for sure. I can't tell you a single thing about the first generation. All I can tell you is that these are the forms, and these are the stances, and that *someone* worked them out and passed them on. The history doesn't really matter to me, only the practice.'

THE MANCHU INVASION

In 1644, China was lost once more to foreign invaders. The Ming dynasty, which had ruled for three centuries since the toppling of the Mongols, itself collapsed at the culmination of a series of climatic and governmental disasters. Poor crops, harsh winters, famines and floods combined to fatally weaken its authority, while north of its borders, the rulers of Manchuria began ominously shadowing China's institutions.

The old Manchu capital, Shenyang, still retains traces of this long-term exercise in political stalking. Rulers of Manchuria were buried in tombs designed to mirror those of the Ming emperors. A 'Forbidden City' was constructed in Shenyang, mimicking the institutions and architecture of the similarly named citadel in Beijing. In China's north, the Manchus began spreading the word that the Ming dynasty had lost the mandate of heaven. It was, instead, the fervently martial Manchus who deserved to rule all under heaven: a military aristocracy divided into eight all-encompassing legions or 'Banners', endlessly preparing for war. A generation before the Manchu conquest, they had already co-opted many northern Chinese defectors into their regime.

Matters came to a head when a revolution within China toppled the incumbent Ming emperor. Holding the Great Wall with nothing but charisma to keep his unpaid men at their posts, a Chinese general heard that the usurper in Beijing had killed his father and raped his lover. Giving up on help from his own side, he signed a fateful pact with the Manchus, inviting them into China to help him retake the capital.

The Manchus would never leave. Their army took Beijing and rolled southward, eventually sweeping across all of China. Those Chinese who had defected without a fight were bought off with dukedoms and sinecures, but the new boy-emperor, Shunzhi, was a Manchu. For the next two and a half centuries, China was a country under occupation, with garrisons of Manchu bannermen in every city. Male subjects were expected to show their allegiance by shaving the front of their heads and wearing their hair in a long braid – infamously, this was a sign of slavery in Manchuria, imparting each man with the look of the backside of a horse.

Hair was a huge issue among the newly conquered Chinese. Many loyalists went to their deaths over their refusal to adopt the odd and oppressive hairstyle, while art and literature swiftly looked back to a past where characters were not immediately identifiable, by their tonsure, as victims of Manchu oppression. But the hair directives swiftly led to a new form of subtle rebellion – the adoption of a monk's status. Monks, of course, had shaven heads, which meant that officially joining a temple allowed an anti-Manchu figure to have the same hairstyle he would have had under the previous regime. This simple fact may have led to a massive swelling of temple ranks with former fighting men and Ming rebels with a questionable interest in religion, and every interest in fomenting rebellion and preparing for revolution.[2]

The era of Manchu rule is usually referred to as the Qing dynasty, using the name the Manchus came up with for their own imperial reign. The concept that China was occupied by 'foreigners' is vitally important for understanding the mood of the times, but increasingly difficult to discuss in today's People's Republic, where government policy specifies that the Manchus are a 'Chinese' ethnic minority, and that Manchuria has never been a separate territory.

This has led to severe curtailments on academic discourse, to the extent that some scholars are fearful to even quote faithfully from seventeenth-century accounts that describe the Manchus as 'invaders.' In dealings with modern Chinese academics, I swiftly learned never to say *Manzhou* (Manchuria), but to always refer to the area as *Dongbei* (the Northeast).

Such hand-holding nationalism is far removed from the mood of the seventeenth century, when the Manchus were regarded as brutal, heartless and, yes, *foreign* intruders, ruthlessly punishing any attempts to stand up to their authority, and regarding the Chinese as a slave class to be dominated and oppressed. When discussing the zeitgeist of Qing-era China, it is vital to understand that it was a time when the Chinese, both the uneducated peasantry and the disenfranchised upper classes of the old order, sought coded and oblique ways of resisting foreign influences, not just of the widely publicised European invaders, but of the Manchus who had seized control of their country.

The ruling Manchus were well aware of this resentment among their population. One might expect trouble to have died down by the 1700s, but the reign of the Qianlong Emperor (r.1736–95) saw dozens of literary inquisitions, censorship sweeps, and executions for treason. Initially under the guise of a grand cataloguing of all available books for the assemblage of an ultimate encyclopaedia, agents of the Qianlong Emperor travelled from door to door to make sure nobody was harbouring any unwholesome works. Over 150,000 books were destroyed and wiped from public knowledge during this period, for reasons including disparaging comments about earlier 'barbarian' dynasties (thought to be an oblique criticism of the Manchus), comments about flowers that alluded to the 'crimson' colours of the departed Ming dynasty, any reference to the word 'brightness' (i.e. *ming*), and plays on words that were regarded as disrespectful of the imperial family.[3] Sometimes, even *The Water*

Margin fell foul of the censor, with officials threatened with the loss of their job if they were found with a copy.[4]

In an effort to ensure that certain pronouncements were no longer set in stone, the government inquisitors were also authorised to destroy any stone tablets that did not fit the Manchus' personal narrative – specifically, they were not to be buried so that they might be re-erected when troubles had passed, but actually destroyed or defaced in an attempt to annihilate their contents from human memory. There were further drives against references perceived to be anti-Manchu in theatrical plays. It is likely that many important historical documents were lost during these purges, although equally likely that later fabricators have hidden behind such censorship as an excuse for the non-existence of any evidence for their martial arts' histories. Notably, the southern provinces of Guangxi and Guizhou offered no materials worthy of inclusion in Qianlong's encyclopaedia, which could mean they were merely last on the list, but equally might suggest that they suffered particularly badly at the hands of his censors.[5]

THE EPITAPH OF WANG ZHENGNAN

One such piece of writing, scheduled for destruction but fortunately never quite erased, was *The Epitaph of Wang Zhengnan*, a document that recognised a 'new' martial art – new in the sense that it had never been mentioned before, although its own documentation swiftly drew centuries-old links.[6] Under the strict pressures of the new regime, which was even regulating hairstyles, forms of protest were often subtle or archaically oblique. One such protest came in the form of an epitaph written for a martial artist of whom nobody had previously heard, which began by telling the reader everything that he was not. 'Shaolin is famous for its boxers. However, its techniques are chiefly offensive, which creates opportunities for an opponent to exploit. Now there is another school that is called "internal", which overcomes movement with stillness. Attackers are effortlessly repulsed. Thus we distinguish Shaolin as "external".[7]

The late Wang Zhengnan (1617–69) had a lifespan that encompassed both the last days of the Ming and the conquests of the Qing. He had supposedly been an accomplished archer and boxer. As a dead man, he could offer no real threat to the new order, allowing the father and son writing team of Huang Zongxi and Huang Baijia to make several pointed attacks on the Manchus in the guise of his eulogy. One such insult included the date of his death, which was given in old-fashioned Chinese zodiacal form in order to avoid using the reign title of the hated new rulers. The Huangs got away with it at the time, but within a generation such literary jibes could, and would, not only be punished by death, but also by the exhumation and mutilation of corpses (to damn the soul for eternity), and the wiping out of relatives.

The Huang family had been prominent in a discredited court faction of 1620s China. Zongxi had spent five years fighting with the Ming resistance before giving up and returning to his country hometown, turning his back on his previous life, and going into quiet retirement. In writing the obituary of a man who may never have existed, he alluded to his own life, noting that the heroic Mr Wang had repeatedly refused to serve the new dynasty, and that he had concentrated on a special, supreme martial art that cultivated inner strength.

It was claimed that Shaolin kung fu, so treasured by the defeated Ming, had been wiped out in the Manchu conquest, its temples burned and its surviving practitioners scattered. Shaolin was an 'external' show of prowess that was no match for the turncoat-recruiting armies of the invading Manchus. It was, noted the Huangs, also 'foreign', rooted in Indian mysticism and alien Buddhism. China had suffered its fill of 'foreign' things. It was time for China to pursue a quietly, stoically *Chinese* philosophy, rooted not in Buddhism but in the ancient, home-grown wisdom and mysteries of the Dao. Huang Baijia was very clear about how this 'supreme' martial art could even trounce Shaolin, with this note about Wang Zhengnan's alleged teacher. 'The external school of pugilism reached its highest development with Shaolin. [Zhang Sanfeng], having mastered Shaolin, reversed its principles, and this is called the Internal School of martial arts. Acquiring even a smattering of this art is sufficient to overcome Shaolin.'[8]

Among an underclass of defeated Ming loyalists, the unlikely tales of this new, mystery martial art came to symbolise a quiet, long-term resistance to Manchu rule. It was not the first time that foreigners had conquered China; writings like this gently suggested that the Manchus, like several other dynasties before them, could be defeated by the yielding, waiting strength of character of the Chinese themselves.

And who was this Zhang Sanfeng, the figure who had reverse-engineered Shaolin kung fu to find some new martial art? Depending on which Qing dynasty book you believe, he was either born in the early or late Song dynasty, was seven feet tall, possibly wore a cymbal for a hat, and had a beard with whiskers shaped like spear blades. Legend held that he had lived for over two hundred years (how else could he have lived long enough to train someone who had died in 1669?), and had the power to travel more than five hundred miles in a single day.

The historian Stanley Henning divides the development of the Zhang Sanfeng legend into three phases: 'Phase I (prior to 1669) merely claims that Zhang was a Taoist immortal; phase II (after 1669) claims that Zhang originated the "internal" school of boxing; and phase III (post-1900) claims that Zhang originated Taijiquan.'[9]

In other words, it is the only in the Qing dynasty, specifically the past 150 years or so, that has seen Zhang credited with the authorship of a manual of this internal martial art, unseen for nearly five centuries, but conveniently rediscovered soon after his name was first mentioned. It was this manual that referred to his secret art as 'the supreme ultimate fist', or *taiji quan*. 'The internal energy should be extended, vibrated like the beat of a drum. The spirit should be condensed in towards the centre of your body. When performing [taiji], it should be perfect; allow no defect. The form should be smooth with no unevenness, and continuous, allowing no interruptions.'[10]

Taiji quan's sudden flourishing in the Qing dynasty, from an entirely unmentioned martial art to a widely popular pastime, saw the mushrooming of several splinter groups and sects. Its basic positions and exercises bore a suspicious resemblance to many of the forms recorded in Qi Jiguang's *New Manual on Military Efficiency*; the difference between it and the 'external' forms lay largely in the philosophy and mysticism associated with the cultivation of *qi*, or life force.[11] Historians outside the world of *taiji quan* seem largely in agreement that it is a fabrication of the late 1800s, but it should be noted, for example, that the term taiji was also part of the name of the father of the first Qing emperor. In deference to the imperial ancestor, this meant that the term 'taiji' was redacted from all books published for decades to come.[12]

This is an annoying historical gap, which even irritates the taiji faithful. As author Yu Zhijun protests in his history of the martial art, there are glimpses of something that resembles taiji at various moments and in various sources stretching back two thousand years, making aficionados extremely reluctant to concede that their 'founder' was alive in the seventeenth century. Suggesting that he might have been immortal might solve this dilemma, but is not much help to historians looking for solid evidence.[13] The possibility remains that Zhang Sanfeng may have been an entirely fictional invention of his obituarists, since not actually existing would have been the perfect defence to ensure his relatives and descendants were kept from harm. Yu prefers to believe that both Zhang and 'internal' martial arts were real, but that for political reasons, *The Epitaph of Wang Zhengnan* overstated Zhang's role in the *invention* of 'internal' martial arts. Better perhaps to suggest that he had refined, codified and recorded a pre-existing tradition, rather that creating it.

We might observe, with something of a weary sigh, that although this explanation does make sense, it requires the reader to not only accept the incontrovertible proof of a message literally set in stone, but also then to doubt roughly half of it.

THE HEAVEN AND EARTH GATHERING

Not only is the Qing dynasty coterminous with our sense of the 'early modern era', from which mass-printed sources are most likely to have survived, it is also a regime that creates a crucial context for understanding the development of the martial arts. After the traumatic conquest in the 1640s, the Qing and their Chinese collaborators embarked on a series of expansions and conquests that propelled China to its largest land area in history. But the transition into the modern period would create fatal ruptures in the Qing/Chinese system. From the beginning of the 1800s, China fell remarkably, noticeably behind in world affairs, subject to constant pressure from the bullying European powers.

The pressure on the Chinese state did not merely come from within. China also faced the very real threat of European invaders, most notably the British in the south, whose traders had forced deadly opium on the locals in return for tea, a somewhat less addictive drug in demand back in Britain.

As part of his efforts to shut down the opium trade, Commissioner Lin Zexu organised for the training of a number of southern Chinese men to form a militia. A report of their training regime, written by a British sailor in 1842, observes that they are being drilled in a number of traditional weapons.

March 21st, Lin was busy drilling 3,000 troops, a third portion of which was to consist of double-sworded men. These twin swords, when in scabbard, appear as one thick, clumsy weapon, about two feet in length; the guard for the hand continuing straight, rather beyond the 'fort' the sword turns toward the point, forming a hook about two inches long. When in use, the thumb of each hand is passed under the hook, on which the sword hangs, until a twist of the wrist brings the grip within the grasp of the swordsman. Clashing and beating them together and cutting the air in every direction, accompanying the action with abuse, noisy shouts and hideous grimaces, these dread heroes advance, increasing their gesticulations and distortions of visage as they approach the enemy, when they expect the foe to become alarmed and fly before them.[14]

The weapons described are clearly 'butterfly swords' (*hudiedao*), the paired daggers common to many modern martial arts of southern China. However obscure or particular they might have been in the 1830s, a decade later they had formed the basic weapons training of an entire division of Lin Zexu's army – a group that, upon defeat, dispersal and falling into ever harder times, was sure to form the nexus of the next generations' brawlers, criminals, bodyguards and martial arts instructors, if not soldiery in other campaigns.

It should not, then, come as any surprise that the Qing period becomes a crucible of so much of what we understand about the martial arts. The Manchus in particular have a lot to answer for. It is thanks to their climate of fear that so much early modern Chinese literature remained ossified and hidebound, petrified of offending the ruling class. We owe the modern stature of *Journey to the West*, *The Water Margin* and *The Romance of the Three Kingdoms* in part to their creation before the days of the Manchu purges, when any innovation in an arbitrarily defined wrong direction might meet with the desecration of one's ancestor's graves, and the beheading of one's children. Fearful of government censors, Chinese writers and artists turned to subjects from the distant past, valorising the knights-errant and wandering heroes of a half-remembered dreamtime. If so much martial arts lore seems steeped in mysticism and schlock fiction, we should at least concede that the restrictions of the Manchu era often left the Chinese with little else to work with.

Meanwhile, the resistance movement of Ming loyalists faded into the shadows as the years passed. Decades, sometimes centuries, later, new organisations would attempt to associate themselves with the forgotten heroes of the past; it is usually impossible to say for sure how genuine such associations were. When we hear of a Chinese criminal fraternity that treasures a box containing a single straw sandal, the attentive reader will immediately note the allusion to the legendary life and death of Bodhidharma. But does this suggest, as some have argued, a secret link to the lost arts of the Shaolin Temple, or is it simply a symbolic allusion to traditional stories of old philosophies? *The Shaolin Grandmasters' Text*, a chronicle of kung fu, is at least honest when it states: 'The history of the Shaolin Order during the [Qing] dynasty is a complete mess. There are two primary reasons for this. One, keeping historical records has never been seen as very significant or important within the Order. Two, as Shaolin gained some notoriety, a plethora of secret societies and martial stylists began tracing their lineage to monks of the Order. And of course, their "historical" accounts all differ.'[15]

Merely because the Qing dynasty is closer to our own era, we are not spared the historical problems of rumour, forgery and apocrypha. 'Secret' societies in the Chinese record can range from everything from alleged revolutionary organisations founded by underground Ming sympathisers, to gambling dens with predictable underworld connections (the so-called Triads), to simple clubs offering savings schemes for labourers without access to banks or state welfare. The traditional organisation of many Chinese institutions often implies that higher-ranking members are privy to some kind of inner knowledge or institutional secrets, regardless of whether any such secrets existed. Examining the foundation myth of several Triad groups, the author Barend ter Haar uncovered a bizarre epic of kung fu allusions, beginning with the conquest of China by the Manchus, and the co-option of the Shaolin Temple, by the Manchus, to provide soldier-monks to help defend the north-west from an incursion by (other) barbarians. For this service, they were granted a special triangular seal by a grateful emperor.

Mere imperial approval, however, turned out not to be enough. Jealous courtiers sought to ruin the Shaolin monastery and sent an army to destroy it. Only thirteen monks escaped the subsequent conflagration, their numbers dropping even further to just five on their long flight to the south. In a moment of dire peril, they suddenly had a vision of an incense burner, rising from a nearby river, with instructions that their new mission was to 'resist the Qing and restore the Ming'.[16]

This group of newly minted Ming loyalists, so the story goes, subsequently fell in with a survivor of the Ming imperial family, becoming embroiled in an abortive attempt at restoring the Ming dynasty to power. When this failed, the five fled to different parts of China, where each of them founded a new cell of an organisation devoted to resurrecting the power and the promise of the three-sided seal: the Triads.

This, at least, is what new recruits to certain south Chinese organised crime fraternities were supposedly told on their initiation, establishing them as the inheritors of a lost order, not merely of loyalists to a departed, *Chinese* regime, but to the occult knowledge of one of five Shaolin warrior-monks. The story first came to light in the 1780s, when a society calling itself the Heaven and Earth Gathering (*Tiandi Hui*) attempted to overthrow the Qing governor of Taiwan. The account summarised above formed part of an oath found on the person of a slain rebel. It forms part of the founding myth of a coalition of organisations in the Chinese-speaking world, some of which persist to this day as the inner organisations of Chinese friendship organisations and political parties.[17] Suspecting further revolts, the Qing dynasty attempted to purge the society from China, but failed to do so in places outside Qing authority – Hong Kong, Singapore and other parts of the Chinese diaspora.

The story seems doubtful in the extreme. There is no destruction of the Shaolin Temple recorded at the particular time when it is supposed to happen. Some apologists have claimed that this is because the reference is to the previously unmentioned *Southern* Shaolin Temple, which nobody had heard of before. Moreover, this story is most often told in the overseas Chinese communities – in Thailand, Malaysia, Singapore and elsewhere – most of whom hail from the south and hence speak dialects in which the pronunciation of 'Shaolin' and the generic place name *xiao lin* ('small forest') are almost identical.[18] It also seems oddly coincidental that a dozen monks should escape, recalling the dozen monks thanked on the Shaolin Temple Stele, and then for that number to be whittled down to five, one for each of the animal methods mentioned in early callisthenic routines.

Barend ter Haar asserts that the term 'secret society' itself was a foreign concept, introduced in a sensationalist English book in 1900 and only subsequently translated back into Chinese and Japanese, where it became a catch-all category for bogeymen and anarchists.[19] But the folklore of martial arts holds that there were indeed secret societies, and that some of them preserved and refined the knowledge of earlier fighting arts. Unfortunately, such assertions often lead us into recursive, inescapable mazes of attribution – the secrets are *secret*, therefore there is no proof of their existence before the Qing dynasty. The absence of proof, to some apologists, is merely further proof of secrecy and hence of truth. Amid the already shaky foundations of martial arts history, China in the eighteenth and nineteenth centuries remains a place of whispers and boasts.

WHITE CRANE AND WING CHUN

It is, for example, notable that *The Shaolin Grandmasters' Text* offers a series of stories about the destruction of the original Shaolin Temple, and the migration of several survivors south to Fujian in 680 [sic].[20] This, claims *The Shaolin Grandmasters' Text*, is the oral tradition of the order, although the historian is apt to immediately wonder if the oral tradition hasn't dropped a digit. Disruption and migration around 1680, during the upheavals of the Ming–Qing changeover, would be entirely believable, and would then dovetail neatly with other traditions about the transmission of kung fu southwards.

According to the *Bubishi*, a collection of martial arts treatises preserved among the karate community of the Ryūkyū Islands, the Shaolin Temple served as a sanctuary for the resistance during the Qing conquest. There were certainly historical precedents for wanted men to fade into the shadows by shaving their heads and taking holy orders, so it should come as no surprise that Ming loyalists may have done so. Nor should it come as a surprise that the Qing authorities were vigorous in their pursuit of such underground refuges, burning the original temple to the ground in 1674.[21]

But this would come as a surprise to the Shaolin Temple's own chroniclers, who list no such attack in their own records, but bear with me for a moment as we endure yet another of many conflagrations in the Shaolin Temple's history.

This particular disruption, it was said, caused the migration to the south of several survivors, including one Fang Zhonggong, a 'master of Eighteen Monk Fist Boxing' (*sic*). Notably, Fang was a family man; his 'monk' status is doubtful, since the *Bubishi* also mentions a daughter, Qiniang, whose name implies that she had at least six siblings. Whatever martial arts skills Fang may have had, they were no match for local toughs in Fujian, who left him mortally injured after a fight over control of their adopted village.

Qiniang would commence but not complete a quest for revenge. In the process of three years of martial arts study, she would perfect a new style, White Crane kung fu, but would also acquire enough of a sense of proportion not to use it in anger. The name supposedly derived either from a temple where she hid, or from the two birds that she unsuccessfully tried to dislodge from her garden, the flapping wings of which concealed the actual attacks by claws, and which seemed to instinctively anticipate each other's attack before it could get properly under way.

Fang Qiniang's White Crane style seems to have been a refinement of the pre-existing eighteen positions of Shaolin kung fu. She sold it to her local disciples as an import – i.e. as something that used breathing, moral guidance and philosophies derived from outside Fujian. She also lifted an element of Mohist philosophy, telling her students that their newfound martial skills were only to be used in self-defence.

Most notably, of course, Fang Qiniang was female. According to the old-time chauvinism that even infected the Chinese language, 'woman' was a synonym for weakness and powerlessness, and yet she was somehow able to defeat male opponents who relied on brute strength. Her most famous opponent, the strongman Zeng Cishu, would become her most famous pupil, impressed with her ability to evade his attacks and turn his own momentum against him.[22]

There are, perhaps without coincidence, a surprising number of parallels between the story of White Crane kung fu and those of certain other martial arts. Take, for example, the Indonesian fighting art of Pencak Silat, supposedly learned by a woman, Rama Sukana, who came up with the idea while watching a tiger fight a 'large bird', and who then uses her new skills to thwart a band of drunken rapists. She then teaches it to her husband. The origins of martial arts in Indonesia stem from a number of influences – not only the Indian styles that arrived by sea, but also *kuntao* (Chinese: *quan dao*; English: 'fist-way'), the Indonesian term for the martial arts practised by the Chinese community in the archipelago, largely descended from the same Fujianese place of origin as White Crane kung fu. There are parts of Indonesia where the term *kuntao* is indistinguishable from *pencak* (a term for local traditions, particularly popular in Java).[23]

The story is even closer to that surrounding the origin of another famous style, Wing Chun. Legends of this particular martial art usually begin in a garbled fashion somewhere around the turn of the 1700s, with the destruction of a Shaolin Temple – the original or a mythical southern branch, nobody can say for sure – and the flight of a paltry handful of survivors. One such refugee was the nun, Wu Mei, who fled south; as a result, stories of her usually refer to her with the Cantonese pronunciation of her name: Ng Mui. Hiding out at a White Crane institution, the nun befriended a local tofu seller, a Mr Yim, whose daughter was enduring sexual harassment at the hands of a local criminal. The daughter, whose name was Yim Wing-chun, learned kung fu from the nun, and returned to the village to defeat her harasser and marry her betrothed, who in turn taught the newly formed martial art to a travelling performer from an opera company, who in turn pooled his knowledge with someone else who had learned staff fighting from another Shaolin refugee.

The opera troupe, the Red Boats, sometimes called the Red Junks, is particularly important in the story of Wing Chun because it comprised a band of travelling performers. This associated them both with acrobatic training, a repertoire thought to comprise up to 70 per cent of stories of heroic derring-do, and a vested interest in protecting themselves from local toughs when travelling between venues.[24]

'The southern [operatic] tradition,' wrote the historian Lin Yu: '. . . is full of showy forms such as Fist, Sword, Staff, 108 Style Fists, Six and a Half Point Pole, Monkey King Staff, Nunchaku, Broadsword, Sudden Thrust, Monk Stick, Buddha Palm, Double Whips, Sword Whip, Long Thread Fist, Flower Fist, Triple Forks, Double Spears, and Cynache Spear.'[25]

Not all of these skills were necessarily real martial arts. 'Monkey King Staff', for example, sounds like a set of moves from a production of *Journey to the West*, rather than a practical combat skill. Others are sure to have been arcane styles entirely unsuited for life in the age of gunpowder. Regardless, there were forms taught to the troupe, and some of them may have retained vestiges of, or even concealed true aspects of, real martial arts.

Legend claims that Li Wen-mao, a leader of the Red Boats, fell in with the Heaven and Earth Gathering at a critical juncture of the 1850s, and ended up leading an open revolt in Foshan after an altercation with a Manchu tax collector. He did so, because this story is not surreal enough already, with an army of fighters dressed in Cantonese opera costumes. 'By adopting the personas of easily-identifiable folk heroes,' explain Judkins and Nielson in *The Creation of Wing Chun*, 'they argued symbolically that it was they, and not the government, that represented the forces of social order and justice that the long-suffering people of the region yearned for.'[26]

Unfortunately, this also associated his opera troupe indelibly with forces of dissent. When this Red Turban Uprising in Foshan, of which Li Wen-mao was but one small part, began to falter before government retaliation, the tables soon turned. Li Wen-mao and his rebels fled across the provincial border to Guangxi, where he proclaimed himself the Lord of Peace and Order, and briefly declared a new, independent kingdom. One would be forgiven for thinking that this 'Red Turban Uprising', like the earlier one that overthrew the Mongols in the fourteenth century, was related to restoring the Ming dynasty, but the red turbans here were merely a symbol of anti-foreign sentiment. Li Wen-mao certainly gave up any pretext of restoring the Ming when he set himself up as the kinglet of a rebel state in the Canton area for several years, before dying in 1858 from wounds sustained during a retreat from Guilin.

The unrest would continue elsewhere. Associates of the Red Turbans would find greater success south of the border, as the Black Flag Army, and further north, where the revolt flourished into the full-blown civil war of the Taiping Rebellion. It is these pendulum swings of disaster, suggests the Wing Chun historian Danny Xuan, that explain odd ellipses in Wing Chun's history, when parochial villagers, whom one might expect never to stray more than a day's walk from their birthplace, suddenly decide to travel for a thousand miles.[27]

Meanwhile, around the heartland of the original revolt in Foshan, Manchu enforcers descended *en masse*, determined to wipe out all sympathy for the revolutionary movement. Vagabonds and drifters were executed, just to be sure, suspected of being former rebels fallen on hard times. Theatrical troupes were arrested and killed for their likely sympathies with the costumed rebels. Even people whose sole crime had been to pay extortion money to the rebels were executed for being 'sympathisers' with the rebel regime. Meanwhile, a culture of collaboration ensured that anyone with a local score to settle would inform on his neighbours for being rebels in hiding. There was little in the way of trials or due process – up to a million southern Chinese died in the purges that followed the Red Turban Uprising.[28]

They took much of their culture with them. Performances of Cantonese opera were banned for a full decade, during which entertainment was provided by out-of-towners speaking Mandarin. Whatever martial arts tradition may have previously existed was certainly stamped out almost completely – even if some former students did crawl out of the woodwork years later, there is no guarantee they had retained their teachers' full panoply of knowledge.

However, according to kung fu lore, at least a couple of Red Boat performers survived, and ended up teaching their martial art, or what they remembered of it, to a traditional Chinese doctor in Foshan. Now cobbled together into the Wing Chun style, this newly formed martial art was passed on to a traditional Chinese medicine man in Foshan, who taught it to his sons and a money-changer from his village. The money-changer would eventually take on sixteen students of his own, the last of whom was a boy called Ip Man. Ip Man's own adventures are covered later in this book, but they would subsequently become a matter of legend, not the least because of the later celebrity of his most famous pupil, Bruce Lee.

Even on the page, the story looks preposterous, as the secret martial art of one obscure villager begets another, which begets another. But it presents a very realistic and persuasive image of the precarious nature of transmission of martial arts, and of the incredible dangers and reversals of fortune of the Qing dynasty.

One of its own chroniclers makes the bold but plausible assertion that the story of the origins of Wing Chun is a deliberate lie, concocted some time in the Qing dynasty to throw Manchu inquisitors off the scent and protect local people from persecution.[29] That would certainly explain why the facts seem embedded in complete fictions, and why it does not hold up to prolonged scrutiny.

Even its factual elements are muddled, with further talk of the destruction of a temple that does not seem to have existed. Nor is a Qing dynasty purge against the Shaolin monks particularly likely, since the Shaolin Temple famously enjoyed the *support* of the Kangxi Emperor (r.1661–1772), to the extent that its front gate still bears a sign written in his own calligraphy. Nor is there reference in any historical source to a Wu Mei, described variously by Wing Chun practitioners as the abbess of the Shaolin Temple, or even as the daughter of a general from the defeated Ming Dynasty – although she would have to be at least in her sixties by 1700 if that were the case. In fact, there *is* a reference to a Wu Mei in the literature of the late Qing period, but that is to a woman in a potboiler novel from 1893, a cackling bad-girl who causes the destruction of the Shaolin Temple in the floridly titled *The Sacred Dynasty's Tripods Flourish Verdant for Ten Thousand Years.*[30] It is this fictional book, incidentally, that contains the first extant mention anywhere of a 'southern' Shaolin Temple – in the interests of editorial sanity, researchers and critics usually refer to its title simply as *Everlasting.*

Everlasting presents two initially unrelated narratives of life in late-Qing south China. One details the wanderings of a bunch of self-important Cantonese brawlers, righting wrongs and taking on even bigger bullies in a series of picaresque adventures. The other, the nature of which probably explains why the author chose to remain anonymous, tells of another wanderer in south China, the disguised Qianlong Emperor, who is smugly touring his southern domains incognito, fighting crime, toppling corrupt officials and otherwise enacting super-heroic kung fu justice at a grass-roots level, when the real-world historical figure of Qianlong rarely left a groove between Beijing and his Summer Palace, composing poetry, issuing censorship orders, and largely failing to notice the immense amount of bribery and corruption that was already fatally undermining his own Forbidden City.

Wu Mei appears as one of the undercover emperor's henchmen, the 'White Eyebrow Daoist', who closes the book by hunting down the brawling anti-heroes of the south, aiding her fellow collaborators in killing off the people's heroes, and presiding over the destruction of the Shaolin Temple.

However, there are circumstantial elements within Wing Chun itself that have led some to argue that there must be something in the claims that it was a martial art created by and for women. Leung Yitai, the surviving actor who passed on the secrets of the martial art to the Foshan doctor, had formerly been the Red Boats' female impersonator, which may go some way towards explaining a certain femininity in the Wing Chun forms. But Danny Xuan in his *Tao of Wing Chun* goes much further, arguing that the basic ergonomics of Wing Chun favour the female build, and that Ip Man himself, the greatest Wing Chun master in modern memory, benefited from his own slightness of form and relative lack of muscle tone.

> I have no doubt that the art is more conformed to a woman's structure and mindset than to that of a man's. For this reason, men tend to struggle to master the art or even to do well against martial artists from other systems today . . . When you look at Wing Chun's . . . postures and concepts, they are all very strange and contradictory to male structure and thinking. Women have no obstacles between their legs, and so can comfortably press the knee inward (which is the basic stance in Wing Chun). Also because of their proportionately wider pelvis . . . their femurs (thigh bones) verge naturally inwards towards the knees . . .[31]

Xuan's assessment is serious – he goes on to cite basic differences between the shape of male and female arms, the *lordosis* (lower vertebrae) and posture, of all which supposedly make Wing Chun more ideally suited to female practitioners.

THE BOXER UPRISING

Women, however, were not the target recruitment market for the martial arts in Qing-era China. Up north in Shandong, the fictional home of the heroes of *The Water Margin*, a real-life censor wrote a report in 1808 about worrying activities among local ne'er-do-wells. 'In this area there are many vagabonds and rowdies who draw their swords and gather crowds. They have established societies of various names: the Obedient Swords, Tiger-tail Whip, the Yi-he Boxers, and Eight Trigrams Sect. They are overbearing in the villages and oppress the good people.'[32]

Originally filed as gamblers and gangsters, some of these sects were soon associated with religious groups affiliated to the anti-Manchu 'White Lotus' beliefs. In particular, they became known for splitting their recruitment into 'civil' and 'military' divisions, using the lure of martial arts lessons to attract young male followers who might be employed in intimidation and gang violence.[33]

Stories of the martial artists of Shandong and its neighbouring provinces have a ring of familiarity – we hear of tough guys, medicine sellers and entertainers, whose snake-oil rituals and secret-society cant are soon implicated in attempted rebellions. In 1813, rebels proclaimed that the leader of the Eight Trigrams sect was a 'true prince of the Ming', leading a terrorist attack on the Forbidden City itself, where they were repelled from the inner sanctum by, among the guards, a thirty-one-year-old Manchu prince with a musket – the future Daoguang Emperor.

Only a few dozen Eight Trigrams rebels were involved in the assault, although some 200,000 alleged supporters would die in Manchu reprisals. None of them seemed to have been particularly well served by their Armour of the Golden Bell, a series of spells and breathing techniques that supposedly left them invulnerable to edged weapons. Some would infamously claim that their spirit armour would protect them even from bullets – when this inevitably failed, it was blamed on imperfect mastery of qi. *True* believers, it was claimed, would be invincible.

A similar magical defence formed part of the performances of the Patriarch's Assembly, a religious organisation purveying circus tricks and quack medicine in north-east China in the 1820s. Reports from Qing investigators mention village-square shamans who could withstand edged weapons, pass needles through their flesh without feeling pain, and heal the sick by applying magical paper charms. The Patriarch's Assembly oddly insisted that no branch could set up in a new town without first stealing the ancestral tablets of another branch, thereby dooming itself to remain small and subject to inter-necine squabbles and turf wars. It did, however, claim that its conjuring tricks were the result of a form of spirit possession.

Many similar sects rose and fell throughout in the region, including the Spirit Boxers, whose name recalled that of earlier sects elsewhere in China, and whose acolytes claimed that they could call down divine beings to shield them from harm and aid them in performing superhuman feats. One could 'leap straight up and do spirit boxing', others were known for their super-human athletic feats, and their ability to commune with spirits that fed them prophecies.[34]

Georg Stenz, a German missionary in Shandong province, observed that even supposedly benign village cults seemed to draw on a martial and somewhat fictional tradition, such as in a ritual he observed himself around the time of the turn of the twentieth century, when local village toughs were brought to a temple shortly after Chinese New Year, and would call down the spirit of the Monkey King, hero of *Journey to the West*, to possess one of them in order to demonstrate martial arts skills. However, by the time he was writing, Stenz was well aware that his presence was part of the problem, as the people of the Shandong region began to push back against the largely German missionary population disrupting local *feng shui* by spreading un-Chinese ideas and erecting churches with pointed steeples. So, too, was Japanese belligerence, with the Sino–Japanese war of 1894–5 depopulating the area of its soldiers to fight on the front in Korea, leaving a vacuum that was soon filled by paramilitary organisations like the Big Sword vigilantes, an offshoot from the supposedly invulnerable Eight Trigrams society of the previous generation. Defeated in Korea, the supposedly modernised Chinese army returned home with tales of their decimation by Japan's modern guns, causing a backlash among the grass-roots in the villages that favoured belief in the power of 'traditional' sorcery to fight such threats.

'Religion' is a misnomer, since many of the 'spirit possessions' invoked by these later rebels were clearly fictional characters. Some, admittedly, would claim to call down the God of War – in China, a real historical personage posthumously deified – and adopt the mannerisms and gait of the character as depicted in popular plays. Others would invoke unquestionably fictional inventions, such as Monkey and Pigsy from *Journey to the West*, and charge into battle yelling their catchphrases.[35]

Such craziness echoes the costumed rebels of the Red Turban Uprising of the 1850s, but possibly without its political message. Instead, the men of the Big Swords seemed more likely to be unable to distinguish between fact and fiction in their entertainments. However, the most crucial difference between them and other movements was the lip service they paid to the Manchu order. The

Big Swords targeted *foreign* invaders, but did not include the Manchu government in that category. Instead, their battle cry, when not impersonating an immortal monkey or an amorous pig, was: 'Support the Qing, expel the foreigners.' Even though they were not above getting into skirmishes with government troops, and even though their actions rather implied that they were carrying out duties where the authorities had failed, they identified themselves as militia in the service of the Manchus.

It is these intrigues behind the scenes that are responsible for modern arguments about the name used to describe them. These vigilantes, who eventually turned on foreigners, massacred missionaries, burned down churches and besieged the Legation Quarter in Beijing, were usually known in English as the 'Boxers' – named by the missionaries in recognition of their mystic, coordinated physical displays of the martial arts, particularly Plum Flower boxing (*Meihua quan*), a martial art that has been variously attributed to Zhang Sanfeng (the supposed founder of taiji!) or Wu Mei (the fictional inventor of Wing Chun!). Sweeping aside the vague boasts of street-corner conjurors, Plum Flower boxing's genuine provenance still has every appearance of a mix-and-match style, deriving a little from the old Long Fist, and a little from the Shaolin techniques of its native Henan province. It supposedly got its name from the likely foliage to be found around spring festivals, where its techniques were most likely to be performed by travelling showmen.[36] The style comprised a number of basic techniques, including eight punches and eight kicks, liable to lift at least the numerology, if not the actual attacks from the Eight Trigram Palm (*Bagua Zhuang*), a taiji-derived martial art that flourished in northern China in the nineteenth century.[37]

This has led many popular accounts to refer to their reign of terror as the Boxer Rebellion, although the historian Joseph Esherick protests that the term 'rebellion' was a largely successful attempt by the Manchu authorities to imply that the Boxers acted without their approval. Esherick prefers the term 'uprising', since he, and almost everyone else who has studied the matter, concludes that whatever the origins of the Boxers, their putsches against foreigners in 1899 were conducted with the collusion of a sizeable faction within the Manchu government, which only disowned them when they ran out of control in Beijing itself, and eight foreign powers retaliated by invading China.[38]

Meanwhile, the Boxers' name for themselves was the *Yihe tuan*, the Unity of Righteous Harmony – it is unclear whether they also believed their basket of techniques was a new martial art of its own, the *Yihe quan* (Righteous and Harmonious Fist), or if this was a name applied by outsiders as a catch-all title for the combination of incantations, poses and forms they employed. There are Chinese documents from as early as 1774 that suggest that the *Yihe quan* had *once* been adopted by some White Lotus rebels as a new name for their order, but it is difficult to draw a direct line from that usage of the term across over a century, to the one used by the fighting men of 1900.[39] In particular, this is because there is documentary evidence that the 1,900 Boxers actively persecuted people from White Lotus sects, sentencing them to execution.[40] It may even be that some observers misheard *tuan* as *quan*, and that there was never a specific martial art by that name. As with so many other martial arts, the name itself is so generic that it is entirely feasible that similar terms are adopted entirely independently by groups unaware of each other's existence. We might note, for example, the existence of a religious group called the *Yihe Menjiao* (the Teachings of Righteous Harmony), reported in the Tianjin area in 1813, which concentrated on meditation, breathing exercises and healing, and which Manchu investigators reported as entirely benign.[41] This is particularly worthy of note because within thirty years, martial artists in northern China would reportedly be teaching a martial art called the *Yihemen quan* – the Fist of the Gate of Righteous Harmony. The *men* part is problematic – it literally means 'gate', but in the name of the 1813 cult, it appears in a compound that transforms its meaning to 'teaching'. Was it misheard or misinterpreted a century later? Did someone think it meant a literal gate, like a temple gate? Or was it still intended to be a poetic word for school or style?

'I would argue,' writes Esherick, 'that those who have attempted to trace origins by following a common *name* have been following a false trail.'[42] Such confusions would become particularly endemic in the twentieth century, when north-east China in particular became the site of chaotic contention, and a melting pot of several different races speaking mutually unintelligible languages. Japanese imperialism, eagerly imitating the model set by the Europeans, seized Taiwan in 1895, Korea in 1910, and Manchuria itself in 1932. This created an incredible period of fervid interchange in the cultures of East Asia, as both conquerors and conquered were cross-pollinated with ideas and discoveries. Chinese martial arts ideas, long nurtured in the Ryūkyū Islands north of Taiwan, swept up the archipelago and took root in modern Japan. Japanese martial arts were forced into the Korean curriculum, lingering and evolving after the colonial period was over. In Manchuria, a Chinese man would teach something he called the Fist of the Gate of Righteous Harmony to a Japanese spy, who would return to his home country in 1947 and use it at the basis of a new martial art.[43] But before we can get to the fertile chaos of the twentieth century, we must take a step back to observe how the martial arts had developed along their own, separate path in the isolated island nation of Japan.

The Way of the Warrior

············

It *could* be Japan. Sixty or seventy years ago, this *was* Japan, and vestiges of five decades of colonial rule have endured since 1945. But this is the Republic of China now, also known as Taiwan, and the pronunciations reflect that.

This is not a judo hall, it is a *roudao* hall.

Feng does not have a second-*dan* black belt; here, he is second-*duan*.

When the teachers yell that it is time to begin, they do not shout '*Hajime!*' They say '*Kaishi!*'

The characters are written the same, they are just pronounced differently. Better that, perhaps, than some of the linguistic car crashes I have run into in Europe, where locals struggle with oriental phonemes. I once encountered a taekwondo instructor who couldn't pronounce the name of the thing he was teaching.

I don't see the appeal of judo. Someone, admittedly a novice, once tried to throw me, and became increasingly annoyed that I didn't cooperate. He needed me to attack him before he could use my weight against me, and by standing and waiting for him to make the first move I ruined his day.

Feng is singularly unimpressed by this, and reminds me that I had been talking to someone who had probably only had a single lesson.

'Do you know there is no first strike in karate?' he says. 'You'd be standing in front of a karate guy waiting for him to make the first move, because he doesn't want to hurt you. And if a judo guy wanted to tie you in knots, the first you'd know about it would be when you hit the ground.'

'All the same,' I say. 'A lot of it seems like glorified falling over. I'm surprised so many people even study judo, rather than, you know, aikido or karate or something with a bit more flair.'

'No,' says Feng, trying to control his horror. 'Judo is the basis for every other martial art! There are many you can't even start until you're a teenager, but you can begin judo when you can barely walk. You can start when you are just a little kid, when your centre of mass is much lower, and falling is less likely to hurt. And more than anything else, it teaches you how to fall. It teaches you how to land. It trains you until you are ready to learn any other technique without injuring yourself.'

He suddenly drops in front of me, hurling himself at the ground but somehow *missing* it. Instead of smacking into the floor, he rolls into his shoulder, transferring the deadly momentum of his downward force into a horizontal movement. There is enough energy in it for him to roll back up into a crouch. He stands up, completely unhurt by a fall that would have probably put me in the hospital.

'I can fall,' he beams. 'I can land. I can hit the ground without being hurt. That's the ancestor of every other fighting form, because *not getting hurt* is one of the main aims. Right?'

I nod meekly.

'If I were inventing a new martial art from scratch,' he muses, 'I would *start* with judo. Everybody should start with judo.'

He looks me up and down.

'Now,' he says, 'do you want me to throw you?'

THE SAMURAI ERA

The martial arts enjoyed a very different form of evolution and development across the sea in Japan, where local conditions created a flourishing environment for combat skills. Japan's samurai class started out as the servants and spare younger sons of the imperial court, packed off to the north of the country to busy themselves on border wars with the local aborigines, marchland politics and similar endeavours. However, by the medieval period, these samurai had acquired and tamed the Kantō plain, the largest and most productive area of flat land in the entire mountainous archipelago. Once beholden to the imperial court, the samurai came to dominate it, ushering in several centuries in which the Japanese emperors were mere figureheads, controlled or fought over by warring clans.

Ancient warfare in Japan derived initially from Chinese models, although many elements of Chinese craft were unsuitable for Japan's geographic conditions. Chariots were useless without flat land, causing the samurai to favour mounted cavalry and archers. Shields were done away with; their function passed on to boxy armour with a hard helmet top and flared neck guards, all the better to allow for a head-down charge at full gallop into a wall of archers. Although the ancient Japanese prized Chinese crossbows, they soon ran out of the technical support to maintain them, and the weapons became matters of legend. Instead, they adopted the curved swords of their aboriginal enemies, the Emishi, which proved to be better for use on horseback.

Chinese military thought was still highly prized. Although many Japanese soldiers would write their own meditations or variations, there was little to challenge the original classics. Most famously, the medieval Japanese hero Yoshitsune would quote Sun Tzu at opportune moments, and seduced a lovelorn lady in the northern provinces while trying to get a peek at her father's copy of *The Six Secret Teachings* (*Liu Tao*), a Chinese manual that was already some two thousand years old.[1]

Notably, the medieval chronicle that relays this story is extremely confused about *The Six Secret Teachings*, mixing its contents up with those of several other military manuals, and offering tall tales, peculiar to Japan, about the various generals and heroes who have put its wisdom to practical use. The modern English reader can access *The Six Secret Teachings* in literally seconds – it is contained in Ralph Sawyer's *Seven Military Classics of Ancient China*, a mere Kindle click away – but for the medieval Yoshitsune and the fifteenth-century author who wrote up his life, it was an arcane manuscript, jealously locked away by clan nobles, who believed that it 'made military geni-uses of all who mastered its contents'. It, like many martial arts, remained a closely guarded secret knowledge, imparted only to loyal retainers of particular clans.

The samurai knew about sumo wrestling, since that was a public event and had been for several centuries. Wrestling, however, had diverged into two distinct forms, the heavily ritualised sport of sumo, and the more practical applications that remained a battle-field technique for dealing with murderous opponents.[2]

Samurai from each clan were also trained in particular forms and styles of weapons usage, particularly archery with the graceful, super-tall Japanese longbow, the use of spears and, of course, swords. Arrows remained the most common cause of death on a samurai battlefield until the sixteenth century, when musket balls took over. Close-quarter grappling was a distant fifth or sixth place. Samurai women were not usually found on the front lines of battles, but were expected to have sufficient martial prowess to defend the home in case of enemy attack. For this reason, many of them were also trained in the bow, and in the use of the *naginata*, a pole-arm well suited to unhorsing enemies.

Grappling was certainly an issue that many samurai had to face, not the least because the basic method of counting achievements on a battlefield came from the tallying of human heads – a particularly gruesome piece of Japanese vocabulary is *kubinejikiru*, usually trans-lated as 'beheading', but literally 'twisting off and cutting' to denote the butchery of a samurai battlefield. There are plenty of accounts of samurai battles that imply the victim was still alive when this operation was performed, suggesting that grappling with a short sword in one's hand was a regularly required skill.[3]

Chinese provenance was sometimes used as a way of implying a certain purity or superiority to a Japanese item or method. According to *The Secret Book of Martial Arts* (*Kenpō Hisho*), a samurai manual dating from the mid-seventeenth century, jujutsu originated as a dialogue between three masterless samurai and a Chinese jack-of-all-trades, Chen Yuanbin, regarding 'the Chinese method of seizing a man [without weapons]'. Chen was a man from Hangzhou, who spent much of his later life in Japan as a retainer in Owari, a domain directly beholden to the Tokugawa clan, where he variously wrote scholarly tracts (including *The Concise Teachings of Laozi*), wrote poems and advised on the firing of new pottery kilns. Apparently, he knew all about martial arts, too.[4]

There is no reason to doubt the existence of the all-knowing master Chen, who seems to have been highly prized by the Tokugawa for the foreign knowledge he brought in to enrich the clan's industries. But even his biographical entry in *Eminent Chinese of the Ch'ing Period* sounds a note of caution that he was the 'creator' of jujutsu. A sharp-eyed reader might suggest that the phrase '*Chinese* method of seizing a man' could have been deliberately coined in opposition to an unmentioned skill already known to the samurai, which is to say a pre-existing *Japanese* method of seizing a man. Unfortunately, our understanding of the form this art may have taken is confused by the sumo lobby, which has claimed many incidences of 'wrestling' in old accounts to be direct references to sumo as it is known today, and not some earlier incarnation, devoid of the all-important ring boundary, with a lesser emphasis on bulk and a greater emphasis on technique.

What possible use would the samurai have for grappling? The clues are there in the various words used for it during the samurai era, which include *jūjutsu* (the gentle craft), *yawara* (softness) and *torite* (the catching hand). It is reasonable to assume that the samurai skillset included at least some discussion of the best way to fall off a horse, of soft landings, of ways to immobilise or disarm an opponent after the loss of one's own weapons and of taking a hostage alive. Empty-handed combat with a fully armoured samurai would be a pointless affair – it is unlikely that any punch or kick would penetrate his armour. But throws, evasions, arm-twists and wrestling-holds might successfully immobilise such an opponent for long enough to save someone's life.

THE HOUSES OF GO

Discussions of this so-called jujutsu also enter Japanese discourse at the end of Japan's centuries of civil war, and the beginning of the long rule of the Tokugawa shogunate. From 1603 until 1868, a single clan monopolised the rank of shogun or 'barbarian-suppressing supreme general', effectively ruling Japan in the name of the emperors.

The Tokugawa period was unprecedented in Japanese history. For the first time since the middle ages, Japan was plunged somewhat unexpectedly into a long run of relative peace. One might even suggest that the Japanese were entirely unprepared for this, lumbered with a huge, top-heavy military aristocracy, dedicated to warfare but with nobody left to fight. There was presumably some intimation of this in the closing years of the sixteenth century, when the warlord Hideyoshi tried to dispel as much of the strength of his former enemies as possible by flinging them against foreign soil in a futile invasion of Korea.

By the early seventeenth century, particularly after the massacre of the last Christian rebels in 1638, the samurai were facing an increasingly idle existence. Many provincial castles were dismantled, and the former warrior class found itself increasingly occupied with court ritual, accountancy and managerial tasks. This period saw the slow decline of the former, practical *jutsu*, which is to say battlefield crafts, into more ritualised, safety-conscious forms that bore a greater resemblance to sports. The word *jutsu* was replaced with the more artistic *dō*, the Japanese pronunciation of Laozi's *dao* (see Chapter One), as in *chadō*, the 'Way of Tea'. *Kenjutsu*, the craft of fighting with a sword, was reformed into *kendō*, the 'Way of the Sword', in which the ritual was separated so far from reality that most practices usually favoured hitting each other with sticks.[5] *Kyūjutsu* (archery) became *kyūdō*, the 'Way of the Bow'. Eventually, some time after the time of the shogunate was over, Japanese even stopped talking of *bujutsu* (the martial arts) and instead favoured *bushidō*, the 'Way of the Warrior'.[6]

Discussions of the martial arts in Japanese often incorporate a number of strategic and tactical skills. One of the *jutsu* was the skill of being able to swim in armour (*sueijutsu*); it, and the art of spitting needles into an opponent's eye (*fukumijutsu*) are just two of many samurai-era martial arts that have been quietly laid to rest in the modern age.[7] One hears of siege warfare described as a 'martial art' in Japan, which would have pleased the ancient strategist Mozi. Espionage, too, drawing on the dedicated chapter on the subject from Sun Tzu's *The Art of War*, was taken to be a knowledge base required of the all-round warrior. Even board games sneaked into the repertoire of the Tokugawa-period samurai, who was expected to be a whizz at *shōgi* – a chess variant in which pieces could transform and even switch sides – as well as that strategy game that is both the most simple and the most complex: Go.

The Shogun Tokugawa Ieyasu plainly held Go in high regard. Only a year after he came to power, he appointed a Buddhist monk as a 'Minister of Go', charged with overseeing contests and promotions, and assessing new ranks of players. This odd governmental position would remain on the books right through Japan's Tokugawa era, as would the four Houses of Go – contending institutions that would train and nurture new players, and pit them against each other in annual contests. The Houses of Go are particularly notable because their foundation included a system designed to match players with opponents of equivalent ability, and to chart improvements in those abilities. For this, the Japanese looked to the ancient Chinese manual *The Classic of Arts* (*Yi Jing*), which suggested categorising players on a nine-rank system derived from the levels of courtiers in attendance on the Chinese emperor. These began at the lowest level, of 'being stupid', before advancing through better gradations such as 'merely inept' to 'fighting strength', 'ability', and then ever more complimentary levels recognising advancements in wisdom, appreciation and true enlightenment.

The samurai era came to an end in the latter part of the nineteenth century, when the last of the shoguns proved unable to perform their basic job description – there was little point in having a 'barbarian-suppressing supreme general' if he was unable to prevent foreign gunboats from sailing into Japanese waters and demanding trade concessions and treaties. Japan was jolted out of its time warp by the severe culture shock brought by American and European contacts, but resolved not to be carved up into imperial concessions like China. In the last days of the samurai, Japan erupted into a multi-sided civil war between supporters of the shogun, opponents who believed the shogun should be replaced with someone more capable, and supporters of the emperor, who believed that he should be 'restored' to genuine authority as the constitutional monarch of a modernised state. All factions claimed to be loyalists; all were arguably samurai clans seeking to put their own particular puppet in charge. In a war that saw the shogunal faction pushed ever northward, until its final days on the windswept shores of Hokkaido, the imperial faction slowly gained ground. Victory was announced in the form of the 1868 Meiji Restoration, in which the young Meiji emperor was supposedly handed back his country, and issued a bunch of proclamations that would disestablish much of the old order over the ensuing decade. Not all of the samurai had truly appreciated the implications of modernism, and there were several flurries of dissent as they were stripped of their influence. Their skills, too, were swiftly outclassed and outmoded by the creation of a modern military. As a result, martial arts of the samurai era came to be known as *kobudō* (classical martial arts) or *koryū* (old styles), and regarded as ossified traditions that were no longer of direct relevance.[8] In Japan today there are seventy-eight 'classical' martial art schools that preserve these ancient traditions, but this number represents a precipitous drop in affiliates since the founding of the Nihon Kobudō Association in 1979. As for modern, approved styles, today's Budōkan organisation recognises only nine today, of which five are chiefly unarmed:

Judo
Sumo
Karate
Aikido
Shorinji kempo
Naginata – pole-arm
Jūkendō – bayonet
Kyūdō – archery
Kendō – swords (or sword-substitutes)

In the generation after 1868, Japan embraced modernity at a frightening rate, while dismantling much of the old order. The samurai were gone within a decade, deprived first of their iconic hairstyles and dress, then of their right to carry swords in public. The lucky ones scrambled to enter the new, modernised army and navy, where they formed a deadly, poisonous officer class of belligerent men spoiling for a fight. Others faded into the urban populations of artisans and workers. The martial sector of society, maintained for centuries as an adjunct to the samurai, was similarly dissipated and forced to diversify. Some, of course, could find employment with the armed forces or police, but most were forced to demilitarise their abilities – swordsmiths became cutlers, armourers into saddle-makers; some specialists in unarmed combat were forced to rebrand themselves by using only a portion of their skills, as masseurs, bone-setters or physicians.

The creation of a national standing army in 1873 also turned many secretive schools and styles into anachronisms. Single domains could easily favour a particular form of martial art and, indeed, were incentivised to do so in order to give them a notional upper hand against potential rivals. But a nationally trained, nationally recruited army required a nationally agreed standard of physical training. For a generation, government committees argued about the requirements of a curriculum in martial arts, emphasising both physical training and a cultural philosophy. The banning of swords in 1876 had effectively destroyed the relevance of any weapons-based martial art as anything but a sport or hobby. The Satsuma Rebellion of 1877, fomented among four suspicious 'schools of swordsmanship', left the authorities wary of any activity that gave dubious characters the right to assemble with offensive weapons. The time was right for the promotion of empty-handed forms of martial art, such as the old grappling style of jujutsu.

FROM JUJUTSU TO JUDO

The speed with which jujutsu took hold can be tracked through the observations of Basil Hall Chamberlain, a lecturer at Tokyo University whose *Things Japanese* was about as close as you can get to a late-Victorian encyclopedia on Japan. The first edition in 1890 does not mention martial arts at all. The second edition of 1891 adds a new entry on 'Wrestling' that deals with the history and culture of sumo.[9] In the third edition of 1898, Chamberlain augmented his 'Wrestling' entry to include jujutsu, reportedly practised by the police and numerous academies, and with details of its cunning means of defeating an opponent by 'yielding to strength, in other words, by pliancy'. By the fifth edition in 1905, Chamberlain wearily notes that 'an unusual amount of rubbish appears to have been circulated abroad on the subject . . .'[10]

But jujutsu was itself undergoing a modern transformation at the hands of Kanō Jigorō (1860–1938), an educator and martial artist who would use his various government positions to push a particular school – his own – until many of its precepts were adopted as the national standard.

Kanō was the third son of a shipping clerk. Sent to top-class schools, including a private European academy where he studied German and English, Kanō had received the best education that money could buy, but still suffered from something of an inferiority complex because of his relatively small stature – he stood at 5 feet 2 inches and only weighed 90 pounds. In his late teens, he was introduced to the idea of jujutsu by a former member of the shogun's guard, who demonstrated that it was a fighting art where small stature was not an impediment.

It had already been a decade since the collapse of the shogunate and the beginning of Japan's modernisation. In his determination to find a jujutsu teacher, Kanō had to search among the 'bone-setters' – backstreet physicians who eventually pointed him at several old instructors who could still be encouraged to give private lessons.

It has been suggested that at least part of Kanō's success owed a debt to his 'European rationalism', imparted to him in his schooldays.[11] Kanō, a university student destined to become an influential educator, was unimpressed with his instructors' emphasis on learning by rote. Students were thrown repeatedly until they learned through the experience of constant defeats. Only then were they taught some of the basic forms. Nor was Kanō taken with the insistence on a limited number of kata; his teachers had combined two different schools of old jujutsu, but even this hybrid form was riddled with gaps and blind spots. Faced with an apparently unbeatable senior opponent, Kanō turned to the library, experimenting and failing with some tricks from sumo. He found better success with a treatise on Western wrestling, which taught him the 'fireman's carry' move in which an opponent is levered over a wrestler's shoulder. Successfully throwing his rival with this move, Kanō called it the *kataguruma* (shoulder wheel), and kept it in his own repertoire thereafter.[12]

By 1879, the teenage Kanō was accomplished enough to be one of the jujutsu fighters who gave a personal demonstration for the visiting former US President, Ulysses S. Grant. By 1881, he had inherited the manuals of two schools, after the deaths of his instructors – conferred with the valuable scrolls by their widows. He continued to train at a third school, where he eventually received a certificate of accomplishment – his only qualification of record in jujutsu.

It was at this third school that Kanō began to supersede his own teacher.

> Now, instead of being thrown, I was throwing him with increasing regularity. I could do this despite the fact that he was of the Kitō-ryū school and was especially adept at throwing techniques. This apparently surprised him, and he was quite upset over it for quite a while. What I had done was quite unusual. But it was the result of my study of how to break the posture of the opponent. It was true that I had been studying the problem for quite some time, together with that

of reading the opponent's motion. But it was here that I first tried to apply thoroughly the principle of breaking the opponent's posture before moving in for the throw.[13]

Student and teacher discussed this odd turnabout, and Kanō expressed his opinion that the key to his sudden superiority was his concentration on exploiting his opponent's own lack of balance. His teacher agreed, somewhat petulantly observing that he had nothing left to teach him, and by 1883 had handed over his own teaching scrolls. The pupil had become the master.

Kanō stopped teaching simple jujutsu. His combination of the teaching materials of three schools, leavened with ideas lifted from wrestling, deserved a new name, leading him to call it *judo* ('the pliant way'). The -*dō* suffix, as ever, implies a sport rather than a practical means of fighting, since Kanō was determined for his new martial art to have other components.

Throughout the 1880s, Kanō had parallel careers. In the martial arts, he was a proponent of jujutsu, and particularly his own brand of judo, with the establishment of the Kōdōkan, a dedicated judo school in Tokyo in 1882. Meanwhile, he bounced between the Ministry of Education and several positions in the educational establishment, beginning his postgraduate career as a minor professor at the Gakushūin, a notoriously high-class school for the children of the aristocracy. Despite eventually serving for a time as the principal of the Gakushūin, Kanō was far from impressed with the attitudes among the schoolboys, many of whom he regarded as insufferable snobs, riding in rickshaws all the way to the school doors (a privilege denied their teachers), and treating the staff as if they were servants. He pushed, along the lines of the teaching philosophy of John Dewey, for students to respect their teachers, and for the teachers to set a moral and intellectual example – he frowned upon drinking, fraternising and weak will. As the head of the Tokyo Teacher Training

College, he was able to instil his philosophy, and his personal martial art, into an entire generation of educators, sowing the seeds for judo's later adoption as part of the Japanese school curriculum.

But Kanō's double life as a mainstream educator would come to influence his attitudes towards judo, which he hoped to establish as a tripartite discipline. As he explained in an 1888 lecture to the Asiatic Society of Japan, judo combined a basic regimen of physical exercise not only with the original grappling techniques of the samurai martial art, but also with 'the cultivation of wisdom and virtue'.

> I therefore anticipated that practitioners would develop their bodies in an ideal manner, to be outstanding in matches, and also to improve their wisdom and virtue and make the spirit of Judo live in their daily lives. If we consider Judo first as a physical exercise, we should remember that our bodies should not be stiff, but free, quick and strong. We should be able to move properly in response to our opponent's unexpected attacks. We should also not forget to make full use of every opportunity during our practice to improve our wisdom and virtue. These are the ideal principles of my Judo.[14]

Notably, however, Kanō's philosophy was secular. The only Chinese philosopher he was apt to call on was Confucius, who similarly suggested a series of mundane regimes and activities that would combine to instil a greater physical, moral and mental virtue. Like Confucius, Kanō had no interest in discussing the supernatural, making his judo curriculum easily adapted through changing times. There was, for example, no obvious reason to deny the establishment of a judo school in a hardline Christian, Muslim or Buddhist country, since none of its precepts required acceptance of a particular religious belief. This was to allow Kanō's curriculum a degree of international flexibility, and often (but not always) helped it get through changing political climates even in Japan.[15]

Kanō's plans for judo required him to consider aspects that had not troubled earlier martial arts teachers. In 1883, he awarded his first pupils with the rank of *shōdan* – the first level. He adopted the ranking system from the Houses of Go, which recognised that a period of training would result in the graduation of novices to a new, basic level of accomplishment that would lead to further ranks of achievement.[16] In order to distinguish those students from novices, he got them to wear black belts, a deliberate choice of colour to evoke the black-and-white contrast of *yin* and *yang* from ancient Chinese thought.

He also devoted considerable thought to the way that his students should dress while training. Kung fu practitioners in traditional China simply wore their everyday clothes, or stripped down to their underwear to practice – the modern 'uniform' seen in taiji is merely a reproduction of how Chinese people used to dress in the nineteenth century. Kendo practitioners, however, got to wear the broad *hakama* trousers of a samurai warrior, with impressive armour and protective headgear. Kanō was savvy enough to realise that judo's image would suffer if it did not come up with a similarly iconic uniform that would be both recognisable and practical. By 1907 he had begun dressing his pupils in loose-fitting trousers and a white top, modelled on the Japanese fireman's traditional hemp jacket or *hanten* – this was a particularly tough material, and would lend itself well to being repeatedly grabbed and tugged in throws.[17] These outfits, in pure Zen-influenced white, would come to be known as *keikogi* ('practice garb') or *dōgi* ('way outfits', or more sensibly, '[martial] arts kit'). With the widespread adoption of judo into the Japanese school curriculum, such *dōgi* became the default attire for any martial art that aspired to judo's crown as a national enterprise. Like all uniforms, it created a sense of community and unity, but also levelled the differences between pupils of different social classes. Although thinner or softer materials were sometimes substituted, the basic look of judo gear, including its remarkably tough material, would become commonplace in most subsequent Japanese martial arts, and those in other countries that derived from Japanese ancestors.[18]

Many of these innovations would become standardised across all the martial arts after the foundation in 1895 of the Greater Japan Martial Virtue Society (Dai Nihon Butoku Kai), an organisation under the auspices of the Ministry of Education, charged with rationalising the Japanese martial arts, promoting the virtues of the samurai, and running exhibitions and tournaments. In other words, the old supervisory capabilities of the Houses of Go were now being applied across the martial arts, in order to ensure that there was a centralised system to rate and oversee them. Kanō was not named in the documentation of the early organisation, but considering his position both inside and outside the Ministry of Education, he is liable to have influenced many of its decisions. Whether Japanese martial artists chose to study judo or not, they were often beholden to a system of organisation, vetting or ranking that derived in some way from judo.

In the 1890s, Kanō briefly taught at the institution that was to become Kumamoto University, inadvertently exposing his particular school of martial arts to a far wider international audience through his contacts with a foreign colleague. Quite by chance, one of Kanō's fellow lecturers was the famous journalist Lafcadio Hearn, newly hired to teach English. Before long, Hearn was drawn to write an essay on Kanō's practice hall, noting that he himself was too old to embark upon the 'seven years of constant practice' required to become proficient. However, since photographs survive of Hearn's eldest children in judo gear, it is reasonable to assume that he had ample contact with Kanō's lessons.

Under Hearn's observation, Kanō becomes a master of 'the art of war', described in reverent admiration.

> By some terrible legerdemain he suddenly dislocates a shoulder, unhinges a joint, bursts a tendon, or snaps a bone – without any apparent effort. He is much more than an athlete: he is an anatomist. And he knows also touches that kill – as by lightning. But this fatal knowledge he is under oath never to communicate except under such conditions as would render its abuse almost impossible. Tradition exacts that it be given only to men of perfect self-command and of unimpeachable moral character.
>
> The fact, however, to which I want to call attention, is that the master of jiujutsu never relies upon his own strength. He scarcely uses his own strength in the greatest emergency. Then what does he use? Simply the strength of his antagonist. The force of the enemy is the only means by which that enemy is overcome. The art of jiujutsu teaches you to rely for victory solely upon the strength of your opponent; and the greater his strength, the worse for him and the better for you. I remember that I was not a little astonished when one of the greatest teachers of jiujutsu [i.e. **Kanō himself**] told me that he found it extremely difficult to teach a certain very strong pupil, whom I had innocently imagined to be the best in the class. On asking why, I was answered: 'Because he relies upon his enormous muscular strength, and uses it.' The very name **jiujutsu** means to conquer by yielding.
>
> I fear I cannot explain at all; I can only suggest. Every one knows what a 'counter' in boxing means. I cannot use it for an exact simile, because the boxer who counters opposes his whole force to the impetus of the other; while a jiujutsu expert does precisely the contrary. Still there remains this

resemblance between a counter in boxing and a yielding in jiujutsu – that the suffering is in both cases due to the uncontrollable forward impetus of the man who receives it. I may venture then to say, loosely, that in jiujutsu there is a sort of counter for every twist, wrench, pull, push, or bend: only, the jiujutsu expert does not oppose such movements at all. No: he yields to them. But he does much more than yield to them. He aids them with a wicked sleight that causes the assailant to put out his own shoulder, to fracture his own arm, or, in a desperate case, even to break his own neck or back.[19]

Hearn regarded judo/jujutsu as a crucial lens through which to view Japan's modernisation, noting that Japan had adopted hundreds of ideas and technologies from the west, propelling itself into the modern age in merely a generation. However, he cautioned his Western readers against any sense of smugness or superiority, for his observations had reminded him that Japan was merely absorbing the strengths of its enemy. Japan had, in his estimation remained 'just as Oriental today as she was a thousand years ago'. '[Japan] has been able to remain herself, and to profit to the utmost possible limit by the strength of the enemy. She has been, and still is, defending herself by the most admirable situation of intellectual self-defense ever heard of, — by a marvellous national jiujutsu.'[20]

Hearn's analogy for jujutsu as the key to the Japanese spirit might have been admiring, but also somewhat alarmist, drifting into Yellow Peril premonitions of the Japanese successfully 'underliving' the European races, adopting the best of their culture and technology, breeding faster and accepting a lower standard of living. He posits that 'they would scarcely regret our disappearance', any more than Europeans might mourn the death of the dinosaurs.[21] His article first appeared in 1894, but was swiftly reprinted in book form a year later, making it one of the most widely read pieces of his journalism in its day. Perhaps because of what would now be regarded by some as racist undertones, it is oddly uncelebrated today in the canon of his work, despite a theme that seems to have been oddly prescient about Japanese attitudes in the ensuing forty years.

Hearn was not the only journalist to write about the practice and application of the Japanese martial arts, but he was one of the most widely read, and ensured that the names jujutsu and judo would be carried far and wide. Kanō, meanwhile, scored an even more impressive coup on his home turf when he was appointed by the Ministry of Education as the head of primary education in 1898. Although he did not enjoy a dictatorial authority, he was soon in a prime position to steer government policy, both through his own arguments at the table, and through his power to cram committees with judo supporters. In 1906, according to his memoirs, he consulted with a committee from the Greater Japan Martial Virtue Society on the adoption of a nationally standardised curriculum. In fact, he was in charge of the committee and packed it with members of his own Kōdōkan organisation, effectively wiping out many rival schools.[22] In 1908, a new law made it compulsory for students at Japanese schools to enrol in either judo or kendo classes. Both appear to have been chosen as physical exercises with a specifically Japanese cultural cachet, but as Kanō himself was once heard to scoff: 'Who walks around with a sword?'[23] Kanō made no efforts to marginalise kendo, but his objections to it were eminently practical – kendo was far less applicable to everyday life, and moreover, alienated poorer schools and practitioners by the insistence on expensive kit.

That is not to paint Kanō as a devious manipulator. His passion for judo was heartfelt and genuine, and when he argued that its moral compass made it superior to other physical exercise activities like soccer and baseball, he was speaking from the heart. Kanō also pursued judo as a largely voluntary, charitable effort, subsidising many elements of his Kōdōkan organisation with his own money. In this regard he was the first, but by no means last, modern martial artist to struggle with the ethical nature of charging money for training and upkeep. Nor did Kanō push judo into places where he felt it would not belong – as the head of Japan's Olympic committee from 1909, he was in a perfect position to engineer the adoption of judo as an Olympic sport. Instead, he refused to involve himself in the discussion, partly out of a sense of conflict of interest, but largely because he felt popularising judo as a mere 'sport' would be to the detriment of its other aspects.[24]

In creating judo, he also brought to life something of a syncretic juggernaut that overwhelmed many of the older schools of martial arts, and threatened to even absorb the newer ones before they had the chance to grow. Relations between judo and other modern martial arts like karate and aikido were cordial and cooperative, albeit wary. Funakoshi Gichin, the great populariser of karate, came to teach at Kanō's judo hall, only to see Kanō appropriate some of his best moves. This was precisely how judo grew and improved, but it left Funakoshi with the concern that his own particular school risked being swamped by the ever-expanding rival. Offered the chance to teach full-time at Kanō's school, Funakoshi declined.[25]

FROM CHINA-HAND TO EMPTY-HAND

Karate was a late arrival in Tokyo, although something like it had been part of the fabric of daily life in its home islands for several centuries. The period of the Tokugawa shogunate had brought the Japanese into increasingly close contacts with the people of the Ryūkyū Islands, stretching from the coasts of southern Japan in a long archipelago all the way down to Taiwan – the largest island being Okinawa. The Ryūkyū Islands were occasionally used as a trading route, allowing sailors in relatively small boats the opportunity to hop from island to island in relative safety, rather than making the direct ocean crossing to China.

By the medieval period, the Ryūkyū Islanders were mentioned in Chinese dynastic chronicles as a subject people, particularly after the fourteenth century, when migrants flocked to the island from south-east China. However, stuck between China and Japan, and remote from the power centres of both, the Ryūkyū Islands came to occupy a unique, liminal position. When eventually conquered by the Japanese, the Ryūkyū Islands became a portal by which many elements of Chinese culture, including the martial arts, were preserved and introduced to the Japanese mainland.

The islands were united under a single king in 1429, when the ruling Shō family was recognised as such by the emperor of China. It is at this point that the history of martial arts in the islands not only begins, but does so in several contradictory strands, each of which may contain some element of the truth.

The mass settlement of 'thirty-six families' of Chinese emigrants is widely thought to have brought certain martial arts to the islands, particularly variants such as the White Crane style from Fujian, elements of which bear a certain resemblance to many later karate moves. However, considering the fact that the islands had been fighting each other for centuries before unification, it is entirely reasonable to assume that there was also some sort of native tradition, practised by the *pechin*, or island aristocracy. The degree to which this was a native tradition, a copy of earlier Chinese styles, or introduced directly with the styles of the thirty-six families, is open to debate.[26]

Other stories of the martial arts on the Ryūkyūs place their origins substantially later, after the unification of the separate islands, relating in particular to a ban on weapons imposed by King Shō Shin in 1507. In this version of events, Ryūkyūan martial arts diverge again, into either combat techniques studied by the aristocracy, or illegal underground peasant rituals designed to teach self-defence using household implements. This explains the prevalence in certain modern martial arts of weapons such as the *sai*, a dagger-like fork used to disarm opponents, but also of the *nunchaku*, a rice flail (or possibly horse-bit) repurposed as a weapon.

The disarming of the Ryūkyūan people was twofold, since the islands were invaded and occupied in 1609 by the Satsuma clan of Japan, which ran them for the next two hundred hundred years as a vassal state. The Satsuma clan also imposed a weapons ban on the locals, leading to the rise of a unified local unarmed fighting system by 1629, using elements of Chinese styles, and usually practised in secret to avoid the attention of the samurai overlords.[27]

In his history of this martial art, Bruce Haines comments that its clandestine nature was significantly different from the teachings of the various samurai grappling techniques. This Okinawan martial art was now an underclass pursuit, taking on many of the 'secret society' elements that we see in Qing-era China, but also lacking any 'flowery' attributes. As a result: 'it became extremely violent since the sole purpose of its practitioners was to maim and kill'.[28] This seems like something of an overstatement – after all, the practitioners did not intend to maim and kill *each other* in training, so sparring was still possible without murdering one's fellow students. Its underground nature, however, did ensure that many elements of its history became garbled or matters of mere legend. Whatever links it may have had to Chinese sources would soon become as unclear as those of the Chinese sources to each other.

This 'China-hand' martial arts system – in Japanese, *Tō-te* or more commonly *Kara-te* – gradually came out of hiding in the late nineteenth century, after the samurai era was over. In 1879, the last king of the Ryūkyū Islands abdicated at the order of the Tokyo government, moving to the mainland and accepting the commiseration prize of becoming a marquis in the Japanese honours system.

The islands were turned into one more domain of the Japanese empire, and the last king's secretary, Itosu Ankō, either lost his job or found his position substantially eroded under the new regime. Ankō became intimately involved in the education system of the swiftly modernising islands, and was instrumental in getting the local Kara-te adopted in all Ryūkyū schools in 1901. However, this system, like Kanō Jigorō's judo, represented a substantial refinement and modernisation of several disparate forms. As noted by his most famous pupil, Funakoshi Gichin (1868–1957), his martial art combined elements of at least two Chinese systems: 'In Okinawa in olden times there were . . . two schools, Nawate and Shurite, and these were thought of as being related to the two schools of Chinese boxing, called Wutang and [Shaolin] . . .'[29]

Funakoshi goes on to describe the two supposedly rival traditions of Chinese martial arts, the 'external' kung fu that he believed to have been invented by Bodhidharma, and the 'internal' taiji that he believed to have been invented by Zhang Sanfeng. He is also, however, keen to stress that these origins are merely matters of 'legend', and that as far as he is concerned, the only crucial element is that 'there is little doubt that Chinese boxing did indeed cross the sea to Okinawa'.[30]

As a teacher at an Okinawan school from 1905, Itosu simplified several elements of the training process to streamline its use in teaching classes of young children. By 1908, when a new law obliged Japanese schools to choose between judo and kendo for compulsory martial arts training, Itosu wrote a letter to the Ministries of Education and War, pushing Kara-te as a reasonable alternative. Seemingly concerned that many elements of Kara-te were just about to be swamped, not only by attrition and ignorance, but also by the imposition of the two state-mandated martial arts, he listed the advantages of Kara-te in a persuasive article known as the Ten Precepts. Many were designed to hammer home to the ministries that they risked wiping out a valuable local tradition that might be better employed in the heartland. The second, in particular, appeals to the ongoing Japanese state trend for growing a generation of martially minded young soldiers: 'The purpose of [Kara-te] is to make the muscles and bones hard as rock and to use the hands and legs as spears. If children were to begin training naturally in military prowess while in elementary school, then they would be well suited for military service. Remember the words attributed to the Duke of Wellington after he defeated Napoleon, "Today's battle was won on the playing fields of our schools."'[31]

Kara-te, however, was still a mixture of 'schools' in its native islands, and Itosu's suggestion that it was a unified system was an attempt to impose his own rules on a number of rival styles. Nor had some of his fellow practitioners given much thought to the nature of their style until such time as they were asked to define it. Miyagi Chōjun (1888–1953), for example, a Ryūkyū islander who had previously trained in Fujian, only started to call the martial art he taught *Gōjū-ryū* (the Hard-Soft style) after one of his own pupils was asked at a competition what school he was from. One of Itosu's own pupils, Chibana Chōshin (1885–1969), developed the habit of referring to his martial art as *Shōrin-ryū* (the Shaolin style). Many such distinctions were really only externally defined – among the Ryūkyū Islanders themselves there was extensive cross-pollination, swapping and comparison of techniques.[32] Even today, most karate systems share the same forms at their basic levels.

Kara-te's ambassador in Tokyo was the plain-speaking Funakoshi Gichin, founder of the Shōtōkan school, a young man from a bullishly traditional family. His parents were so set in their ways that they had refused to allow him to cut off his topknot in his youth, thereby keeping him from his chosen career of studying at medical school. Instead, he drifted into a career as an assistant teacher, in which role he had become a follower of Itosu's rationalised system. He gave a demonstration in Kyoto in 1915, and published a book on Kara-te in 1922, the year that he officially moved to Tokyo.[33] Despite being Okinawa's greatest champion in the capital, Funakoshi's moves to popularise Kara-te were not necessarily greeted with a warm reception in his home islands. In particular, his controversial decision in 1936 to rename it *karate*, the 'empty hand' was regarded as a step too far by many of his colleagues. This, however, made the martial art much more palatable to an increasingly nationalist Japanese government that was busily purging foreign elements from its culture. The emphasis on 'emptiness' not only accentuated karate's value as a form of unarmed combat, immensely more useful than a martial art that required the acquisition of a bow and arrow or a spear, but also allowed him to push for a Zen-influenced philosophical component – the full name remains *karate-dō*, with that all-important suffix denoting elements beyond the physical.

Back in the Ryūkyū Islands, the attentions of the mainland were not always welcome. We see in the histories of the local martial arts schools a period of bluster and one-upmanship, as a formerly *ad hoc* regime of fighting styles is suddenly subject to the scrutiny of a national association, the Greater Japan Martial Virtue Society. In particular, there was a period of fervent credentialism, as village teachers suddenly saw themselves conferred with official ranks within a standardised curriculum, and class conflict, as a hierarchy formerly reliant on birth and wealth suddenly placed higher value on a notional meritocracy.

Funakoshi's attitude to such politicking was refreshingly realist. In particular, he was scathing about martial artists who claimed that their training allowed them to focus their *qi* and perform superhuman feats. 'Perhaps in the distant past there were karate experts capable of performing such miraculous feats,' he wrote. 'To that I cannot testify ... but I can assure my readers that, at least to my

THE WAY OF THE WARRIOR

fairly wide knowledge, there is no man living who . . . can exceed the natural bounds of human powers.'[34]

Funakoshi dismisses as 'nonsense' any claims of punches that can shatter rocks, fingers that can penetrate human flesh and muscle, or a death-grip that can do any more than pinch an opponent's skin. But while such remarks seem lucid and welcome, they possibly mask continuing feuds behind the scenes among the great teachers of karate. We might infer, for example, that Funakoshi's comments are not a general assertion of realism, but a chiding reference to the likes of his fellow karate master Miyagi Chōjun, who made a name for himself in Tokyo with performative stunts such as tearing the bark off trees, or ripping apart hunks of meat with his bare hands.[35] And we might note that while Funakoshi is often commemorated today as the 'founder' of karate, and certainly as its leading populariser on mainland Japan, his rival Motobu Chōki took great pains to pretend he did not know who he was: 'When I came to Tokyo [in 1927] there was another Okinawan who was teaching karate there quite actively. When in Okinawa, I hadn't even heard his name.'[36]

It is, in fact, highly unlikely that Motobu genuinely was ignorant of Funakoshi's identity, but his acid comments on the subject make it clear how much of the prevailing narrative in any martial art is often formed at the finishing line after a race between many contending opinions and practitioners.

CHAPTER SIX

Nationalism and Modernism
....

'Don't believe everything you hear,' says Park. 'Karate isn't from the Ryūkyū Islands at all. It's from Korea. Korea!'

He takes another swig of his drink.

'Korean sailors taught it to the people in Okinawa in the middle ages,' he says. 'Then they brought it to Japan.'

I ask if he's sure about this, because everybody in the world outside Korea seems pretty certain that karate came from China, up the Ryūkyū Islands to Japan.

'There's evidence in the chronicles of the Yi dynasty!' he scowls, as if everybody ought to know that.

Yes, of Japanese sailors in Korea, not that they learned all their martial arts there. And then, and I know I am going to regret this even as I say it, karate was brought from Japan to Korea during the period that Korea was a Japanese colony, 1910–45.

'No!' says Park, slapping the table for emphasis. 'We took nothing from Japan. They took it from us. And Korea had martial arts before China!'

Once again, I say, wincing a little at how deep the hole is already getting, general opinion concurs that the Chinese martial arts—

'No! Korea!'

But Shaolin—

'Korea! There are Korean tomb pictures of taekwondo from centuries before the Shaolin Temple was built. Koreans invented it. The Chinese stole it, too!'

But wasn't taekwondo only invented in the 1950s . . . ? How can it be—

'KOREA! We took nothing from Japan. We took nothing from China. They took from us.'

I'm ready to accept the possibility of a little cultural interchange, but Park's position, derived directly from the taekwondo federation's own, is aggressively (or rather, defensively) independent.

'We've had martial arts in Korea for more than two thousand years,' he continues, slurring a little bit now. 'There are pictures and everything. Of people fighting . . . Korea.'

He stares at two of me, his eyes a little crossed, daring me to disagree.

The nationalist ideal in Japan was a vision of martial strength, occasionally manifesting as 'pan-Asianism' – a declaration that Japan was destined to lead the nations of Asia in a unified resistance against predatory Western powers. This was unwelcome news to the other nations in Asia, who had little desire to shake off foreign colonialism only to find themselves under Japanese hegemony.

Japan's encroachment on China proceeded in ever larger increments. It began in earnest in November 1871 with some Ryūkyū Islanders, blown off course and seeking shelter on the east coast of Taiwan. There, they got into a fight with local aborigines, and a number of them were killed. In a cunning diplomatic move, Japan demanded reparations from China; simply by engaging in negotiations over this matter, China tacitly acknowledged that the Ryūkyū Islands were part of Japan, even though an imperial Chinese envoy had looked in on the vassal archipelago only four years previously.[1] Seeking to avoid the blame for the deaths, the Chinese claimed that while Taiwan was part of China, the eastern part of the island was not yet under Chinese control, leading the Japanese to set off on an ill-fated punitive expedition against the aborigines in 1874, in which Japan lost several hundred soldiers to disease.

With the Ryūkyūs now established as 'Japanese' territory, the islands were incorporated into Japan proper in the 1880s, as discussed in Chapter Five. By 1876, Korea had been forced to open to Japanese trade, and in the war that broke out between China and Japan in 1894, Japan seized and retained Taiwan. Korea itself became a Japanese colony by 1910, with strong Japanese influences soon established over its border in the form of the railways leading out to China.

At least partly as a result of such land-grabs on Chinese territory, the 'last emperor' of China was finally overthrown in 1911, replaced by a shaky Republic already creaking under the influence of warlords and corruption. Throughout the first three decades of the twentieth century, Japanese agents swarmed over East Asia, in multiple attempts to secure even more territory on the mainland. These included an abortive invasion of Siberia under cover of coming to the aid of the last of the White Russians, agents posing as anthropologists and educators, securing support for Japan as far west as Xinjiang, and the eventual seizure of a huge swathe of territory in north-east China, which formed the puppet state of Manchukuo from 1932–45.

The role that this long project played in the martial arts has many aspects. As already implied in Chapter Five, it saw an increasingly militaristic attitude in Japan towards the need to educate a martially minded generation to conquer Asia. Among the Chinese, it inspired numerous efforts at nationalism, designed to push the notion of a uniquely Chinese response. The troubled Chinese state, a republic after 1911 but split into several warring factions, tried to pursue a programme of modernisation that denied Japanese influences, rediscovering or reinventing Chinese traditions worth keeping in the modern world. Meanwhile, Japanese expatriates, particularly in the areas either directly or indirectly under Japanese rule, brought with them the fruits of the modern Japanese curriculum, including an emphasis on the athletic properties of the martial arts, particularly judo. The youth of Korea and certain parts of China were exposed to these modern variants of the martial arts as everyday features of their school life. But so, too, were the Japanese, as colonists in Manchuria, Korea and Taiwan learned of local traditions. By the time the tide of Japanese imperialism ebbed in 1945, it had created new 'traditions', not only in Korea and China, but even back home in Japan.

JINGWU, IP MAN AND GUOSHU

The Jingwu ('Pure Martial') Association was founded in 1909 in Shanghai as a school to teach sports, exercises of the mind like chess, the English language and educational excursions. As the name implies, there was also an emphasis on martial arts. The 'founder' Huo Yuanjia (1868–1910) was a martial artist of some repute. More importantly for the Jingwu school's later successes, it was funded by a trio of wealthy businessmen and backed by the Tongmenghui, a society whose president Sun Yat-sen, then living in Japan, was fated to become the first president of the Republic of China only two years later.

Jingwu was also intimately connected with the New Culture Movement, an intellectual drive that argued for the necessity of a modern China. This began as an opposition to the hidebound imperial system, but also as a protest against the mess of warlords and corruption left behind by its collapse. The Chinese of the early twentieth century had a genuine and, as it turned out, entirely justified fear that warlords in the north of the country would happily hand over sovereign Chinese territory to the Japanese. Foreign predators would need to be held at bay by a combination of foreign methods (modernisation, reform, science) and Chinese traditions – it is here, in the assertion of Chinese traditions worth preserving, that the Jingwu school would excel.

Huo Yuanjia's reputation is semi-legendary – there is little or no contemporary evidence of his famous deeds until they were celebrated in later movies. According to popular myth, it was Huo, a practitioner of a form of 'northern' Shaolin kung fu, who accepted the challenge of a Russian or possibly British boxer, who proclaimed that he would 'flatten any sick men of Asia' who would fight him in the ring.[2] This tale has grown with the telling in its most recent incarnations, such as the Jet Li film *Fearless* (2006), in which a fictionalised Huo takes on a Belgian lancer, a Spanish fencer, a British boxer and, in the grand finale, a sword-wielding Japanese, demonstrating on every occasion the superiority of Chinese techniques and attitudes. The folk tale of an Asian hero taking on a Western boxer is a recurring theme in the narratives of China and Japan – Huo Yuanjia's victories are not the first, and we hear of similar matches in the legends of Wong Fei-hong (see Chapter Seven), as well as in numerous Japanese media, from Kurosawa Akira's *Judo Story II* onwards. The multiple occurrences of these tales might seem at first hand to be wish fulfilment, or the remarkable bad luck of a series of bullying foreigners, although it seems far more likely that they have their origins in an entire subgenre of sideshow fights, in which Asian martial artists were pitted against an opponent in boxing gloves on multiple occasions. Known in Japan as *merikan* (from 'American'), such best-of-three contests between rival fighting styles were commonplace at the turn of the twentieth century – it is notable that Huo's most famous bouts are in Tianjin and Shanghai, two cities with the heaviest Japanese presence in that period. The *merikan* fashion only faded around 1925, the year in which an article in the *Japan Times* complained that they merely aroused 'useless racial prejudices'.[3] We might reasonably assume that reports of them, sometimes second or third hand, informed many a pulp novel, comic, or movie account of a plucky East Asian martial artist bringing down a pompous European or American boxer.

The historical Huo was approached by a committee of pro-Republican reformers, searching for a figurehead who could lead classes at their newly founded Jingwu school and function as an embodiment of the 'new Chinese citizen'. Huo served in this role very briefly before dying under suspicious circumstances, seemingly poisoned by his Japanese doctor in revenge for defeating a judo champion (or, less dramatically and more embarrassingly, by the arsenic component of the traditional Chinese medicine he was taking).[4] The Jingwu school's modernist aspects included an insistence on an exam-based curriculum rather than the airy qualifications of multiple martial arts masters, and also the involvement of those parts of society that had previously been excluded, such as the merchant class and, from 1917, women.

By 1915, the second Chinese president Yuan Shikai was advocating 'traditional Chinese martial arts' as an essential inclusion within the country's education system. Martial arts, specifically taiji and some variants on it, had become part of the teacher-training curriculum at the newly founded Beijing Normal University by 1917. The same year saw the adoption of several techniques of grappling, punches and kicks and fighting with swords and staffs, as 'new Chinese martial arts' (*zhonghua xin wushu*), not only for the teachers, but also for trainee soldiers and policemen.[5] This new system, however, soon fell out of favour, largely through its association with the militaristic state principles of Germany, which had done the country no good in the First World War.

The researcher Kai Filipiak acknowledges many early pioneers in martial arts history, but notes that the modernism movement in 1920s China discouraged many academics from undertaking worthwhile research. Martial arts were seen by many as an unwelcome relic of old China, whereas more modern (i.e. Western) sporting activities were believed to be more relevant to contemporary needs, and more likely to pay dividends in physical fitness. The flourishing mass-market printing industry of the early twentieth century also allowed for textbooks to reach a wide audience. Both taiji quan and bagua quan benefited from the publication of how-to manuals, the practicalities of actually teaching taking permanent precedence over any claims of historical veracity.

Chiang Kai-shek, who first became president of the Republic of China in 1928, would restate the political position on kung fu unequivocally as a cornerstone of Chinese culture:

Chinese boxing is not simply a form of physical contest; it is also pregnant with meaning for the physical education of our citizens ... We call our type the 'Chinese national boxing (*Guoshu*),' because we wish to emphasise its significance for the physical and mental health of our citizens. In all our future educational plans, we must regard Chinese boxing as an essential item in the physical education of our citizens, and encourage people to learn it with all the persuasion and authority we can command.[6]

Part of the Jingwu school's remit was to reclaim the martial arts from the bad press it had suffered in recent years. Jingwu publications deliberately confronted several widespread fallacies among the Chinese, aspects of which ironically endure among many foreigners to this day. The chief contentions of the Jingwu school were that:

- The perpetrators of the Boxer Uprising, reviled throughout China, were not true inheritors of the tradition of martial arts.
- True martial arts were nothing like the brawling, licentious, outlaw habits depicted in novels such as *The Water Margin*.

- The warlords who then were carving up China were behaving contrary to the attitudes and ethics of the Chinese martial arts tradition.[7]

Much like the Greater Japan Martial Virtue Society, the Jingwu school both popularised and homogenised the martial arts. By 1919, the Jingwu school had opened a branch in Guangzhou in South China, where its representatives were fiercely critical of the many secretive practices and petty disputes among local martial arts schools. Although the Jingwu school derived much of its financial backing from southern Chinese businessmen, its own curriculum heavily favoured 'northern' martial arts, and roundly ignored many forms popular in the south.[8] Writers on the subject would sometimes characterise this, rather generally, as a standoff in prevailing styles between 'southern fists and northern legs', rehashing similar claims from centuries earlier.[9] We can, perhaps, see an attempt to head off such criticisms at the opening of the Guangzhou branch, where the martial artist Wong Fei-hung (1847–1924), a prominent herbalist and master of the Hung Gar boxing style, was supposedly invited to perform.

Jingwu privileged northern styles and swamped many southern ones, but vastly increased the number of qualified teachers. With an emphasis on attainable goals and clear milestones, it speeded up progress, ensuring that qualified disciples were not left waiting for years for a master's whim to confer them with educator status. It also pushed martial arts into a new bracket of likely students, adopted by young, educated members of the middle classes. Among several dozen Jingwu branches in China, one of the most famous was set up in Foshan, home of the martial art of Wing Chun, in 1920.

Ever since the days of the later (nineteenth-century) Red Turban Uprising, Foshan had been associated with a multiplicity of obscure martial arts and secretive training regimes. Locals did not initially take kindly to the arrival of officious, interfering newcomers from Shanghai, telling them that their long-standing traditions were in need of improvement and rationalising, particularly since the message was often one of the implied superiority of 'northern' techniques. By 1922, the Foshan branch of the Jingwu school only had ten members, the original local chairman had resigned, and recruitment appeared to have stagnated. Out of frustration, one of the few remaining members, a teacher called Yu Lejiang, who specialised in a branch of kung fu called Northern Mantis (based on the praying mantis animal form) began publicising his willingness to demonstrate the superiority of Jingwu techniques by defeating all comers in public matches.

A local pharmacist soon volunteered a policeman friend of his to represent southern styles. Canny local businessmen decided to push the entire event as a big occasion, renting out a local theatre and ensuring they had sewn up the drinks and snacks concessions. On the appointed day, Yu Lejiang took to the stage to prove the value of the Jingwu school, in combat with the newly arrived adversary, Ip Man (1893–1972).

Unfortunately for the crowd, both men had come to fight, not to put on a kung fu exhibition. Real fights, without extensive rules and safety equipment, rarely last long and tend not to be all that visually spectacular, at least not when compared to the popular imagination. Ip family lore states that Yu started by throwing his signature punches, and was quickly engaged and countered by Ip Man who simply [threw him off balance] and threw him off the stage. Yu was hurt by the fall and may have broken some ribs. The fight was called off at this point.[10]

148

The combatants had inadvertently broken the cardinal rule of using performative fighting and 'flowery' kung fu – to keep the crowd happy. The event's backers scurried behind the scenes to Ip Man, who was persuaded to come back to the stage and give a demonstration of his techniques, turning the advertised fight into a prolonged advertisement for the Wing Chun that he had been teaching to a small, local audience.

Ip Man's local celebrity would not serve him particularly well in a restive China. He would eventually permanently relocate to Hong Kong in 1949, when the Nationalist establishment he served was defeated by the proclamation and victory of the Communist-led *People's* Republic of China. In Hong Kong, he would struggle for years as a small-scale martial arts instructor, while his pupils developed a heady mix of tall tales about his younger days. The Jingwu school would suffer similar setbacks, particularly after its main backers lost their fortunes in 1924. Its ideals, however, were sufficiently robust to attract the attention of the Nationalist government, which would inaugurate a research academy into *Guoshu* (the 'National' arts) in the then capital, Nanjing in 1928. Part of the academy's policy was to create a nationally accepted curriculum of martial arts, which it did through experimental sporting events in which male contenders from multiple disciplines would compete for three days, until seventeen 'national champions' were declared. The event was deemed a success, although not for all competitors, some of whom were injured or killed in the proceedings. Some of the survivors ended up as faculty staff at the academy.[11]

The academy organised a second national competition in 1933, showing a growing sense of structure with the division of competitors into weight classes, and an insistence that competitors select three disciplines from a list of wrestling, boxing, swords and spears. There was also an increased 'sporting' emphasis on correct conduct, with points deducted for '"unsportsmanlike conduct" such as low

kicks, eye gouges, attacking an opponent's back in fencing or grabbing an opponent's spear in an attempt to disarm him'.[12] The
Communists, unwelcome but certain to comment from the side
lines, disapproved of it all, decrying it for the 'trophy-ism' that valued
prizes for individual achievements above one's contribution to sport
as a whole.[13]

Such sporting attitudes were less apparent among the staff of
the Guoshu Research Academy itself, where teachers were infamous for settling petty disputes by fighting each other. In particular,
a somewhat artificial faculty division between 'external' Shaolin
fighting arts, and 'internal' fighting arts – now named Wudang,
seemingly with no basis except in potboiler novels – periodically
came to blows, with kung fu fights breaking out in meetings. In one
infamous escalation, the dean of Shaolin and the dean of Wudang
resolved a policy disagreement by attacking each other with bamboo
spears.[14]

The Central Guoshu Academy, as it had become known after
several rebrandings, fizzled out in the 1940s, as the pressures not
only of the Second World War, but of the tensions between the
Nationalists and Communists began to take priority. The high point
of its accomplishments was arguably a demonstration event during
the 1936 Berlin Olympics, which brought several products of the
Guoshu regime to the notice of the European public. According to
the official report of the Berlin Olympiad:

> The gymnastics of the Chinese team introduced the specta-
> tors into an entirely different world. The demonstration of
> 'Chinese Boxing' on August 11th in the Dietrich Eckart Open-
> Air Theatre showed that Chinese gymnastics are based upon
> ancient Chinese conceptions of the universe. The individual
> exercises have the purpose of giving the body the highest
> degree of suppleness and elasticity, with self-defense in view.

In the partner exercises, which must be carried out with great speed, the Chinese displayed an insensitivity to hard and fast blows which was astonishing. The exercises with the sword, spear and pike were noteworthy. These weapons were carried past the body in dangerous proximity. This was nerve-racking for the spectators but it proved the courage and daring taught by these exercises.[15]

The demonstration included one of the last accomplishments of 'Guoshu', in the form of taiji callisthenics (*taiji cao*), a simplified, slowed-down form of taiji, designed to be within the capabilities of literally anyone, including exercising pensioners. Its promoter, Chu Minyi (1884–1946) was a famous Nationalist who had studied medicine in France, and had earned his doctorate in 1925 from the University of Strasbourg. It was Chu, in his role as the dean of Zhongshan University, who encouraged and recruited teachers who would emphasise this particular form of taiji, thereby privileging it ahead of many others. Three years earlier, he had arranged a similar mass demonstration in Nanjing of the exercises that he occasionally called 'national callisthenics' (*Guocao*), reasonably predicting the degree to which they would be taken up in China and across the world's overseas Chinese populations.[16]

A prominent figure in the 1930s Nationalist administration, Chu would later switch sides – marooned in Shanghai after the Japanese takeover, he would agree to help his brother-in-law Wang Jingwei form a quisling government. Chu is hence a complex and difficult figure in Chinese history, widely regarded as a hero of the Nationalist regime, but also as a collaborator in his final years. Arrested and tried for treason after the defeat of Japan, he went to his execution defiantly proclaiming his service to a higher power: 'I am not ashamed for my living, yet my death will make more value. My body should be sent to the hospital to assist the study on medicine.'

RIVERS AND LAKES — EARLY MODERN FICTIONS

Even as the Nationalist government attempted to adopt a realist attitude towards the martial arts, its assumptions were inevitably tainted by elements drawn not from fact, but from fiction. When we read accounts of the histories of the martial arts, we should bear in mind that we are reading records that have been told and retold, fashioned into plays and novels 'based on a true story', pirated and reprinted under different covers, and passed on as 'true', along a chain of readers and audiences, some of whom were illiterate, and others of whom were credulous.

We find stories, for example, like Wu Xuan's *Legends of the Flying Dragon* (1797, *Fei Long Zhuan*), set safely far back at the time of the founding of the Song dynasty. The man who will one day become the first Song emperor is shown wandering the country, righting wrongs, rescuing fair maidens, entering blood oaths with earnest revolutionaries, and learning the many tricks and techniques that will one day be turned into the Long Fist fighting style for which he will be known. In the fictional world, this is what is known as a *retcon* – retroactive continuity. As noted in Chapter Three, there is no historical evidence of the creation of the Long Fist, or even of a genuine association between it and the first Song emperor, but now 'proof' is being supplied long after the fact, in a series of tall tales that will be rehearsed and recycled, passed on in taverns and among conversationalists who are convinced that the novel they have just read is 'based on a true story'.

Such tales also existed in a liminal world in which China was experiencing an ever-widening reality gap between the boastful proclamations of its rulers in Beijing and the grim realities of foreign incursions at the coast. By 1842 Hong Kong had become a British colony. Speakers of Cantonese and similar southern Chinese dialects were spreading throughout the world to form new Chinatown communities, creating a ready audience for tall tales of the heroes and struggles of the homeland. These stories would often reflect a bias that drifted southward, with heroes from Guangdong (Canton) or the south-eastern province of Fujian. They also favoured an idea that China was falling apart, that justice was no longer guaranteed from the Manchu authorities (if it ever had been), and that true heroes would have to be sourced at a grass-roots level. They would be uneducated but heroic; unarmed but unbeatable; born of a noble spirit despite lowly origins. They would be so pure of heart that they would be able to take on corrupt officials and grasping bandits using just the power of their bare hands. They would be champions of a forgotten China, living embodiments of an invigorated and hard-working spirit that would stand against the opium-fogged cronies of the contemporary regime. Like the Confucian gentleman of old, they would first settle matters in their families, among their friends, in their village and in their communities, before expanding their horizons to right wrongs elsewhere. Although rarely stated outright in the nineteenth century, they would be the poster boys of a movement that would eventually overthrow the Manchus, restore Chinese rule to China, and cast out the unwanted European imperialists.

Such a cast list had plenty of precedents in traditional Chinese literature. *The Water Margin*, with its tale of noble outlaws robbing the undeserving rich and giving to the oppressed poor, presented many models. But the heroes of Victorian-era Chinese potboilers were often men of little means, like the implied reader. They had to learn their trade somewhere, and they had to flourish somehow in the straitened times. They dwelt forever in a world of *jiang hu* – rivers and lakes.

A centuries-old poetic term that originally meant turning away from state politics, *jiang hu* first appeared in this new context in the title of a 1921 novel, *The Peculiar Heroes of the Rivers and Lakes*, evoking the placeless expanses of the Chinese hinterland, where mighty rivers and grand canals link inland seas and waterways, offering refuge to small-town crooks and wheeler-dealers, travelling crime-fighters and distressed damsels.[17]

Shanghai, home of the Jingwu martial arts school, was also the location where much of China's early twentieth-century publishing and film-making flourished. In an attempt to cash in on the worldwide success of early Hollywood swashbuckler movies, local film-makers turned to the stories of martial artists and roaming heroes, leading to the first acknowledged *wuxia* film, *Lady Knight Li Feifei* (1925), produced by Shaw Renje.[18] Finding a ready audience for his films not only in Shanghai, but in urban centres of the Chinese diaspora in Singapore and South-East Asia, Shaw continued to invest in similar projects in which heroes championed Chinese tradition in the face of persecution.

Shaw and his siblings – better known today as the Shaw Brothers after the Hong Kong studio they would set up in 1947 – soon faced a backlash from the New Culture Movement, proponents of which regarded a concentration on traditional fantasies as counter-productively old-fashioned. There was, however, no accounting for taste, and their rivals at the Mingxing Picture Company continued to adapt potboilers, most notably with *The Burning of the Red Lotus Temple* (1928), an adaptation of *The Peculiar Heroes of the Rivers and Lakes*, establishing the term *jiang hu* in common parlance. In the years that have since passed, *jiang hu* has taken on an interpretation increasingly related to the criminal underworld. A translator in the early twentieth century would have been well within his rights to render *jiang hu* as 'days of old', or to find some construction reminiscent of the American West – even modern computer games of a *jiang hu* style replicate sentence constructions and vocabulary that we might call 'Victorian' or 'Wild West' in English. But in Hong

Kong in particular, *jiang hu* came to signify a wainscot society of organised criminals – the *hao han* 'good fellows' of *The Water Margin* fame transforming into literal goodfellas with a Mafia twist, echoing the 'secret societies' of old.

As for *The Burning of the Red Lotus Temple*, it came loaded with supernatural feats of mid-air swordplay accomplished by dangling the actors on wires, as well as hand-drawn animation to impart the effects of lightning and energy beams. The film spawned many sequels, imitators and even a cult of would-be martial artists who 'left their homes and took the hills, heading to Mount Emei in Sichuan Province in search of immortals to teach them the supernatural arts'.[19]

The modernist establishment was aghast. The young novelist Mao Dun, a revolutionary realist who would soon become a leading standard bearer of the Communist Party, wrote a stinging broadside against the 'feudalistic petty urban bourgeoisie', disgusted at the degree to which the audience swallowed the illusions onscreen and the imaginary martial arts depicted. 'When they criticise the film, they don't say this or that actor has given a good or bad performance. Instead they criticise the merits or demerits of the Kunlun school or the Emei school. To them, the film is real, not a play of shadows on the screen.'[20]

The left wing was not alone. The ruling Kuomintang Party agreed about the potentially destructive influence of the martial arts film on impressionable young audiences, introducing strict film censorship policies in 1931 that had all but killed off the genre within a couple of years.[21] It would only continue to flourish outside China, among the overseas audiences of the Chinese diaspora, and in the hands of the Hong Kong film industry, to which many refugee film-makers would flock in the 1940s.

FROM AIKIDO TO HAPKIDO

Meanwhile, in Japan, the modernisation of traditional fighting arts continued to generate many refinements and rediscoveries. Just as karate only rose to prominence in the twentieth century, aikido similarly was created in modern times, but came rich with allusions to an ancient past. According to the martial art's own internal history, its 'distant' founder was the medieval samurai Shinra Saburō Minamoto no Yoshimitsu, who flourished in the early twelfth century, and who was regarded in his day at the curator of the ancient traditions of sumo. These, not unexpectedly, were accorded substantially longer pedigrees in Japan than they have been given in this book, since Japan's own folklore, knocked up in the years that followed the arrival of so much Tang dynasty culture, bullishly claimed that sumo had been around since the dawn of time, and had even been practised by the gods who created Japan in the first place.

Whoever invented wrestling – and let us be honest, since it seems to be reinvented by every generation of children, puppies and kittens, it may even be universal – much of the art was in the hands of particular samurai experts by the commencement of Japan's civil wars. Yoshimitsu's descendants within the Minamoto clan continued to refine and repurpose his grappling art, drawing, it was said, on forbidden knowledge that Yoshimitsu had first gained by diligently dissecting battlefield corpses in search of the secrets of joints and pressure points.

By the late-medieval period, Yoshimitsu's descendants were better known as the Takeda family, and their battlefield grappling technique variously known as the Takeda style (Takeda-*ryū*) or Great Eastern style (*Daitō-ryū*). A cynical reader might already be wondering why so many names are required for what is supposedly the same thing – surely a simpler explanation is that later authors are drawing a shaky line between a series of vaguely related dots, and then proclaiming the line to be a *lineage* long after the fact. But let us give them the benefit of the doubt for the moment, and agree that when Tokugawa Ieyasu came to power as the first Tokugawa shogun, he happily incorporated many men, ideas and institutions from the faithful Takeda clan into the running of his state. One of Ieyasu's grandsons even *became* a Takeda, marrying into the family, studying the Takeda-*ryū*, and including many elements of it into his education regime when he was appointed as the lord of the Aizu domain.

Aizu is crucial because it is a lynchpin of Japanese history – the site of one of the last battles of the great civil war that heralded the Meiji Restoration in 1868. Pushed out of the Kyoto area and ever northwards, the forces of the dying shogunate made a prolonged, brave but futile stand at Aizu, before the castle fell in a terrible conflagration, and the last of the samurai fled to make their true last stand, as noted in Chapter Five, on the northern island of Hokkaido. *Daitō-ryū*, and the many other names for grappling forms to which it is linked, is thus indelibly associated with the martial heroism of the 'last of the samurai' – useful not only in branding, but in explaining why it should be in the hands of a disenfranchised group with enough time on their hands to be martial arts teachers.[22] The victors in the Meiji Restoration had other things on their minds, forming the new elite of a swiftly modernising Japan, studying newfangled disciplines like international law, engineering, hydraulics or foreign languages. Tellingly, it is from the vanquished that we draw the ranks of the first generation of *Daitō-ryū* teachers in modern times – an underclass excluded from many roles in the new order. We find them as priests and vagrants, and as settlers in the last samurai heartland of Hokkaido, where many of the shogun's surviving former loyalists were effectively marooned, having lost everything they owned in the south.

Takeda Sōkaku (1859–1943) was a descendant of the Takeda clan, living on Hokkaido and dedicated to a life of martial arts, citing his personal background as the inheritor of the Takeda clan's grappling techniques, and teaching a martial art that, by now, he was calling the 'Great Eastern style combined soft techniques' (*Daitō-ryū aiki jūjutsu*). This is only one of several schools claiming a provenance that extends back into the samurai era, but it is important because two of Takeda's students supposedly started martial arts of their own.

The most famous was Ueshiba Morihei (1883–1969), a veteran of the Russo-Japanese War who became one of the frontier settlers in Hokkaido in 1912. A pupil of Takeda, Ueshiba eventually grew into his most treasured disciple. When forced to move back south by family circumstances, Ueshiba left most of his possessions and his newly constructed training hall with Takeda.

Down in the south, in Kyoto and its environs, Ueshiba fell in with an odd crowd. He became an acolyte of a fringe religious sect, the Ōmoto-kyō, which contained several explosive doctrines nestled among its general proclamations of peace and harmony. One was the belief that in ancient times Amaterasu, the sun goddess, had usurped the throne of Japan from the land's true gods – a claim that brought the cult into conflicts with the authorities, since Amaterasu was believed to be the ancestor of the Emperor. Another oddity was the cult's leader Deguchi Onisaburō, who believed himself to be a reincarnation of Genghis Khan, causing Ueshiba to travel with Deguchi to the edges of Mongolia in 1924, purportedly in the hope of setting up a new Japanese-influenced religious state in the area.[23]

An underhand intrigue, seemingly conceived in collaboration between the Japanese 'Black Dragon' secret society and a group of Chinese bandits, this was merely one of many attempts by the Japanese to interfere in mainland politics – the most successful and infamous of which would come several years later, when Japanese officers staged a terrorist attack and armed response in order to snatch all of Manchuria from China, setting up the Japan-sponsored puppet state of Manchukuo in its place.

However, in the case of the reincarnated Genghis Khan plot, the venture was a resounding failure, ending with the execution of the Chinese collaborators and the deportation of the Japanese, Ueshiba and Deguchi among them. Although Deguchi was imprisoned (he had already violated his bail for a previous crime simply by leaving the country), Ueshiba enjoyed increased contacts with certain military factions – despite misgivings about his association with the cult, he enjoyed enough support among the authorities to be officially invited to Tokyo as a martial arts instructor for the imperial guard.

In 1925, Ueshiba performed a demonstration fight when, unarmed, he successfully disarmed a naval officer wielding a wooden sword. He reported a 'golden experience' afterwards, when resting in his garden, as he experienced a religious vision, in which the universe shook and a golden spirit rose up from the ground, transforming him into a gold effigy, and allowing him to understand the language of birds. It was at this moment, so he would claim, that he experienced enlightenment, and the counter-intuitive realisation that *budō*, the 'martial way' was nothing to do with war or fighting at all, but in fact should be considered as an effort for all to live in peace and harmony.

We can see here the influence of Deguchi's religion, and possibly also an anachronistic post-war aspect, since all Japanese martial arts were banned in 1945, and Ueshiba, like many other teachers, may have over-emphasised pacifism and philosophy in later years in order to have legal training reinstated and avoid associations with the defeated wartime state. Regardless of when such pacifist notions began to creep into his lessons, Ueshiba was valued as a teacher by the military authorities, and prominent enough to be invited on multiple occasions to China, to teach at a Japan-sponsored university in Changchun, then the capital of Manchukuo.

Ueshiba attracted the attention of judo's founder, Kanō Jigorō, who commented of his martial art: 'This is true *budō*; it is true judo.' This caused some consternation among his own pupils, some of whom were heard to ask if this meant that Kanō was teaching 'fake' judo. Several of Kanō's students were known to be simultaneously studying with Ueshiba, and one even pointedly returned his belt to Kanō after Ueshiba had bested him in a bout.[24]

Aikido would continue to flourish after the end of the Second World War, not only in its original form, but in a distaff cousin in a former colony. Following Japan's defeat, the Japanese empire that had taken half a century to assemble was suddenly broken up. Taiwan was returned to the Republic of China, and soon became the only territory claimed by that entity. Manchuria and other mainland possessions ended up within the People's Republic of China, and the colony of Korea was eventually divided into two countries, a Communist north and a democratic south.

The late 1940s and early 1950s in Korea saw many former colonial subjects rebranding their Japanese martial arts or combining them with Korean traditions to create 'Korean' originals. This created a mess of newly formed *kwon* schools (Chinese: *quan*, English: fist), many of which displayed or implied connections to Japanese models, such as *Tang soo do*, the meaning of which echoed the old Kara-te (the 'China-hand way'), or two confusing versions of *tae soo do*, the 'supreme-hand way' and the 'stomp-hand way'. Others studiously disavowed any connection with the colonial period, such as *taekkyon* (kick-punch), whose practitioners claimed it to be a traditional Korean martial art, practised in secret during the Japanese occupation, and now conveniently revealed to the population. If *taekkyon* had any foreign influences at all, it was said, then it would only be to the 'boxing' derived from traditional manuals in the eighteenth century, and hence from China rather than Japan.

We might observe that comments on 'secrecy' may also allude to something that definitely *did* happen during the Japanese colonial period, in that Koreans from 1910 to 1945 were unable to compete in international sporting events as Koreans, but instead had to function as Japanese subjects, often with Japanese names. An ethnic Korean, for example, represented Japan in boxing at the 1932 Olympics in Los Angeles, while the 'Japanese' gold medallist at the 1936 Berlin Olympics marathon was actually a Korean, Sohn Keechung. At his medal ceremony, Sohn refused to acknowledge the Japanese national anthem, and news coverage of his victory created a scandal in Seoul, when a local newspaper blanked out a Rising Sun emblem in a photograph.[25] Hence, sport in post-war Korea was openly regarded as a tool of political reconstruction, and part of a concerted effort to reclaim an ethnic Korean identity that had been swamped and overwritten by the Japanese empire since 1910.

Urged by the South Korean president in 1951 to rationalise the competing factions, the *kwon* community integrated most of them into a single federation. By 1957, this merged style was known as *taekwondo* (kick-fist way), in which form it would spread beyond Korea to the world at large.[26] Before long, the taekwondo federation was making further claims for its provenance, claiming that any pictures of boxers in ancient tombs, and any references to unarmed combat in any chronicle, and any statue of a warrior, were actually references to this taekwondo, even though the word itself had only existed for six years. There were, undoubtedly, earlier schools of unarmed combat in Korea, most memorably that of a General Chok in ancient Baekje, who taught that 'the art of hand is like the use of sword'. It is not, however, clear just how literal this was intended to be, as the same verse claims that 'one single pass of the two hands' will behead an opponent. Nor, of course, is there any clear link between whatever it was that General Chok taught, and the martial arts schools in South Korea a dozen centuries later.[27] Connections to Japan are far more apparent, but unwelcome among the Koreans themselves.

One of several Korean forms that remained outside this federation was *hapkido*, established by Choi Yong-sool (1904–86) in 1951. Choi had spent much of his life in Japan, and would claim (or be attributed to have said) in an interview only posthumously published that he was the adopted son of Takeda Sōkaku, the founder of Daitō-ryū aiki-jūjutsu. This, perhaps, explains why the characters used to write the name hapkido look exactly like the ones used in Japanese to write aikido, although Choi's status in the Takeda family was news to the Japanese. Ueshiba Morihei's son reported that someone fitting Choi's description had attended seminars in north Japan, but had no recollection of having an adopted Korean brother. It has been suggested elsewhere that Choi was a servant in Takeda's house, but there is no evidence or agreement in Japan that this somehow translated into the thirty years of individual training claimed for Choi. Notably, apart from the aforementioned posthumous interview, there is no extant evidence that Choi made any such far-fetched claims during his lifetime. He made no secret that his hapkido was his own invention, heavily inspired by Japanese traditions. The degree to which it is an *inheritor* of a Japanese tradition remains a controversial subject – Korean books continue to insist that it is a two thousand-year-old tradition, practised in secret for five centuries before modern times, and suddenly rediscovered in the twentieth century.[28] Kim Un-yong, a leading light in the taekwondo world, subsequently threw the cat among the pigeons by suggesting that there is evidence enough in the ancient chronicles to suggest that *Koreans* taught karate to the Ryūkyū Islanders.[29] This assertion seems to be trying a little too hard to right the wrongs of the colonial era, although more level-headed scholars do not rule out a degree of cross-pollination.

THE CREATION OF SHORINJI KEMPO

Another young martial art, born from the hybrid connections of twentieth century East Asia, is Shorinji Kempo, founded in 1947 in Japan by Sō Dōshin (1911–80), a former Manchurian colonist. Born as Nakano Michiomi, Sō had a terrible hard-luck story as a child. With Japan reeling from the cataclysmic aftermath of the Great Kantō earthquake of 1923, Sō was shunted from relative to relative after his father's death and his mother's preoccupied involvement in an unspecified religious sect. His grandfather Shigetō was an employee of the South Manchuria Railway, and Sō lived with him from the age of fourteen, becoming one of many Japanese expatriates in north-east China who formed the front line of an unofficial wave of immigration. Sō appears to have adopted his grandfather's surname at some point; notably, as implied by its monosyllabic peculiarity, it is a surname intimately connected with the island of Tsushima, and implies an ancestry on the borderline between Japan and Korea, much as the Ryūkyū Islands permitted permeable cultural contacts between Japan and China.[30] But by the 1920s, Manchuria was Japan's great hope for resources and mainland expansion, and would soon officially secede from China with the establishment of the puppet state of Manchukuo.

Historical memory usually regards the Japanese presence in Manchuria as an oppressive colonial regime, and a predatory land-grab with eyes even further westward on Mongolia and the plains near Beijing. Mention of the *Japanese* martial arts in a Manchurian context is usually limited to gruesome accounts of, for example, judo as a tactic used by thugs and extortionists.[31] This is certainly true, but such broad sweeps of history overlook the many human stories of the period. The Japanese were unquestionably the agents of an occupying power, but Sō's account, like those of many others, also comes shimmering with starry-eyed romance about a wild frontier and a great enterprise to build an Asian utopia. We hear very little today about the Chinese collaborators who welcomed the Japanese presence, the businesses and farms that thrived under their rule, and the citizens who however briefly, enjoyed a respite from the internecine struggles that were tearing China apart elsewhere.[32] Sō's memoirs make no secrets of his misgivings about Japanese imperialism and, indeed, we might even suggest that by the 1930s he had somewhat 'gone native'. He was, however, still working as a spy and surveyor on behalf of the Japanese authorities, and certainly part of an engine of intelligence gathering designed to infiltrate deeply into China, either to conquer it directly or use it as a means of attacking the Soviet Union from an unexpected angle. Common to many imperialists, he regarded his role as ultimately beneficial not only to Japan, but also to China.

Sō had trained in Japanese martial arts with his grandfather, and spent some time undercover as a temple acolyte, learning kung fu from a local collaborator called Chen Lian. His memoirs call it 'Shaolin kung fu', although his account of his training offers a great insight into the slippery nature defining anything taught in remote places by unknown authorities: 'While I lived with Master [Chen] I received an introduction to his techniques little by little in between my duties. However, if a technique I was taught was not systematised, then it did not have a name with meaning and even if I could remember it, it was very hard to do. Some of the moves did not have names at all.'[33]

Sō writes that Master Chen was not his sole teacher, but that in their travels throughout north China, he introduced him to many other martial artists 'in hiding' who taught him other, unspecified techniques. The most important, however, was named – Wen

Taizong, the twentieth-generation grandmaster of something that Sō called 'northern' Shaolin *Yihemen quan* (Fist of the Gate of Righteous Harmony). It is an odd name – he specifies 'northern' Shaolin, even though the Shaolin Temple itself never does so, as the designation is only required if one believes the myth that there was ever a 'southern' Shaolin from which it needed to be distinguished. This was, however, a designation already in use in the Jingwu school in Shanghai.[34] Moreover, as noted in Chapter Four, there is no mention of a 'Gate of Righteous Harmony' during the Boxer Uprising, nor of a specific martial art that draws its name from the Unity of Righteous Harmony. Sō, however, was told not only that Wen was a grandmaster in *Yihemen quan*, but that he had been instrumental in the Boxer Uprising some thirty years earlier.

'I had learned the basics from Master Chen,' he wrote, 'which helped me with my natural intuition. Under Master Wen, I learned the tricks to various techniques as sand absorbs water. Even though the system required three years to become a senior disciple, I was able to do it in less than one.'[35]

This is the comment that modern martial artists would find the hardest to believe. After a decade in deep cover in China, I find it wholly plausible that Sō could be taken in by the Chinese as one of their own; I don't doubt that he was a fast and eager student. Despite the reverence accorded to the black belt among the general public, it is not unknown for one to be attainable in Japan in a single calendar year, assuming daily study rather than the once-weekly lessons commonly found abroad. But there was no such thing as a 'black belt' in 1930s China, and we have no way of really understanding the nature of such a title. It was not unknown, in the days before the standardised issuing of credentials from a national body, for the conferral of rank to be a much simpler matter, often limited to perhaps three levels of accomplishment, with no talk of 'belts' or grandmaster status. Nor was there any particular moment of 'examination', but rather a rolling period of general assessment, at which point a pupil would be informed of his achievement.

Back in Japan, where the Greater Japan Martial Virtue Society had been policing credentials since 1895, such statuses had real meaning. The term 'senior disciple' implies attainment of a level more equivalent to a modern second or third-*dan*. In a remote temple in the mountains of Henan, at the feet of a master whose skills did not come accompanied by any credentials save his observable abilities, it means only what Master Wen says it means, in both a good and bad sense. By 1936, according to Sō, Master Wen was not only calling him his senior disciple, but was prepared to confer upon him the rank of twenty-first senior grandmaster, the highest rank imaginable, in a 'simple ceremony' conducted at the Shaolin Temple itself.[36]

This is not the ridiculous boast that it first appears to be, although some adherents of Shorinji Kempo do take it at face value and brag of their founder's supposed status within the Chinese martial arts community. Sō himself offers an explanation that indicates just how far the martial arts are likely to have fallen during the turmoil of the late nineteenth and early twentieth century. When he writes of his visit to the Shaolin Temple, it is a mural that inspires him the most: a painting on the north wall of the Baiyi Hall, unharmed in the fire of 1928 and still extant today, which depicts monks sparring in the temple precincts, largely divided into pairs in which a dark-skinned, Indian monk is imparting unarmed combat techniques to a lighter-skinned Chinese. He writes that when, ten years later, he founded his own martial art, it was this image of multicultural transmission, and the place where he saw it, that inspired him call his new style *Shōrinji Kempō* (Japanese: Shaolin Temple Fist Law). As to his opinions on original Shaolin kung fu, or what was left of it, and the likely value of being made a grandmaster by an old man on a hilltop, he was substantially less enthusiastic.

I thought that since Master Wen must have held me in high esteem and had been so kind to me, that I might as well accept the honour if it would please him . . . After the succession ceremony, a temple monk gave us a demonstration of his techniques, but he failed to make it as lively as what was depicted in the mural. I felt sad that due to the outlawing of and clampdown on martial arts following the Boxer Rebellion, their skill was forced into decline.[37]

Sō's remarks point to an issue that had already been raised by the Jingwu association in Shanghai, and was surely troubling surviving martial artists all over China – decades of deprivation had reached the point where many martial arts were less being transmitted than salvaged or reverse-engineered from whatever paltry evidence remained of them. As his own writings made clear, Sō did not see himself as transmitting an ancient tradition, but of salvaging the 'scattered remnants' of whatever martial arts had survived Qing purges and Republican discord in the preceding decades.[38]

Sō returned to Japan in 1946, having witnessed the crisis that befell the colonists in Manchuria, who were abandoned by the very same Japanese soldiers who were supposedly there to protect them. The Japanese army fled ahead of the Soviets, leaving the settlers to fend for themselves. Many committed suicide or died in the ensuing battle over resources. His last command was of a group of three-hundred fellow refugees, whom he was obliged to keep together with nothing but charisma and choke-holds to cow the more violent members into submission. With no family in the homeland that he had barely seen since his teens, he settled in the harbour town of Tadotsu, where he tried to rebrand the frontier utopianism that had driven him to Manchuria in the first place as a more patriotic philosophy. With martial arts still illegal under the US occupation, he emphasised his new organisation's religious nature in all dealings with the authorities. Shorinji Kempo thus began in Japan as an offshoot of Buddhist philosophy, emphasising in particular the teachings of Bodhidharma (which happened to include something called the Fists of the Arhats, derived from the Eighteen Hands of the Luohan), and with the acolytes that might otherwise be called 'black belts' attired, as they still often are to this day, in the robes of Buddhist priests. Confucius himself would have been pleased to hear that Sō explained to the authorities that his disciples' worship involved a kind of 'dance'.

Such subterfuges were not uncommon in the 1940s and 1950s, not only to avoid entanglements with the authorities, but to gain the advantages of tax breaks for religious organisations. Shorinji Kempo was founded at a time when reference to *Japanese* martial arts was heavily discouraged. The US occupation authorities proscribed all media that lionised the old samurai order, which was held responsible for dragging Japan into the 'dark valley' of a militarised nation that had pursued an empire in East Asia. As a result, many elements of Japanese culture, which had undeniably been dominated by samurai elements for a thousand years, found strange new ways of flourishing. An exhibition of swords in Tokyo was carefully parsed as an exhibition of the *artistry* of smithing. Kabuki theatres trashed much of their more modern, martial repertoire in favour of the 'parasols and cherry blossoms' school of Tokugawa romance. In the lurid world of potboiler novels and the burgeoning medium of *manga* comics, tales of samurai daring were discarded, replaced instead by historical epics that created a new underclass of shadowy assassins, valorising the peasant subalterns ignored by previous narratives (see Chapter Eight).

The occupation ended officially at the beginning of 1952, returning Japan to home rule, albeit with some divisive legacies – the official absence of a Japanese military, and the continued stationing of US forces on Japanese territory. Martial arts and samurai stories re-asserted themselves in the Japanese media, but the ongoing presence of American personnel in Japan was already creating a new crossover. Servicemen returning home, from the Second World War, the Korean War or simply stationed on the 'unsinkable aircraft carrier' of Japan would arrive in America with personal experience of the martial arts. They were by no means the first foreigners to return from the Far East with an interest in such subjects (see Chapter Five for some of their predecessors). But their influence would be profound all across North America and the world.

CHAPTER SEVEN

Journey to the West

....

'I had that Danish karate team in the back of my cab once,' says the driver. He uses the cabbies' definite article, as if I am supposed to know which Danish karate team he is talking about.

'They were over for that tournament, and they went out on the town afterwards. They drink a lot, you know? I was surprised. I didn't think kung fu people liked beer or whatever. But I picked them up at like two in the morning, in their red tracksuits, and I was driving them back to their hotel, and we was all south of the river. In *Brixton*. And one of them says: "You know what, I want some orange juice. Pull over a second." And I says: no mate, you don't want to stop the car in bloody *Brixton*, not now, not at kicking-out time round all the clubs. And he laughs and says just pull over. So I do. I stops the cab, and all three of them hop out and go into a Seven-Eleven.

'I just know there's going to be trouble, and sure enough, there's three big blokes go in. And one of them is like: give me your money. Give me your money, he says, to this ginger Dane in a tracksuit. Give me your phone and all. And the Danish guy is like: no, leave me alone. And the bloke is like (and he's a big feller, right?) and he's like give to me now or I will eff you up. And the Dane is like: "No. Step away, sir, please." Polite as you like.

'So the bloke pulls back to punch him, and POOF! He's on the ground clutching his head. And the Dane says: really, I am warning you. But he's like: "GET THE LADS!" And the other two run off to the club, and they are back in flash with half a dozen mates, and they all charge at these Danes.

'And these are tired, right, but they train for this every day. They don't even have to think. It's like BOFF! BOFF! BOFF! Kung fu fighting and they knock them all down. A couple of berks try to get up again, and then it's BOFF! Stay down. Then they go to pay for their orange juice, and the police turn up.

'And what do the police see? They see eight or nine big thugs just lying on the ground moaning and hanging on to their arms and that. And these three little Danes having a packet of Wotsits. And the policeman says to me: "Did you see what happened here, sir?"

'And I says: "Them three blokes are the Danish karate team. And them others just found out what that means!"'

I'll save you the trouble, dear reader. I Googled this one. I Googled every possible permutation of Brixton and Denmark and karate. When I came up blank, I tried every other Scandinavian country, as well as the Netherlands, on a hunch. I switched the martial arts, just in case it was kung fu or aikido or judo. But despite such an epic account from my story-teller, despite a midnight riot that was sure to have entered the folklore of south London, despite the implied eye-witness experience of the narrator himself, down to the tracksuit colours and omnipotent view of what was said and done a hundred feet away while he was still in his car, there is not a scrap of evidence online of this supposed event. No court hearing, no police report, not even a snickering comment in the local newspaper.

I Googled it in Danish, too, just to be sure.

Nothing.

But that's the story I heard, word for word. Straight up.

BRITAIN — FROM BARTITSU TO THE BUDOKWAI

Edward William Barton-Wright (1860–1951) was a child of empire, the son of a railway engineer in British India, who worked for railway and mining companies all over the world. He spent several years in Japan, where he studied jujutsu and judo, before returning to London in 1898 and setting himself up as a martial arts instructor. In his Bartitsu Academy of Arms and Physical Culture under what is now the Shaftesbury Hotel on Shaftesbury Avenue, ironically just across the road from the future location of London's Chinatown, he began holding courses in a martial art of his own devising, which he decided to call *Bartitsu*.

Barton-Wright was keen to establish his martial art's Japanese credentials, and would ship in several prominent judo teachers in the next few years. But he also made clear to his pupils that he regarded the pure martial arts as inadequate in dealing with a notional European opponent. 'Judo and jujitsu were not designed as primary means of attack and defence against a boxer or a man who kicks you,' he wrote in the *Transactions of the Japan Society*, 'but are only to be used after coming to close quarters, and in order to get to close quarters it is absolutely necessary to understand boxing and the use of the foot.'[1]

Barton-Wright's fighting school played to a general worry among London's middle classes that their way of life was under threat from hungry urchins and flinty brigands from the East End. He offered instead a touch of imperial superiority – a chance for the straight-backed, cane-wielding gentleman about town to get one over on any would-be robbers. He offered his students 'immunity against injury in cowardly attacks', but also the delicious prospect of being able to 'scientifically attack' weak spots and use an opponent's strength against him.

Bartitsu was a flash in the pan; its creator soon drifted off into physical therapy, outclassed by many of his own instructors. Although Barton-Wright tried to promote his fad in a flurry of magazine articles and public appearances, interest soon waned. The most enduring element turned out to be a misprint in 1901, when Arthur Conan Doyle's hero Sherlock Holmes, returning from the dead after years away from the pages of the London magazines, revealed to

John Watson that he was able to defeat his adversary Moriarty through *baritsu* [sic], 'or the Japanese system of wrestling, which has more than once been very useful to me.'[2]

One of Barton-Wright's instructors, Tani Yukiō, left for a brief side-show career as Apollo, the Pocket Hercules, wrestling for money against all comers before setting up his own Japanese School of Jujutsu on Oxford Street in 1904. Two years later, he co-authored *The Game of Ju-jitsu for the Use of Schools and Colleges*, a book that helped promote him far and wide. The introduction to the second printing, a mere four months after the first, boasts of the swift interest in the martial art as far afield as training sessions at the Royal Military Academy in Woolwich, Eton College and an Admiralty grant to teach at the Navy School of Physical Training. Gamages, the athletic outfitters in Holborn, began advertising 'authentic jujitsu oufits'. Meanwhile, the school's influence had an unexpected impact on Cambridge University, where a Miss Roberts, Tani's 'instructor for ladies' gained a swift following among the would-be suffragettes of the women's colleges. The rhetoric of jujutsu – that size did not matter, and that one might use one's own opponent's weight and momentum against him – was of great interest to a political group who were being excluded from equality on the grounds that they were the weaker sex.

Uyenishi Sadakazu, another of the Japanese brought in by Barton-Wright as an instructor, also tired of his boss's showman-ship and *hauteur*, leaving in 1903 to found the School of Japanese Self-Defence in nearby Golden Square. After Uyenishi returned to Japan in 1908, his school was taken over by two of his students, husband and wife William and Edith Garrud. It was Edith who had the greatest media profile, arguably becoming Britain's first martial arts film star after her appearance in the short Pathé silent movie *The Lady Athlete, or Jiu Jitsu Downs the Footpads* (1907). By 1911, she was teaching classes after hours in an Argyll Street dance school, to an exclusive club of suffragettes.

'We have not yet made ourselves a match for the police, and we have got to do it,' suffragette Sylvia Pankhurst told a crowd in Bromley. 'The police know jiu-jitsu. I advise you to learn jiu-jitsu. Women should practise it as well as men.'[3]

In 1918, the United Kingdom gained its first martial arts training hall, the Budokwai, founded in London by Koizumi Gunji (1885–1965), initially at Lower Grosvenor Place, not far from Buckingham Palace. It was the first in Europe, and represented a toehold for the martial arts overseas that would be built upon by other disciplines, and in other countries. The Budokwai initially offered training in jujutsu, kendo and several non-martial arts, although the name itself implies an emphasis on *budō* samurai spirit – Tani Yukiō, the martial artist formerly known as the Pocket Hercules, was one of his instructors. Koizumi used the same venue to host a society for easing the passage of Japanese immigrants into UK society. The emphasis changed in 1920, when Kanō Jigorō, on his way to the Antwerp Olympics, stopped off in Britain and encouraged Koizumi and Tani to switch allegiance to judo proper. Both men were conferred with official second-*dan* black belts, and Koizumi thereafter pursued the role for which he would be remembered, as 'the father of British judo'.

Koizumi's contribution to Anglo–Japanese relations was not limited to the Budokwai. In 1922, he was called in to the Victoria & Albert Museum as a consultant on lacquerware, subsequently cataloguing the entire collection and writing a book on its appraisal. He kept lessons going throughout the Second World War, at considerable personal expense, determined to prove that judo's internationalist perspective transcended contemporary politics. He was the first leader of the British Judo Association, founded in 1948, and spent the last decade of his life dedicated both to the teaching of judo, and its popularisation through books.

A year after his death, the UK gained its first single-style karate organisation, the Karate Union of Great Britain in 1966.[4] Other martial arts soon followed.

AUSTRALASIA — FROM CECIL ELLIOTT TO THE AUCKLAND JUDOKWAI

Despite the fact that Australia and New Zealand were closer to the Far East than Europe, immigration restrictions severely limited contacts between these countries and Asia in the first half of the twentieth century. Social organisations serving the population of expatriate Chinese workers in Australia were founded as early as 1860, and it is difficult to imagine that some form of martial arts did not form part of their programmes in the ensuing four decades, which certainly included performances of Chinese opera, presumably with attendant acrobatics.[5] A Ballarat newspaper in 1892, for example, reported on a botched foul at a football match, seemingly noting the presence of martial arts skills, without realising what they were: 'A young fellow . . . went for a Chinaman, with the result that he made a mistake. "John", a muscular son of the Sun, seized the offender and well soused him in some adjacent mud amid the applause and laughter of a large section of the onlookers.'[6]

However, if such events occurred, they were not part of any outreach programme, and were simply unnoticed by the Australian colonists of European extraction. Instead, the earliest official contacts in the martial arts came via a circuitous route, brought in by immigrants from the United Kingdom.

Although there are rumours of martial arts events as early as 1878, when Yuasa Takejirō, a student of Kanō Jigorō, gave a demonstration as a visiting naval officer, the first official jujutsu demonstration in Australia, and hence its 'discovery' by the white population, was in 1906, by Cecil Elliott (1875–1963), a former able seaman in the British Navy, who had gained a first-*dan* black belt in Yokohama two years earlier.[7] He arrived in Sydney and found work as a teacher at R. F. Young's School of Physical Culture, which soon added jujutsu to its curriculum. The demonstration was given before an invited audience, including the New South Wales Commissioner of Police. Seemingly in imitation of the model followed by Edward Barton-Wright in London, Elliott shipped in two Japanese to aid in his classes, Okura Jinkichi and Fukushima Ryūgoro, the latter of whom would eventually become an Australian national wrestling champion.[8] Fukushima went on a tour of major Australian cities with a travelling circus, adding a new spin to his promotion of the martial arts by promising a reward to any man he could not throw to the ground within fifteen minutes.[9]

Fukushima was not the only travelling wrestler. A native of New South Wales, 'Professor' P. W. Stevenson arrived in Australia in 1906 having claimed to have studied in New York under a Japanese teacher, and to have won the previously unmentioned and entirely unknown 'White Jujitsu Championship' in America. He staged several wrestling matches that took the form of a circus sideshow, under what he called 'jujitsu rules' that, somewhat to audiences' surprise, included an allowance for biting and eye-gouging. After some scandalised reporting of this apparently savage art, Fukushima was moved to write to the *Sydney Morning Herald*, which printed his letter on 11 May 1909:

I am a certificated Japanese teacher of Ju-Jitsu, and since my arrival here have been teaching for some time in Sydney. I wish emphatically to protest against Mr. Stevenson calling such an exhibition *'Ju-Jitsu.'* . . . In a contest in Japan they do not allow biting, scratching, gouging, or kicking. I may say I challenged Mr. Stevenson some time ago to a real Japanese contest, but he did not accept.

It is not his province to frame rules governing the art. He must be guided by the rules that are recognised in Japan. I should be sorry to think that the public should get its impression of an immensely valuable system of physical culture, and means of athletic sport combined, from the report of what was represented as Ju-Jitsu in a circus tent on Saturday evening.

Ju-Jitsu, as understood and practised in Japan is, in friendly contests, governed by rules which would make it more acceptable as a trial of skill to the average Australian onlooker than either boxing or wrestling, as they have been exemplified of late. At least I think so, and I have seen contest in both countries, and I think understand something of boxing and wrestling, as well as Ju-Jitsu.

I write this to you, as I think it would be a pity for Australians to get wrong notions of an art, the usefulness of which to the individual, cannot well be over-emphasised.[10]

The conflict between Stevenson and Fukushima would escalate in a series of wrestling matches in which each would content to proclaim himself as the 'Jiujitsu Champion of Australia'. However, in the view of historian John Nash, the nature of their competitions diverged far from the practices of judo, and instead formed the early days of a new 'all-in' wrestling, rather than a manifestation of East Asian fighting styles.

Although numbers were small, transmission in the early days of judo in Australia ensued much as in any other country, following the migrations of its teacher. Elliott's move to Queensland caused the opening of another branch there. Fukushima returned to Japan in the 1920s, but came back to Australia in the 1930s, before moving on to New Zealand in 1936, where he became a naturalised citizen. One of his pupils in Sydney, Leonard Noyes, founded the Mercury

Jujitsu Club in 1938, and would be instrumental in the formation of the Australian Society of Jujitsuans in 1956. A British immigrant, George Grundy, would found New Zealand's first judo club, the Judokwai, in Auckland in 1948.

NORTH AMERICA — FROM ROOSEVELT TO RUSTY GLICKMAN

Much as in Britain and Australasia, the first appearances of the martial arts in North America were unseen by the non-Asian community. Despite the many thousands of Chinese labourers in the sawmills of Vancouver or the gold fields of California, the official 'beginning' of martial arts on the continent does not arrive until the twentieth century. Japanese martial arts, particularly judo, as well as several schools of Chinese kung fu, were practised among the immigrant populations of the Territory of Hawaii, forming an important bridge between East Asia and the United States.

In 1903, Kanō Jigorō's star pupil Yamashita Yoshiaki (1865–1935) arrived in Seattle, originally at the request of local millionaire Sam Hill, who had requested a judo instructor for his young son. General accounts tend to draw a veil over the fact that by the time Yamashita arrived, Mrs Hill had already returned home to the East Coast with their children, rendering Yamashita's original purpose almost pointless.[11] A demonstration in a Seattle theatre was hastily arranged for an invited audience, before Hill accompanied his guests east to Washington. In their wake, they left an interest in judo that led to the local Japanese community starting up the first dojo in Seattle.

In Washington, Yamashita gave some lessons to the Hill children over the winter of 1903, and gained his most famous pupil, President Theodore Roosevelt, in the spring of 1904, teaching at the White House that March and April. This was much to the annoyance of Mr Hill, who protested that the president had 'taken away from Harvard my judo man without my permission or even asking'.[12]

By 1905, Yamashita was teaching judo at the Naval Academy although seemingly on Roosevelt's orders rather than the academy's own wishes – the President had to write to the administration to encourage them to rehire him. Yamashita was not the only instructor in the area, 'Jiu-do' was also demonstrated in New York as early as 1905.[13]

The First World War caused a large number of Americans to be enlisted in the armed forces, where jujutsu formed a component of their unarmed combat training. This is liable to have created a more formidable group of interested parties in the post-war period, leading to a rise in available classes in the 1920s. America gained its first intercollegiate judo competition in 1940, by which time the country was already on a collision course with the Far East in the Second World War.

The martial arts had been co-opted into the Japanese war machine, not only for physical training, but for indoctrinating soldiers, with the battlefield philosophies of Zen dragged into arguments over a soldier's mind to be a blank slate, written upon only by the will of his commander. 'The soldier must become one with his superior. He must actually become his superior. Similarly, he must become the order he receives. That is to say, his self must disappear.'[14]

We might expect anything tainted with martial associations to be entirely suppressed by the occupation forces, but the martial arts were oddly resilient. The return of sports to post-war Japan was a remarkable rise from rock-bottom: the banning of martial arts from the school curriculum by the new, America-led Ministry of Education in 1945. Kendo swiftly wriggled around the ban by 'sportifying' – dropping its wooden swords and favouring bamboo *shinai* that emphasised this was more of a game and less of a practical skill.[15] Perhaps judo is to thank, with a well-established tradition overseas and clear pacifist aims – judo was back in Japanese schools by 1950.

Perhaps it was simple practicality, with servicemen recognising the military applications of the martial arts not just among the wartime Japanese, but among the post-war US forces.

In the wake of Japan's defeat, the Occupation of 1945–52, the Korean War of 1950–53, and the continued stationing of American personnel on Japanese soil, particularly in Okinawa, the home of karate, would expose thousands of soldiers and sailors to the martial arts. The effects were not felt back home in the US until the 1950s, particularly after 1953, when a team of ten Japanese martial arts instructors was taken on a tour of American air bases, sponsored by Strategic Air Command – Emil Bruno, head of SAC combative measures, had been a leading light of pre-war US collegiate judo. Teachers of judo, aikido and karate then helped foster an interest on the mainland in the same skills witnessed in the Far East.[16]

Martial arts had become a common fixture in sports arenas and church halls, with the association of the military and Okinawa leading to a rapid growth in karate, alongside the older, more established judo. For a martial art to truly take root, it required a substantial population of teachers and interested students, creating a bias that heavily favoured those martial arts that would not only get a mention in the mass media, but also had an already-established footprint. On the one day in someone's life they went looking for a training hall in a named martial art, it helped if such a training hall actually existed in their home town. Occasionally, this was easier than it looked, since Chinatown associations, previously ignored by non-Chinese, could now suddenly flourish with a more diverse clientele. Less well-known martial arts, such as taekwondo, introduced in 1956, would still require a generation to grow a suitable body of teachers and popularisers. More obscure martial arts huddled on the side-lines. In the case of Wing Chun, for example, training was somewhat inglorious. Bruce Lee, a newly arrived teenage Wing Chun practitioner in Seattle, was obliged to give lessons in a car park.

In Canada, martial arts enjoyed multiple routes to success, both on the west coast, where Vancouver's thriving Asian community gained its first martial arts school, a kendo dojo, in 1906, and through its connections to Britain and France. Bill Underwood, a sometime student of Tani Yukiō, emigrated as a young man to Canada in 1911, where he would teach an unarmed combat system derived from jujutsu. Originally called 'Combato', it was renamed 'Defendo' in the post-war period, when Underwood attempted to remove the more lethal military applications to make it seem more applicable to law enforcement. Meanwhile, karate arrived in Quebec in the 1950s, through connections to the French federation, as well as in English-speaking Canada through connections to the United States. Canada's most prominent martial artist was its prime minister, Pierre Trudeau, who would receive his black belt in judo on a state visit to Japan in 1970.

Meanwhile, merely because the suffragettes had embraced jujutsu with alacrity, women in the martial arts were not necessarily welcomed. In Japan, they were encouraged to stick to the more lady-like pursuits of naginatajutsu (pole-arms) and archery, and training for women was segregated from training for men. In American judo, for example, they were banned from competition throughout the 1960s, despite, or possibly because, of the achievements of the sport's most famous female champions. Throughout the 1940s and 1950s, women's judo's main poster-girl was June Tegner, who frequently appeared in newspapers and magazines extolling judo's benefits for health and fitness.[17] She was eclipsed, however, in the 1950s by a far scrappier and more controversial figure, whose long life in the martial arts packed in sufficient drama for a movie.

Rena 'Rusty' Glickman's story has much in common with those of many other martial artists. Hailing from an impoverished background on New York's Coney Island, Glickman was a gang leader by her teens. She discovered judo at the YMCA in 1955, and by 1959 had advanced sufficiently in the sport to fight on the winning men's team in the New York State YMCA judo championship in 1959. She was, however, immediately obliged to return her medal, after it was discovered that 'Rusty' Glickman was a woman – she had taped down her breasts and cut her hair in order to pass as a man. Shut out of US competition owing to a blanket ban on women, she moved to Japan, where she trained alongside the men at the Kōdōkan in Tokyo. By Glickman's own account, this was because she was considered too tough for the women's division, although this possibly echoes the findings of the Kōdōkan's first ever female black belt, Sarah Mayer, who commented as early as 1934 that she preferred to train with the men because the Kōdōkan's women's division was nothing but a 'finishing school for young Japanese ladies'.[18] Regardless, while training with the men, Glickman met and married a fellow judoist, and returned with him to New York to teach judo in Brooklyn.

> Over the course of her life she sustained a broken nose, a broken arm and 20 fractures in her toes, broke both collarbones and dislocated her shoulder. Why so many injuries? The quantity of injuries she attributes to two things: the poor quality of the mats used back then and the intensity of her male opponents who could not risk losing to a female. 'I was a threat,' she said. 'When they threw me, they tried to put me through the cellar.'[19]

Glickman's fighting spirit extended to mortgaging her house and maxing out her credit cards in order to host the first-ever Women's World Judo Championship in 1980 at Madison Square Garden. She was also instrumental in getting women's judo accepted as a demonstration sport at the Seoul Olympics, for which she was the US team coach. In 2009, two months before her death, she was awarded a gold medal for lifetime achievement by the same New York YMCA that had refused to honour her in 1959.

In each of these cases, however – Britain, Australasia and North America, for men and women – the true watershed moment only came in the 1970s, when popular culture suddenly began to recognise the existence of karate, kung fu and other martial arts. This not only increased the take-up of the sport among pre-existing trainers, but encouraged many Chinatown schools, previously closed to non-Chinese, to open their admissions to outsiders. The reason was a genre of films, and one actor in particular, who inherited a tradition of martial arts cinema stretching back to the 1940s.

FIST OF FURY – THE SPREAD OF MARTIAL ARTS CINEMA

With the banning of martial arts films in the Republic of China in the 1930s, the nexus of production shifted away from Shanghai to the south, across the border to the British colony of Hong Kong. This radically changed the nature of the films, favouring source material and audience interest derived not from Mandarin Chinese, but from the Cantonese spoken in Guangdong province, Hong Kong and throughout the Chinese diaspora.

The first Cantonese martial arts film hero appeared in *The Adventures of Fong Sai-yuk* (1938), played by a Cantonese opera star and centring on the unlikely story of the burning of the 'southern' Shaolin temple, as mentioned in numerous popular novels.[20] This would spawn several sequels in the 1940s, but was soon eclipsed by another franchise, which began with *The True Story of Wong Fei-hung* (1948). It was derived from an article in the Hong Kong press, from which director Wu Pang had got the idea to commission an entire book on the subject, to create a ready-made source for film adaptation. The article was already somewhat over-enthusiastic; now the original author Zhu Yuzhai was expressly hired to sensationalise the 'true' story of Wong Fei-hung (1847–1924), a native of Foshan and the son of an itinerant medicine pedlar and martial artist. Initially trained in Hung Gar (a martial art associated with the 'secret socie-ties' of the Qing dynasty), Wong's life spanned some of the greatest periods of unrest in Chinese history, including the Sino-Japanese War of 1894–95 – in which he was alleged to have been a paramedic with the Black Flag Army resisting the French in Indochina and the Japanese in Taiwan – and a stint as a bodyguard and military trainer in the chaotic Canton area following the founding of the Republic. Actor Kwan Tak-hing (1905–96) would go on to play Wong in seven-ty-seven films from 1949–70, turning movies about this specific historical character into an entire subset of the Cantonese film industry. It was only after Kwan's retirement from film in the 1970s – when life imitated art and he became a martial arts teacher and herbalist – that stories of Wong Fei-hung would return to his younger days with younger actors, such as Jackie Chan in *Drunken Master* (1979) and most famously, Jet Li with *Once Upon a Time in China* (1991), both of which spawned their own sequels and remakes.

The films about Wong Fei-hung, as one might imagine, had already diverged far from the historical record, even before the ongoing franchise generated the need to come up with new stories. Wong would dispense Chinese traditional medicine along with training in various forms of kung fu to his disciples, and right wrongs in a series of Cantonese villages, replaying the narrative of the wandering hero. Real-world politics would also intrude; the historical Wong died conveniently before the rise of the Communists, allowing his life to reflect a Chinese resistance to predatory foreign-ers and the glory days of the early Republic, and not, say, a slow decline of back-stabbing Mao-era betrayals. Amid much sensation-alisation of imagined conflicts between multiple schools of kung fu, the Wong films would push for a sense of 'real kung fu' (*zhen gongfu*) – falsely suggesting that they offered a grittier and more real-ist depiction of the development of the martial arts at the turn of the twentieth century.[21] Eschewing the obvious wirework and special effects of more fantastical shows, the Wong films instead concen-trated on what was claimed to be a truthful depiction of the 'southern' schools.

Demand from overseas Chinese communities, particularly in South-East Asia where so many traced their ancestors to south China, was so great that most new Wong Fei-hung films could be financed largely with pre-production bids by overseas distributors.[22] Among those overseas distributors were the Shaw brothers, that same cabal of Shanghai haberdasher's sons who had sewn up much of the overseas Chinese theatre market in South-East Asia. Quitting the mainland Chinese market ahead of the Communist takeover, the Shaws relocated their own business to Hong Kong, with Run-run, the youngest brother, establishing Movietown, an inte-grated production facility, up and running by 1961. The Shaw Brothers studio would also muscle in on Wong Fei-hung with *The Master of Kung Fu* (1973), claiming once again to be pushing for historical realism, even though the Shaws' output in the 1960s became progressively less realist, and depended increasingly upon fights. The Shaws had identified a market outside the audience of Chinese descent, who cared less for history and more for spectacle. This would increase the likelihood of kung fu films making it to a foreign audience, but would also lead to a rise in the number of made-up martial arts, schools and splits, and vendettas between temples that never truly existed.

Shaw Brothers' main competitor in the 1970s was Golden Harvest, an upstart studio whose leading man, Bruce Lee (1940– 73), had rejected the contractual terms of a career in the Shaw star system. Lee was a liminal figure – although raised in Hong Kong, his American birthplace allowed him to slip between the two countries, and he had spent the 1960s in the US as a student, martial arts trainer and actor. He had appeared as Kato in the TV series *Green Hornet*, obliged at first to portray a Japanese character, although Kato's ethnicity wavered a little and ended up as a more generic 'Asian'. Lee had also briefly taught his own, syncretic martial art, Jeet Kune Do in several locations. A beloved fighting trainer among several big-name stars in the Hollywood community, Lee was in negotiations to star in his own TV series, in which he planned to portray a Chinese fighter in the world of the Wild West. In the meantime, he was flitting between Hong Kong and the United States, hoping to establish a paradigm whereby he would work for four months of every year in Asia, before returning to Hollywood to groom a different audience.

His first film for Golden Harvest was *The Big Boss* (1971), a story aimed at a modern, overseas audience, with its tale of a Cantonese youth who inadvertently uncovers a drug ring based in a Thailand ice factory. Although the film made use of Lee's abilities in Wing Chun, it was the follow-up that would establish him indisputably as a hero and populariser of the martial arts. This next film was released internationally as *Fist of Fury*, although in America it was retitled *The Chinese Connection* in a marketing-inspired effort to associate it with *The French Connection* (1971). Its original Chinese name, however, carried far deeper resonance, as it was called *Jingwu Men* – a double-meaning referring either to the *Gates of the Jingwu School*, or more literally as *Understanding Pure Martial* – that same tricky *men* character that confuses accounts of the Righteous and Harmonious Fists in Chapter Four. It hence had substantially greater meaning for a Chinese audience, familiar with the history of the Jingwu school, than for overseas audiences who simply saw it as a story of suicidal revenge against the Japanese.

The film had powerful resonances for any Chinese martial artist, alluding as it did to the early days of the Jingwu school in Shanghai, and its careful interweaving of fact and fiction. Shortly after the suspicious death of Huo Yuanjia, the much-lauded founder of the Jingwu school, his fictional star pupil Chen (Bruce Lee) returns for his funeral. A group of Japanese martial artists gatecrash the ceremony, challenging the Chinese to a duel, and presenting them with a mocking sign that proclaims them to be the 'Sick Man of Asia'. Despite admonitions not to provoke any conflict, Chen is unable to resist, dropping in on the Japanese martial arts school, defeating its entire complement of students, and forcing two of the leading disciples to literally eat their words by cramming the 'Sick Man of Asia' calligraphy into their mouths. He then attempts to walk home through a Shanghai park, where he is prevented from entering by a Sikh policeman, who points to a sign on the gate that reads 'No dogs and Chinese allowed'. When it becomes clear that dogs *are* actually allowed in, a passing Japanese man offers to lead Chen in as his pet, and is subsequently beaten up.

After this diversion, Chen returns to the Jingwu school to discover that the Japanese martial artists have already ransacked the place, beating up many of his fellow students and demanding that Chen be handed over to them. An escalating series of tit-for-tat murders ensues, particularly after Chen overhears two Japanese agents admitting that they had poisoned Huo Yuanjia. Eventually, Chen hands himself over to the police, only to charge a line of armed soldiers waiting outside, immortalised in a freeze-frame as their guns fire.

The film was a crossover hit with international audiences, although its biggest footprint was among Chinese communities who welcomed the film's anti-colonial aspects. Robert Clouse, who would later direct *Enter the Dragon*, reported seeing the film in a cinema in Hong Kong, a city which had endured a period of occupation not unlike that of Shanghai's. 'Bruce . . . went to the Japanese headquarters to confront the murderous villains. He single-handedly laid waste to the entire organisation, sending the audience to hysteria . . . Following a dramatic pause he said: "The Chinese are not the sick people of Asia." Pandemonium! Everyone rose to his feet. Wave upon wave of earsplitting sound rolled up to the balcony. The seats were humming and the floor of the old balcony was shaking!'[23]

Nor was Clouse's account mere hyperbole. Half a decade later, Craig Reid found Chinese audiences were still cheering at screenings of the film. 'It is no wonder that Chinese crowds reportedly cried and gave standing ovations at every showing. I saw this film in Taiwan in 1979, and even seven years after its initial release, the normally quiet Taiwanese movie-goers were still cheering during the moments when Bruce Lee was beating the crap out of the Japanese.'[24]

Fred Weintraub, who would go on to produce the TV series *Kung Fu*, regarded Lee's popularity as transcending the Chinese community, and offering a sense of empowerment and accomplishment to all non-whites (and who knows, to whites, too).[25] The film also contains multiple subtle messages that will only resonate with a martial arts audience. The victorious Lee, for example, pauses in front of an out-of-focus picture of a dour old man, which appears to be a portrait of Funakoshi Gichin, the founder of Shōtōkan karate – although if true, it would be an odd thing to see in a Shanghai judo hall ten years before the real Funakoshi even demonstrated karate in Tokyo.[26] But when Lee fights the leader of the dojo he chooses to do so with a nunchaku – an Okinawan rice flail, thought by some to be a subtle dig at Japanese appropriation of the Ryūkyū Islands, formerly 'Chinese'.[27]

Fist of Fury, along with the other works of Bruce Lee, tapped into a rising interest in the martial arts in overseas audiences. Not everyone bought the hype – judo champion Jon Bluming infamously wrote off Lee as 'a movie star who could not beat his grandmother'.[28]

But for most of the world, it became a symbol both of racism and resistance to it. The infamous sign that he vandalises, 'No dogs and Chinese allowed', has entered popular myth, although there was never a real-world analogue – a much more detailed list of restrictions was once posted at what is now the Huangpu Park, in the International Settlement at the north end of Shanghai's Bund, which did include proscriptions against dogs and Chinese, along with bicycles, unaccompanied children and those 'inappropriately dressed'. The film scholar Craig Reid also identifies a powerful legacy for the film. Among film production personnel asked to express their feelings about the film, the vast majority agreed with the statement: 'It gave our country an identity.' Among actors, the more common response was: 'He made me proud to be Asian.'[29]

Fist of Fury's influence would endure in many forms. It was seen by Liao Chengzhi, a Communist Party cadre charged with reviving overseas Chinese contacts during the economic reforms of the early 1980s, who suggested that a similarly 'patriotic' film would help bring in tourists and foreign capital to the People's Republic. The result was *Shaolin Temple* (1982), a feature film retelling (or rather, imagining the gaps in between) the events carved into the Shaolin Temple Stele, with monks supporting the future Tang emperor Taizong as he wars against the murderous Wang Shichong. One monk in particular is Jue Yuan (Jet Li, in the role that made him a star), intent on avenging his father's death at the hands of a usurper.

It was Liao who made it possible for this Hong Kong film to be made on location in China, and who pulled a number of strings to establish ideal conditions for its success – a release during the spring vacation; hype about real-world martial artists in prominent roles; pre-sales to Japan. In particular, Liao was able to draw upon Shaolin's nominal connection to Shorinji Kempo, luring several prominent Japanese martial artists over to appear in walk-on roles in the film, and even arranging for Sō Dōshin to visit the temple.

The trip was breathlessly reported in both China and Japan, but was far more influential in the former, where the upcoming ceremonial welcoming of a martial arts grandmaster from Japan prompted the Chinese authorities to lift a ban on the wearing of monks' robes that had been in effect for almost twenty years. It was hence a movie's depiction of the martial arts that would led to the thawing of government policy towards the monks who supposedly invented them. After the release of the movie in 1982, tourists visiting the actual temple multiplied by a factor of ten.[30] They were lured not by its associations with the history of Buddhism, but with its questionable centrality in the history of kung fu itself.

THE PRC, *WUSHU* AND MARTIAL AMNESIA

The release of the *Shaolin Temple* movie represented a return of martial arts cinema to the People's Republic, from which it had been effectively banned for a generation. It also saw the culmination of a series of transformations in sports policy that had seen varying fortunes for Chinese martial arts since the proclamation of the People's Republic.

Originally, the rise of the People's Republic saw the martial arts co-opted into a Soviet-inspired project to 'discover, systematise and raise standards' of physical culture.[31] 'Guoshu', the National arts, were now forever associated in Communist eyes with the Republic of China, which now only occupied the island of Taiwan. In the realm of the martial arts in Communist China, Guoshu was replaced by *wushu*, literally 'martial arts', an attempt by the state to encompass all variant forms into a single, certifiable federation.

The Republic and the People's Republic would joust with each other, and are still jousting, over who got to call themselves what at international sports meetings, leading to such neologisms as 'Chinese Taipei' and 'Formosa China'. Matters would become remarkably tense, with such espionage coups as that of 1956, when a Communist agent managed to switch the flags at the Melbourne Olympics, so that the Taiwanese team was forced to watch a red flag with Communist stars raised while they listened to their national anthem, or of 1964, when Communist agents drugged the orange juice of a Taiwanese decathlete.[32]

Among many hiatuses in the transmission of martial arts knowledge in China, it has been observed that the twentieth century brought cataclysmic damage to many elements of Chinese culture. It was not merely a matter of decades of civil war and Japanese invasion, but also the deprivation and rearrangement of priorities that such upheavals caused. The private practice of martial arts, long regarded as a crucible of dissent, was temporarily banned,[33] and the landlord caste was purged and often killed. Danny Xuan observes that the depredations of the Great Leap Forward (1959–62) left the people of China struggling merely for food, commenting: 'You can be certain that no one was practising Tai Chi in the parks or pounding on Ip Man's wooden dummy in Foshan (Fatsan) during this period.'[34] And yet, the Great Leap Forward saw a massive rise in popularity of taiji, which had been promoted since 1949, the year of the proclamation of the People's Republic, as a medically approved and yet traditionally Chinese form of exercise. Under the name *qigong*, taiji exercises became commonplace all over China, until their association with 'tradition' led to their fall from favour in the early 1960s, and their outright ban just before the Cultural Revolution.[35] Mao's China saw a great flowering of open-air exercise facilities, although, of course, that would require publicly acceptable, State-approved callisthenics or *wushu*, not specific martial arts. Mao's martial arts were not necessarily the martial arts practised by his ancestors, although they are certainly the martial arts most likely to be practised by his descendants.

The real damage came in 1966, with the implementation of the Cultural Revolution, a nationwide pogrom against anything associated with the old China, and open war on traditions and heritage. Even as 'model' Chinese operas like *The Red Detachment of Women* added martial poses and forms to the dancers' steps, the heritage of the actual martial arts itself was being destroyed.[36] Academics and teachers were murdered or sent to perform menial slave labour in the countryside, cutting many off from any disciples likely to pass on their knowledge. Meanwhile, campaigns against 'ancestor-worship' led to the destruction of many family chronicles and lineage lists, wiping out much of the heritage of the martial arts.

With evident bitterness and impish provocation, Anthony L. Schmieg writes:

> Over the last fifty years there has been a complete upheaval of Chinese society. Not by accident: the Communist Chinese Cultural Revolution . . . eliminated the foundations of Chinese culture. Yet the attraction of ancient Chinese civilization is so potent and alluring to both Chinese and Westerners alike that the government of the People's Republic of China has relentlessly postured to don the mantle of Chinese civilization. For many reasons this façade is not only illegitimate, but the historical revisions supporting it are also fraudulent. There is no doubt that the conclusive disjunction of Chinese civilization occurred during the Cultural Revolution. Consequently, I do not consider the Chinese cultural institutions that have been modified and promulgated by the Chinese Communist government to be traditional, despite their unfailing use of the word.[37]

Schmieg has a point, although I would argue that the damage done by the Cultural Revolution is easily matched by that of the Century of Humiliation that preceded it – Opium Wars, Japanese invasion, famines, revolution, civil war and all. Blaming the current administration for forgetting some of its forerunners is rather like blaming the janitor for the mess he is cleaning up.

Some did survive. Miraculously, at the very height of the Cultural Revolution in 1971, the cancer survivor Guo Lin was regularly meeting a class in a Beijing park to practice *qigong*, which she believed to have cured her. Following the death of Mao, she found the authorities substantially more amenable to her activities, and *qigong* became one of the most widespread modern sights in post-Mao China. It was, however, only partly a martial art – only 47 per cent of modern Chinese qigong teachers regarded its origins as 'martial', while over 50 per cent regard it as founded on medical-religious principles.[38] These would eventually take over by the 1980s, as the Chinese government became increasingly fretful about the religious nature of *qigong* literature, and the likelihood that claims for medical healing powers amounted to illegal superstition. A 1989 law attempted to regulate *qigong* therapies, while Yan Xin, a *qigong* celebrity who claimed to be taught by a student of a former Boxer Uprising veteran, left for the United States two weeks after the Tiananmen Square incident.

Other, more *martial* arts were not so lucky. As Danny Xuan asks in *The Tao of Wing Chun*, how could any of the former teachers and masters have survived the purges? Where were the Buddhist monks to retrain the next generation of acolytes? 'The truth of the matter is that those who were not killed or persecuted before and immediately after the Communist takeover of China had escaped to Hong Kong, Macau, Taiwan, South-east Asia and to the West. These refugees were the ones who truly preserved the Chinese culture and Chinese martial arts.'[39]

This is not merely true of the martial arts, but of many other aspects of Chinese culture. It is depressing, for example, to wander around the museum that sits at the centre of Shanghai and realise that so many of the examples of local culture that it features have been loaned by overseas Chinese – the people of Shanghai having broken much of their own heritage up with hammers during the Cultural Revolution. But the somewhat happy ending that Xuan posits prompts another possibility, which is that the heritage return-ing to China is not necessarily proportionate.

In faithfully repeating the locations of the main repositories of Chinese culture, Xuan provides a list that is largely *southern*. Guangdong and Fujian, in particular, are prominent among the places of origin of overseas Chinese, with the Cantonese and Hokkien dialects vastly outweighing Mandarin in most Chinatowns. Although the efforts of those communities in preserving Chinese heritage are much appreciated, to what degree have they preserved Chinese culture with an inadvertently southern bias? The people of the Chinese diaspora may have successfully prevented certain aspects of their ancestors' culture from becoming extinct, but may have done so by repopulating Chinese heritage with biased accounts from a mere fragment of the original sources.

After 1979, the State Commission for Physical Culture and Sports initiated a special taskforce to arrange for the teaching and practice of *wushu*. We might call this project a salvage effort in all but name, as commissioners tried to enlist the survivors of many martial arts that had been all but wiped out. In the unarmed combat classes, modern *wushu* is divided into three main forms, the Long Fist (Shaolin and several other 'northern' styles), the Southern Fist (forms found south of the Yangtse, including Hung Gar and Wing Chun) and Taiji. Scores are often determined by the practitioners' ability to perform a number of difficult moves, within a set number of steps, and to the correct degree of form. A dozen or so subsidiary forms, which gain fewer points and are hence marginalised, amount to a list of many minor martial arts.

In addition to the exhibition category, modern *wushu* also features a combat category, although this has been heavily sportified, with numerous powerful locks, holds and chokes forbidden. By 1998, there were protests in China that modern *wushu* had entirely defanged and over-written the vibrant forms and martial arts of old, replacing it with what one critic called 'flowery postures', seemingly in allusion to the 'flowery kung fu' of ancient reports.[40]

However, such complaints reflect less the ruination of martial arts than the double standard between practical martial arts in the service of the state and a sporting spin-off deprived of many original applications. According to the *LA Times*:

> In the meantime, more practical martial arts training is reserved for the military and police, who hire martial arts masters to drill their riot-shield-and-baton-wielding phalanxes.
>
> Also demoralizing to martial artists is the corruption that has permeated a field once known for its code of chivalry. In China's state sports machine, coaches' pay depends on their meeting quotas for how many of their athletes win in competition.
>
> As a result, referees say that they are commonly bribed to inflate scores and that the outcome of some competitions is decided in advance according to which athletes are to be groomed for stardom.[41]

The evolution of martial arts in the People's Republic of China is not merely a case of forgetting. It is also a case of studiously not remembering certain elements that were once considered vital to the martial arts tradition. Religion and superstition are both frowned upon by the Communist state, encouraging all modern *wushu* arts to emphasise simple exercise and competition forms above any discussion of immortality or magic. There is no talk here of bullet-resistant Boxers or the secret of Daoist eternal youth, although *qigong*, ironically, remains at least partly shielded by its role within traditional Chinese medicine, still supported as an alternative to Western medicine. Attempts within the *qigong* lobby to reassert its old religious or magical status, such as the millenarian cult Falun Gong, have been swiftly quashed by a Communist state that will tolerate no truck with 'superstitions'.

But the last and arguably most influential factor on the shape of modern Chinese *wushu* is the potential it offers for overseas expansion. No single nation, not even the populous People's Republic, is immune to such a temptation. Martial arts that become more like sports are rendered easier to quantify, rationalise and export. A 'journey to the west' is implicit in the future of any modern martial art, as are the problems soon likely to arise.

CHAPTER EIGHT

Ball of Kungfusion

....

It was called the Feel Good Fair, although with admission at €3, a coffee at €4 and parking at €8, I had trouble working out how anyone in the Finnish town of Jyväskylä would feel good about it. All the organisations in town, from newsagents to health food shops, had stalls in the main hall, informing the people of the community about the goods and services on offer.

Because the emphasis was on health and exercise, the martial artists dominated the central display area. A bunch of taekwondo practitioners, mainly in their teens and under, kicked each other and thin air in a flurry of multi-coloured belts. When their allotted time arrived, the judo people rolled around in their customary fashion. The Thai boxers seemed a little meek, unable to really let rip at each other at a mere demonstration. At one point, the local aerobics club took the stage and half-heartedly went through a dance routine that included some punches and kicks. After an hour of real martial artists, it all looked risible.

The Shorinji Kempo club seemed out of place. At least one member had been mistaken for someone dressed up as a Jedi, since the higher belts are allowed to wear Buddhist priest's robes that seem somewhat science-fictional. When it came to the onstage demonstration, their options were straightforward *randori*, which just looks like a bar-room brawl, or the performance of an *enbu*, a series of matched and duplicated moves designed to show off teamwork and mastery.

Their biggest problem was being recognised. For every possible recruit, wandering past with a fistful of fliers, a dozen may have never even made it to the stand, having been lured away by the bigger, more populous martial arts elsewhere in the hall.

'Are you the karate people?' asks a girl with blue hair.

'No we're not,' scowls a man dressed as a Buddhist priest. He gruffly doesn't volunteer any more information, and his questioner soon wanders off again.

No, Shorinji Kempo isn't karate. It isn't kung fu or judo or taekwondo. It isn't any of the dozen brands most likely to be on someone's mind on that day in their life when they wake up and decide that for a New Year's Resolution they are going to get fit and do a martial art. And in a small university town, it faces the problems of being the unpronounceable option, lacking numbers and name recognition.

'We have a recurring problem,' confesses Vesa, a visiting branch master from Kajaani. 'If we're lucky, we can sign up new arrivals at the beginning of their college years. If they stay the course, going to a couple of training sessions a week, we can get them to black belt by the time they graduate. But then what happens? They're not necessarily going to stay in town. They *might* go to another town that also has a Shorinji Kempo club. But if they don't, that's it, we've lost them.'

All martial arts have trouble with dropouts. People lose interest; they have kids; they move away – these issues plague any hobby organisation requiring weekly attendance. But the smaller, less well-known martial arts can suffer problems of recruitment and competition. It's not just a case of the novice who asks for karate because it's the only thing she's heard of. It's the novice who asked for it five years earlier in a different town, and decides to continue with it when she moves. She has a better chance of starting, and of carrying on to a level where she can contribute herself.

'That's not all,' continues Vesa. 'Because a black belt is just a *shōdan*. It's just the beginning. You need to be third-*dan* before you can become a branch master. We could be a factory churning out first-degree black belts, but none of them can go to a new town and start their own branch. We can't expand without third-*dans*, and for someone to be in the game that long is really a matter of luck. And don't think this is just a problem here in Finland. It's a problem in England; it's a problem in Germany. It's a problem all over.'

GAMIFICATION AND SPORTIFICATION

In 1956, the eighty-seven-year-old Funakoshi Gichin looked back over his long life. Born in the year of the Meiji Restoration, 1868, he had seen Japan rise from a medieval time warp, through rapid modernisation, a terrifying generation of war, occupation, and now modern reconstruction. His personal martial art, karate, had been caught up in the sudden rise of Japan, survived its fall, and travelled even further afield. 'So Karate-dō which, in my childhood, was a clandestine local Okinawan activity, had finally become one of Japan's martial arts before it took wing and flew to America,' he wrote. 'Now it is known all over the world . . . Still astonished by the number of people who have heard about karate, I now realise that once this book is finished I shall have to start a new project – that of sending Japanese karate experts abroad.'[1]

Funakoshi's words are caught up in the zeitgeist of post-war Japan, a dream of export that hoped Japanese products and culture would become profitable commodities in global exchange.

As a corollary of the number of martial arts that were only truly created, or perhaps rediscovered, or codified in the twentieth century, generational loss has been a major issue since the 1950s. As with any organisation founded through the willpower and charisma of a single visionary, the issue of succession can cause multiple splits and scandals. In the case of Funakoshi Gichin, already a controversial figure with certain karate teachers back home in Okinawa, his own Shōtōkan organisation erupted into arguments over the best way to commemorate him at his funeral in 1957. The funeral was not the true cause, but it was certainly a catalyst that exposed several factions that would soon diverge into two new organisations.

What do martial arts organisations argue about? Sometimes it is a simple matter of succession – should the son take over the organisation from the father, even though he is not the best of the martial artists? If there is no son, should it be a daughter? Does a son-in-law take precedence? If there are three (or four, or ten) able disciples, which one should become the new leader? And what if they have different ideas about the future direction of the discipline? In a textbook case in 2003, the death of the UK Shōtōkan karate chief Enoeda Keinosuke led to a succession dispute between his highest-ranking British pupil, Andy Sherry, and his Japanese deputy, Ōta Yoshinobu. It ended with a split between the Karate Union of Great Britain under Sherry, and JKA England under Ōta.

Sometimes, the matter seems clear, until the next major disruption or doctrinal dispute, at which point the new leader's ruling is interpreted by someone as going against the spirit of the founder. What would the founder do? One of the most contentious issues in modern martial arts is often sportification – the transformation of what was once a form of combat into a marketable, teachable form of competition.[2]

Unsurprisingly, considering the head start it had on other martial arts in the modern global market, judo was the first to face many of these perils. Judo (for men) was introduced as a sport at the 1964 Tokyo Olympics, where Japanese pride at its adoption came accompanied by internationalist proclamations delivered through gritted teeth, when the Dutch Anton Geesink won the open championship. Guttman and Thompson, historians of Japanese sport, observe that Kanō Jigorō would have been immensely proud to have seen contestants from seven different nations winning medals for judo at a Tokyo Olympics, but . . .

Kanō's spirit, however, might have been troubled by the fact that the sport contested in 1964 was not exactly the sport he had invented some eighty years earlier. Jūdō, which Kanō had created as a balanced synthesis of modern and traditional elements, had become markedly more modern. This has meant, in part, that the trend towards increasing rationalization, specialization, bureaucratization, and quantification has continued.[3]

Modern judo has a set number of specified skills, and set levels required, to advance to a set rank. There are watchmen who watch the watchers, to make sure that judging in one country is the same as judging in another, and there is an increased emphasis on competition. The *Encyclopedia of World Sport* notes that in becoming a sport, judo favoured tournament competitions over much of the philosophy of its founder, now dismissed by some as mere 'mumbo jumbo'.[4]

Sportification begins with the systems put in place, at first by judo in the nineteenth century, to aid categorisation and assessment, turning almost every martial art into what is now known as a gamified process – a loyalty scheme.

The first and most visible sign of this came as early as 1927 when judo trainers in the United Kingdom began ranking students at the *kyū* levels below black belt with a system of coloured belts.[5] This innovation spread to Paris by 1935, and was soon adopted by many other martial arts. However, Danny Xuan observes that belts today can serve a more insidious purpose, often working less like badges of achievement than as lures to investment: 'The belt (ranking) system that is in play in most martial arts, although originally intended for grading and goal-setting, is nowadays often used as bait to keep students hooked as ongoing paying customers.'[6]

There is even a pejorative term for such enterprises in modern Japanese – *karateya*, with the *ya* indicating a shop or place of business, rather than a true training hall. As early as 1975, C. W. Nicol was sounding dire warnings about the drift of karate into a sport: 'I think that Karate as a sport is very fast developing, and we will end up with weight divisions, rounds, fouls, champions (actually we already have those), heroes, and worst of all, spectators . . . armchair Karate men who have never stepped on a dojo floor.'[7]

Simple issues in management and commercialisation have also altered the nature of training – sportification arguably proceeds before any contest even begins:

> In the new martial arts studios one will typically spend the first twenty minutes warming up, and then spend another twenty minutes on drills, another twenty minutes on kata or forms, and then, perhaps, fifteen minutes will be devoted to technique training. Finally, sparring might be done, but if it is, only for about ten minutes or so . . . There is nothing wrong with this approach – if your goal in taking up a martial art is simply to exercise your body . . . However, if you are serious about learning martial arts, shouldn't you be spending more time on it in class?[8]

Danny Xuan's complaint above is a pedagogical issue. He notes that golf classes do not waste time doing aerobics, but with regard to martial arts itself, in his case Wing Chun, he observes that much of the exercise component in such training involves impractical, repetitive drills with a dummy opponent that serve no practical purpose, even in sparring. With all the fervour of a true convert, he rants: 'You should do fitness exercises on your own; there is no sense in spending your time doing them in Wing Chun class.'[9]

Sportification, however, is a step further. For its supporters it is a natural part of the process away from combat and towards competition, opening a martial art to the potential for funding from athletics bodies, the publicity and prestige of appearing at sporting events, and a probable increase in admissions. But even Kanō Jigorō was reluctant to initially conceive his judo as a mere sport – he felt that the sporting element would come at the detriment of philosophy, and on the basis of the *Encyclopedia of World Sport*'s comments on 'mumbo jumbo', he was right. *Wushu*, of course, in China, is studiously sportive, since that helps it seem modern and untainted by associations with religion. But, for example, Shorinji Kempo still *is* a religion – its upper ranks are Zen priests; its philosophy favours cooperation over competition. It should hence come as no surprise that one of Shorinji Kempo's first big splits was occasioned shortly after the death of its founder, Sō Dōshin, when the new management expressly forbade the entry of Shorinji Kempo fighters into martial arts tournaments. Sugihara Masayasu, who had been doing so for several years while the authorities looked the other way, blatantly flouted this new rule, entering a karate competition with a made-up martial art. Deriving his pseudonym from the White Lotus bodyguards of the founder, he called himself a practitioner from the White Lotus Association (*Byakuren Kaikan*). Within a year, he had split to form Byakuren 'karate', heavily derived from Shorinji Kempo, but without the original's anti-sport directives.

We can, perhaps, now see why so many martial arts were so small in the nineteenth century, and subject to so many ruptures. When a martial arts teacher was focused solely on his village, there would have been relatively little incentive to attempt to exercise control over far-flung branches and franchises. But with the introduction of systems and rules, size suddenly matters, leading governing bodies to exert a stronger grip on their members. Shorinji Kempo itself has begun to legally defend its very name as a brand that cannot be co-opted in Japan by anyone who feels like calling themselves an adherent of the Shaolin Temple – there are at least a dozen martial arts in Japan that claim descent from Shaolin: ironically, Shorinji Kempo is not really one of them.

Such issues can go far deeper than mere names, quite literally into the very fabric of a martial art. In 1986, organisers at a Dutch judo competition controversially decided that alternate competitors would wear blue judo outfits in order to help judges and TV audiences tell them apart. There were rumblings of disapproval in Japan, where Kanō Jigorō's insistence on the purity of white clothes was seen to have been brushed aside. When the blue uniforms appeared to be a hit in Europe, the Japanese federation threatened in 1993 to boycott any competitions that used them, but by 1996 had glumly agreed to play along.[10]

In 2011, the International Judo Federation introduced a quality label to judo gear, designed to make sure that competitors were wearing uniforms with identical properties. There would, henceforth, be no off-white *dōgi* spoiling the group photographs; no splitting of poor-quality seams; no material that was too stiff or too soft, modifying an opponent's grip. However, such quality marking serves another purpose, directly involving the International Judo Federation in the approval, manufacture and sale of its uniforms. This makes sound sense to a brand manager or a marketing consultant; it makes sense to a sportsman, but is it really what Kanō Jigorō had in mind? Would he have approved of such changes if he were still alive today? Such is the nature of doctrinal disputes, when the actions of a founder in a very different time are subject to debates over what they *would* have done, if they were presented with the facts of global competition and literally millions of adherents.

The debate over sportification conceals a problem that arguably runs even deeper in many martial arts: financing. The Kōdōkan struggled financially throughout Kanō Jigorō's lifetime, even after the establishment of a Kōdōkan charitable foundation in 1909, intended to offset the cost overruns. In 1932, facing a genuine risk of bankruptcy, Kanō even proposed the drastic measure of advancing all 40,000 black belt holders one rank, and then charging them a registration fee. This plan was rejected, but serves as an indicator of a

problem that would thereafter be endemic in many martial arts –
how to keep financed without openly running one's martial art as a
business.[11] When even the 'first' and most established of the modern
martial arts struggled to monetise, the prospects are not good for
smaller disciplines, particularly those that rely upon the goodwill of
their teaching bodies to remain voluntary. Several martial arts have
been split by disputes over finances, as prominent teachers are found
to be cooking the books in order to keep themselves from running
into debt. There are often elaborate legal acrobatics over the nature of
'mat fees' paid to training halls, but sportification can bring with it a
more open approach to business and finance.[12]

ENTER THE NINJA

If the current organisation does not do it for you, why not form your
own? This is, after all, how every martial art appears to have formed.
Even the 'originals' began as splinters from some forgotten ancestor. It should hence come as no surprise that martial arts continue
to evolve and transform.

The Occupation period's clampdown on the depiction of the
samurai, and on the martial nature of the martial arts, would lead to
the creation of a new discipline: *ninjutsu*. Many samurai manuals
from the Tokugawa period, aping one of the thirteen chapters of
Sun Tzu's *The Art of War*, included chapters on espionage.
Skulduggery and double-crosses, night assaults and tunnelling,
targeted assassinations, poison and traps were all within the skillset
of historical samurai, although the prolonged peace of the Tokugawa
period created an element of cognitive dissonance. After telling each
other for two hundred years that they were honourable sportsmen,
great philosophers, appraisers of tea and players of Go, the samurai
class had essentially talked themselves out of taking responsibility
for any of the dirty work of war. Any discussion of spy-craft, viewed

through the lens of twentieth century Japan, seemed difficult to believe. *Who would carry out such missions?*

Many a military manual of the Tokugawa era spoke of the need to employ spies, scouts and people of stealth: in Japanese, *shinobi-mono*. In the twentieth century, a meteoric trend in popular fiction would use an alternative reading for the same characters, claiming that instead they were supposed to be pronounced *nin-ja*. 'People of stealth,' it was suddenly argued, was not a general term for any scouts or hired thugs, but a specific, identifiable brand. Ninja, it was now claimed, were an actual group of super-human assassins, drawn from certain remote communities whose samurai-era manuals were heavy on the espionage. Although there was no evidence of them from history (or from drama – they are unmentioned in kabuki), their presence could be extrapolated by simply changing any mention of spying operations, assassination or Fortean phenomena from the history books and suggesting that it was the work of ninja.

Such circular, credulous reasoning does not belong in a serious history book, but did not actually originate in one. The invention of the ninja tradition was a masterpiece of creative, fictional thinking by a number of authors struggling to make ends meet amid drastic restrictions in Occupation media. With a ban on samurai and the martial arts that had been favoured by the wartime population, it might at first seem impossible for a potboiler novelist or manga artist to sell a single page. A handful of writers and artists, however, did find a way through the censorship minefield, creating a new trend that would continue to grow in the decade after the occupation ended.

The reasoning went like this: if the ruling class had duped the population into the Second World War, perhaps there had been other lies in the past. Perhaps, argued the pulp authors of the 1950s and 1960s, there was a whole forgotten underclass in Japanese history – the people who did the real work in the samurai wars, gritty, tough tricksters with gadgets and athletic abilities to match those of TV spy thrillers. Ninja are largely a creation of the twentieth century – black-clad assassins dressed like the 'invisible' stagehands of the kabuki theatre. With the samurai aristocracy blamed for dragging Japan into the Second World War, ninja formed a new, proletarian archetype – honest, impoverished, cunning peasants, literally unseen in the historical fiction that had previously concentrated on the ruling class.

With the Americans gone, 1959 was the banner year for ninja, with the publication of Yamada Fūtarō's novel *The Kōga Ninja Scrolls* (*Kōga Ninpōchō*) – the first of a series that would run for over a decade. It competed against another novel, Shiba Ryōtarō's *Castle of Owls* (*Fukurō no Shiro*) and the first of several ninja manga by Shirato Sanpei.

By 1964, the children's animated series *Fujimaru the Wind Ninja* was tapping into the fad, and would end each episode with a live-action demonstration of ninja skills by Hatsumi Masaaki, an accomplished martial artist and sometime stuntman. Hatsumi, it was claimed, was actually a real-life ninja master, having learned from the last of the real ninja.

A 1964 article in *Newsweek* insightfully identified this for what it was: '. . . the latest craze to hit craze-prone Japan . . . a vogue which sweeps from toddlers to grandparents. Japanese cops are plagued by gangs of would-be ninja, and the Japanese press with discouraging regularity reports the misadventures of youngsters who seek to soar off rooftops or slip through drainpipes in approved ninja fashion.'[13]

Much as Chinese martial arts super-heroics rested on the impossible feats of puppet shows and the stylised combats of Cantonese opera, the ninja fad was fuelled by television, a new arrival that had only been available to the public since 1953. Colour television ownership soared in the run-up to the Tokyo Olympics of 1964, and in the years that followed, dozens of samurai-era castles were rebuilt across Japan. Many had been pulled down in the nineteenth century, but these edifices became the new focal points for many towns, as meeting halls, local museums and tourist attractions. They were not always historically accurate – many were constructed out of modern materials like concrete. Some even retrofitted adornments that owed more to popular fiction, including ninja hiding places as an acknowledgement of a modern fad.

In the publishing world, author Yamaguchi Masayuki tried something similar. His *Life of the Ninja* (*Ninja no Seikatsu*, 1965) shoehorned ninja into every historical event he could think of, twisting every off-hand mention of commoners, spies, stealth, or sneak attacks in ancient chronicles into 'proof' of the heretofore unmentioned ninja clans. The historical equivalent of a Dan Brown novel, Yamaguchi's book was cheekily disingenuous and played freely with the facts, but became the lynchpin of subsequent publications, cited and quoted as if it were a work of unassailable scholarship. Apologists for the ninja also presented a familiar and infuriatingly recursive argument – there had been no direct mention of ninja previously because they were a *secret* society! But once we have established the possibility of ninja, and hence the possibility that they are being discussed, then all sorts of new 'proofs' come leaping out of the woodwork. Take, for example, *The Myriad Rivers Reach the Sea* (*Bansen Shūkai*, 1676) and *The Chronicle of True Stealth* (*Shōnin-ki*, 1681), demonstrably old military texts that mention spying and spies, poison and tools, since creatively edited and repurposed as historical evidence of supposed 'ninja' manuals.

Meanwhile, the ninja boom continued unabated in the world of fiction, fuelled by the tricks and gadgetry of foreign espionage thrillers such as *The Man From U.N.C.L.E.* (broadcast in Japan in 1965 as *0011 Napoleon Solo*) and *Mission: Impossible* (broadcast in Japan in 1967 as *Spy Great Strategy*). But ninja had already moved past their mid-1960s peak, and were now ironically over-exposed. Their finest hour, arguably, was their appearance in the James Bond novel and film *You Only Live Twice* (1964 and 1967 respectively), which carried the idea of the ninja around the world, even as their lustre faded in Japan itself.

Arguably, ninja were killed by their own success, dragging the samurai themselves down to their level. In 1972, Japanese viewers sick of the Vietnam War and the Watergate Scandal settled down in front of their televisions to watch *Monjirō*, the tale of a homeless samurai reduced to vagrant status. The *Monjirō* series was swiftly followed by *Sure Death (Hissatsu)*, another long series that co-opted ninja tactics into the adventures of respectable members of samurai society. A last-gasp gimmick, a sci-fi cartoon starring multi-coloured ninja in avian costumes, *Science-Ninja Team Gatchaman*, was released outside Japan as *Battle of the Planets*. Meanwhile, in the wake of the martial arts boom fostered by Bruce Lee, Hatsumi Masaaki, the pundit and former stunt coordinator on several early ninja shows (a former theatre studies major and occasional osteopath), found fame in the West as the author of *Ninjutsu*, a martial arts manual of ninja techniques. Hatsumi revealed that in 1972 he had been privy to the transmission of the grandmaster-level status from the last of the ninja, who had recognised him, much as Sō Dōshin had been recognised in *Yihemen-quan*, with the conferral of a grandmaster's title and a secret scroll. Hatsumi, according to Hatsumi himself, had been the sole pupil of the last ninja for the previous fifteen years, acquiring a grab-bag of nine grandmaster-ships.[14] For no logical reason, the ancient and secret tradition of the ninja was now open to the public (if it really were a hush-hush espionage conspiracy, wouldn't the authorities want to keep it quiet?), and anyone could come to train at Hatsumi's schools for a fee. Hatsumi's schools were not recognised as 'old' traditional arts, since proof of their relevance and tradition was slow in forthcoming. Nor was ninjutsu recognised as a 'new' martial art, since its founder was busily boasting how old it was. But Hatsumi did not seem to mind, and published several further books outlining the origins of his no-longer-secret tradition. Amid the hysteria over ninja in the 1960s, the fiction and the facts all seemed to get intertwined. Even if Hatsumi wasn't a ninja master, he would go on to play one on TV, appearing as the grey-haired mentor Yamaji Tetsuzan in the kids' adventure series *World Ninja War Jiraiya* (1988).

This is where we came in. This is, in fact, where *I* came in since it was an investigation of the invention of ninjutsu that first led me to embark upon the writing of this book. But when compared to the invention of other martial arts traditions, ninjutsu does not seem all that different.

Hatsumi still teaches a verifiable, quantifiable, visible martial art. He has real high-level black belts from a plethora of organisations, and successful graduates of his school probably know a thousand ways to kill you. The practice of ninjutsu may involve some silly and unlikely weapons, but so does modern *wushu*. Its students also learn palpably practical fighting techniques, practising their moves amid real-world clutter like tables and chairs, rather than the minimalist and unreal settings of a training hall. Despite the hokum that birthed it, many ninjutsu techniques have a pragmatic approach that recalls Jeet Kune Do.

An exposure to ninjutsu inoculates the reader against taking the claims of any other martial art at face value. Much like many other martial arts in earlier chapters of this book, it takes a genuine modern materiality (tell a ninjutsu practitioner that he doesn't exist, and he can swiftly prove you wrong by punching you in the face), and then claims that many previous references in old texts are in fact references to this new invention, or its prototypes. This then establishes the modern form as something with a long history after the fact.

The next step in the establishment of an invented tradition for a martial art is the co-option of historical characters, which ninjutsu swiftly did with the likes of Hattori Hanzō, a samurai-era celebrity notorious for his cunning, who happened to come from the supposed ninjutsu heartland. The use of real historical figures subsequently allows apologists to claim that any appearance by these figures in the historical record is a reference to the martial art. Such incidences can be strung together sufficiently to create an archive of content that can be referred to, as if every reference to Julius Caesar online was suddenly tagged tomorrow with the word *#vampire*. This would not make him a blood-sucking member of the undead, but would spin off some interesting speculations about his origins, his influence and his activities. Even if the rumour were quashed, apologists could now report the quashing of the rumour, and a new conspiracy theory unfolds.

Ninjutsu's sole crime, perhaps, is being so young that its founders are still living, at a time when Internet rumour busting and due diligence can destroy many aspirations to form 'folk history'. Whereas we can only investigate the origins of kung fu or karate through historical documentation, the myths of ninjutsu are emerging before us in real time. Other martial arts have had plenty of time for those scrolls to go missing, and for that chart of grandmasters to be nicely aged and dusty, whereas with ninjutsu, it swiftly seems that the vast majority of the claims for its heritage and history issue from an organisation set up by Hatsumi himself.

Such claims as Hatsumi's, it should be acknowledged, first came at a time when many other martial arts were scrambling to be recognised. There continue to be occasional controversies today, particularly about the conferral of honorary black belts that are then parleyed into bogus qualifications, but the 1950s seemed to be a time of particular struggle, as multiple contending schools fought to establish themselves as anything more than local brands. The intense political ferment of the 1950s was, we now know, the last chance for a Japanese martial art to be properly established – Shorinji Kempo, founded in 1947, is the last and youngest of the nine modern budō arts recognised by the Budōkan organisation. Part of the struggle was over credentials for teaching, but also over the credentials for transmission (i.e. creating a large-enough group of teachers) and for recognition. In the most ludicrous of scandals from the period, a teacher of Okinawan karate in 1959 conferred the once-in-a-generation rank of 10th-*dan* on several of his pupils, including a man of only thirty-four.[15] Such grade-inflation and credentialism is precisely the sort of thing that national, standardised bodies are supposed to prevent, and if it was happening within karate, it should come as no surprise than a newly founded school, outside the purview of the authorities, should strive so hard for attention.

In a sense, Hatsumi beat the system by creating his own, establishing his personal Bujinkan organisation at the beginning of the 1970s. If the Budōkan had nine recognised martial arts, then now so did the Bujinkan, which also recognised eighteen specific 'skills of ninjutsu'. Notably, an Internet search for the 'nine budō', which is to say, the nine martial arts approved by the Japanese authorities, instead returns result dominated by the 'nine *ryūha* lineages', which is to say the nine divisions of ninjutsu defined by Hatsumi's Bujinkan organisation.

It is odd, too, that ninjutsu has flourished so vigorously when so much of its modern materials are literally aimed at children. Japanese television is infested with ninja tales for the kids, including the anime hit of recent years, *Naruto*, in which the eponymous ninja inexplicably wears orange. Such juvenilia even infect the work of respected authors dragged in to write on the topic. I was shocked when I finally obtained a copy of Donn Draeger's *Ninjutsu: The Art of Invisibility* (1971), and discovered that it was neither a serious history nor a step-by-step manual, but a breathless, large-print children's book about 'the original James Bond'. Far too many citations about the truth of ninja may be traced back to such nonsense. There is very little written about the historical ninja that is not methodologically compromised or blatantly recent.

REASONABLE FORCE

Ninjutsu's other big problem comes from its purported origins in a toolkit of assassination. Judo and the other established martial arts have struggled for a century to establish themselves as philosophical exercises, as mental regimes that soothe and tame savage thoughts. Ninjutsu pays lip service to this ideal, and the Bujinkan's own philosophical leanings seem to borrow much from those of aikido and karate, but at the most basic level, ninjutsu's claim for authenticity has forced it to acknowledge that certain of its manuals are concerned with breaking and entering, poisons and sneak attacks. One wonders how long it is liable to survive under increasingly paranoid anti-terror legislations – even those countries that recognise a 'right to self-defence' do not recognise a 'right to attack'.[16]

Legality is one of the recurring issues of martial artistry, not only in the censorious days of the US Occupation of Japan, but in any civilised society that is apt to question the value of any art being 'martial'. A generation ago, David Jones observed that some schools in Japan remained a little *too* martial. 'However, some martial arts really do want you to punch a tree until your knuckles are callused and hardened. Some teachers will assume you will consider it an honour if they blacken your eye or choke you into unconsciousness. Some schools will suggest that you accept broken bones as a requisite of sincere practice.'[17]

Alexander Bennett notes that the first issue with certain martial arts has been policing themselves, and rooting out the more belligerent trainers. 'In the last decade or so, the media has called attention to incidents involving the injury or even death, of pupils due to physical or psychological bullying in sports clubs, leading to a change in social attitudes. Overly zealous instructors who carelessly, or arrogantly, spurn the line between discipline and unadorned abuse are no longer tolerated, and rightly so.'[18]

Sportification, of course, has not merely rationalised the students, but also their teachers, making martial arts safer for everyone. Are they also safer for the opponent that one might fight on the street? I would say yes, since every martial art, even ninjutsu, now seems to come barnacled with warnings about the legal dangers that can arrive on the doorstep of any practitioner who dares to apply them in the real world outside of a battlefield.

It seems to be something of a Hollywood myth that training in martial arts causes a practitioner to be registered as a lethal weapon for legal purposes – folk rumour ascribes the origins of this concept to a wisecrack on *The Andy Griffith Show* in the 1960s. In most countries, the fact that someone has been trained in martial arts does not affect their legal status when it comes to defending themselves.

In practice, however, it does, particularly in Japan, as observed by C. W. Nicol: 'The Japanese police, whom I respect more than any other police force except the British, lean very heavily on anyone involved in a brawl. If the offender is a martial artist, he is in very hot water indeed. On reaching the first *dan* grade [i.e. black belt – JC], the martial artist is registered, and this information is readily available to the police. Misuse of a martial art is considered to be as bad as the use of a weapon.'[19]

Do the Japanese police really have a registry of every *shōdan* in Japan? Wouldn't that be *millions* of people?

Doctrines of 'reasonable force' require a defender to inflict the minimum amount of necessary damage to cause an attack to halt. A trained martial artist is expected to know exactly how much damage that is likely to be, and how to stop. He or she is also expected to see the situation escalating before it begins, and to take steps to move both defender and attacker out of the confrontation. C. W. Nicol regarded 'the most dangerous time' for making fatal errors in karate to be at the brown belt level, when fighters have learned many lethal techniques,

214

but not necessarily the 'calmness and tolerance and the state of empty mind that is brought about by further intensive practice'.[20]

I have witnessed such considerations at work at a martial arts training hall, where the teacher was discussing what to do if someone snatches your phone.

'Let it go,' he said. 'It's just a phone! Not worth dying over.'

This might seem counter-intuitive – surely the study of martial arts is undertaken so that we are not the archetypal wimp who has sand kicked in our face, but the admonitions of the teachers and the law recall the earliest adages of Sun Tzu in his *Art of War*. Fighting is only a last resort, even for fighters. What were you doing on the beach next to the idiot kicking sand?

Even the highly apocryphal karate Danes, in the story as told to me by a Brixton taxi driver, took great pains to give their assailants every opportunity to walk away, and indeed, were themselves cornered among the shelves of a convenience store. Otherwise we might expect them to have run away. Time and again, among the most competent of martial artists, we see the maxim: 'Escape is the best option.'[21]

When someone is really trying to kill you, they won't play by any rules. As Anthony L. Schmieg wrote:

> Al Hall, my first martial arts teacher, once said that the most dangerous opponent alive is a drunk, toothless redneck. 'You can't hurt him. You can't make him any uglier. And tomorrow he won't remember anything.' The most dangerous adversary is one who abides by no rules, has no limitations to his actions, and does not care about the consequences of those actions.[22]

Martial arts might instil modern practitioners with confidence, but usually not the swaggering, belligerent braggadocio of many a kung fu film. Instead they instil their students with the confidence to walk away, to de-escalate, to sense trouble before it brews and prepare to be somewhere else. Every dojo has a cautionary tale about a friend of a friend who discovered that knowing kung fu was not enough to keep them out of hospital. 'As some of those students later discovered to their dismay,' writes Dave Lowry in *Autumn Lightning*, 'the flaw in their instruction was that muggers and rapists have always had the disconcerting habit of assaulting victims in ways that have not been covered in self-defense courses ... trainees found that their tactics could be a lot more difficult to execute with an armful of groceries in tow, or while bent over, loosening the nuts on a flat tire.'[23]

Modern martial artists might know how to kill, but they hope never to have to use that knowledge. At the upper levels, they learn to envisage not the movie-style quick hit of a victory at fisticuffs, but the blood and carnage, pain and inconvenience, and legal entanglements likely to follow soon behind. Sun Tzu would have approved: the best form of self-defence is not to fight at all.[24]

INTERNATIONAL FRICTIONS

Funakoshi Gichin did not live to see karate become the world's most popular martial art. When he wrote his memoirs in the last year of his life, he saw only the prospects for good, and had little to say in terms of predicting likely areas of conflict. It has taken a generation or two for the expansion of East Asian martial arts overseas to create new issues – problems with establishing the credentials of foreign aspirants, in disciplines that previously prided themselves on their nationally, even racially defined exclusivity. Among the schools of classical Japanese martial arts overseas, writes Alexander Bennett:

> Some are authorised by the corresponding school in Japan and its current *sōke* (head of the tradition), but the lion's share are Frankensteins – totally fabricated and supported by

216

bogus claims of historical legitimacy . . . In addition, some of these small schools are plagued by incessant squabbling and infighting over matters of authentic sōkeship. The modern budō arts are a thousand-fold healthier in terms of the number of practitioners, although a degree of political factionalism exists in these federations as well.[25]

Alexander Bennett observes that the Budōkan, Tokyo's huge martial arts hall, was originally built for the 1964 Olympics, when judo achieved the international honour of being included as an Olympic school. But today, 'on alternate nights small armies of scalpers [are] illegally selling concert tickets to legions of eager groupies'.[26] Unsurprisingly, as with any other sporting venue, there is not enough interest in the martial arts for the Budōkan to be used solely for martial arts occasions – it runs a profitable and necessary sideline in hosting rock concerts.

Bennett also points to the racism implicit in the Budōkan's own charter, the translation of which he revised in 2004, removing the 1977 suggestion that 'the erosion of budō's cultural integrity was partly catalysed by its growing popularity overseas. For the sake of international goodwill, I convinced the Budōkan to allow me to gloss over the sentiment in my revision.'[27] Nor was Bennett being overly careful, since as he himself reports, snide comments about the dilution of martial arts through the arrival of foreign practitioners is not unknown in the Japanese media. It was, after all, Ishihara Shintarō, shortly before he was thankfully ousted as governor of Tokyo, who commented during the 2012 Olympics: 'Westerners practising judo resemble beasts fighting. Internationalised judo has lost its appeal . . . In Brazil they put chocolate in *norimaki*, but I wouldn't call it sushi. Judo has gone the same way.'[28]

International success, after all, is the means by which Japanese martial arts can truly grow, with varying claims for the popularity of certain forms. There are, it is claimed, at least fifty million people doing karate worldwide and five million doing judo. Such expansion can lead, however, to the very real possibility of what post-colonial studies calls hybridity and what the layman might call 'blowback', with some martial arts becoming dominated by foreigners. Most notable among these is sumo, supposedly Japan's national sport, but dominated by foreigners for the last decade. Sumo in the late twentieth century had suffered from declining achievements among local talents, and ever-more impressive wins by foreigners. Hawaiians caused particular stress to the sumo authorities, with Jesse 'Takamiyama' Kuhaulua winning victories in the 1970s that would have surely propelled a local boy to the champion rank of yokozuna. The desire to keep foreigners out of the top rank, particularly an attempt to prevent the meteoric rise of Salevaa 'Konishiki' Atisanoe, may have led to the pre-emptive promotion of a number of lesser Japanese wrestlers in order to crowd out the ranks. Mealy-mouthed excuses in the 1990s focussed on *hinkaku* – the stipulation that a champion in sumo needed a certain ineffable and handily unquantifiable sense of dignity or character, which these foreigners conveniently lacked. Sumo, however, was becoming increasingly sportified by this point, with the Sumo Association insisting on specific, quantifiable criteria for advancement. We might even suggest that the attempts to use such ethnically questionable 'mumbo jumbo' to keep perfectly good wrestlers from the top spot, when Japan itself was failing to provide any contenders, seemed increasingly untenable. In 1993, the Hawaiian-born Chadwick 'Akebono' Rowan became the first identifiably 'foreign' yokozuna champion – the first of many.[29]

A story of Ueshiba Morihei, the founder of aikido, recounts his arrival in Hawaii to teach a class, his greetings and thanks for the invitation. 'But after that, he would talk about fire and water, and we translators were lost'.[30] How many other martial arts traditions have stumbled at foreign borders, lost in translation?

It should come as no surprise that, in both China and Japan, organisations that have been developed and grown as nationalist enterprises should face difficult dilemmas when they gain foreign members. This becomes particularly problematic at the levels above third-*dan*, when many martial arts begin to incorporate philosophical concepts and managerial responsibilities. For many martial artists in the upper echelons of such organisations, progression above fifth-*dan* implicitly requires not only mastery of a martial art, but fluency in a foreign language. Foreigners excluded from further advancement are liable to feel swindled or shut-out, which only increases the chance of splinter groups that deny much of the cultural elements of a discipline, instead pushed ever closer to sportification.

The favouring of Asian candidates is not necessarily a matter of racism, although it sometimes is. It is a common occurrence in any organisation that develops a faction of overseas adherents that do not speak the common language, and possibly do not share the common culture of the founders. I have witnessed teachers from the Far East, not merely in the martial arts but in other fields, giving presentations that rely on visual puns from Chinese or Japanese, intelligible to any native teenager, but wholly baffling to non-linguist Europeans. I have observed legal spats over the financing of foreign branches, which demand a Japanese manager but cannot find a means of ethically reimbursing him for 'free' tuition. From Kanō Jigorō onwards, many founders of martial arts have tried to keep their vocation *voluntary* – a noble sentiment that can often place severe demands on the time and resources of teachers. Is it any surprise that the sumo wrestling *hinkaku* dispute should reappear, tacitly and no so tacitly, in many other martial arts?

Long gone are the days when the likes of Sō Dōshin would be conferred with a grandmaster's status whenever his teacher felt like it would be a good idea. It is more normal now for advancement through the ranking system to take a substantial and more uniform time. In Japan and China, where daily classes are more likely, it is theoretically possible to reach the level of first-degree black belt in a single year. '. . . followed by a 2-dan one year after passing *shōdan*, 3-dan two years after 2-dan, and so on. For reference, a strong university student would usually graduate at age twenty-two with the rank of 4-dan.'[31]

In other words, students in the Far East are far more likely to finish their tertiary education with a ranking in a martial art suitable to allow them to teach it. Although many might give up, there is a ready supply of new teachers, and if someone moves to a town without a dojo, he or she is already qualified to start one. This pattern is not repeated in the Western world, where fewer opportunities and a less fanatical concentration on a single hobby is liable to leave the average, dedicated twenty-four-year-old looking at a *shōdan* – a first-degree black belt, impressive but not suitable for independent teaching.

Many martial artists reach a glass ceiling at the upper grades, confronted by materials that only exist in a foreign language, creating a vibrant and confusing sub-genre of privately translated manuals and glosses designed to help colleagues get through the next stage. This linguistic dilemma has caused some Asian orders to spare their foreign members the effort of more philosophical pursuits, calving off their overseas branches into sporting societies, divorced from the historical context of a martial art. In other cases, the foreign practitioners have struggled through, leaving handwritten notes and mimeographed manuscripts for the next generation.

Similar problems endure even in the Far East. Twentieth-century Japanese guides pastiche or summarise Chinese manuals, themselves of debatable provenance. The vast explosion of military-manual publishing in Japan's Tokugawa era has created an archive of books that are old but not ancient, drawing on a Chinese original that makes a similar claim for itself. All too often, a purportedly ancient tradition will turn out to be based on a dusty manuscript, itself a copy of a lost original, but without any real evidence stretching back more than a hundred years.

Meanwhile, many modern martial arts are facing the greying of their early generations and the thinning of their adherents. Although such conditions are likely to have been repeated on innumerable occasions throughout history, most modern martial arts are now facing them in real time. For any martial art founded (or 'rediscovered') in the twentieth century, the generation of elders who can remember the direct transmission of the founder is now dying off. As with any organisation, there are sure to be debates over policy and arguments over what the founder *would have wanted*, and how the founder's mind *might have changed* in accordance with new circumstances. A founding generation, largely of men with military experience or memories, must now contend with grandchildren who have grown up in affluent society, with the acceptance (or lack of it) of female participants, with an influx of foreign disciples who stand little chance of understanding the more localised and exclusive ideals. Martial arts, the ruling councils of which once comprised men who had literally killed in their military days, are now packed with descendants and new recruits who have studied marketing and international relations. Such new blood can often bring fresh ideas, but not necessarily to a discipline's objective improvement. *Maybe we should make the exams easier? Maybe we should drop the exams in Buddhist philosophy? Maybe we should rebrand ourselves as a community outreach organisation, and forget about the kung fu stuff? Maybe we should become a sport? Maybe we should fund a movie that makes us look good? Can we monetise the uniforms? Shouldn't we have a theme song? What should our logo be . . . ?*

Owing to such generational issues, martial arts in the twenty-first century are poised on the brink of another set of transformations. Some will turn into sports, others will fracture on ideological lines, turning a strong, single federation into a bunch of spin-offs too small to thrive alone. Some will succeed and thrive, perhaps transformed by an unlikely boom in admissions – a sudden wave of interest in Indonesia, perhaps, or an American wave of new adherents, inspired by a particular movie. The martial arts worldwide are facing another shake-out, much like the Tokugawa-era competition that saw only a few *budō* disciplines survive the nineteenth century; much like the contention of the sixteenth century that saw only a few forms of kung fu make it into *The New Manual of Military Efficiency*; much like the tribulations of the Cultural Revolution, that wiped out so much knowledge. In our lifetimes, there will be new forms of old disciplines, and new 'traditions' invented out of whole cloth. Some contemporary forms will be unrecognisable; others will inexplicably have endured.

This is not the end of martial arts history. Thanks to the wider availability of documentation and almost a century of scholarship, we face the future knowing (and able to know) substantially more about the development of the martial arts than any previous generation. Examining the origins, and confronting the issues arising, is going to become both easier and less liable to misunderstanding. I leave you with the words of one martial artist who popularised the entire field as an actor, and created a syncretic version of his own, a champion of the East, a proponent of international understanding, and one of the few figures to truly unite the opinions of rival practitioners. For it was Bruce Lee who once said:

> I hope martial artists are more interested in the root of martial arts and not the different decorative branches, flowers or leaves. It is futile to argue as to which single leaf, which design or branches or which attractive flower you like; when you understand the root you understand all its blossoming.[32]

Chronology

....

220

Chen Qun, a minister of China's Northern Wei dynasty, suggests that courtiers be ranked on a nine-level system.

496

Foundation of the Shaolin Temple on behalf of the Indian monk Buddhabhadra.

547

A Record of the Buddhist Monasteries of Luoyang claims that Bodhidharma visited Luoyang around 525 AD.

577

Destruction of the Shaolin Temple.

580

Reconstruction of the Shaolin Temple.

607

First recorded contact between China and the Ryūkyū Islands.

618

Destruction of Shaolin Temple, again.

621

The 'Prince of Qin's Instruction' on the Shaolin Stele thanks the monks of the temple for their military assistance.

622

Shaolin Temple site abandoned.

624

Shaolin Temple restored by imperial decree.

632

Shaolin Temple is ordered dissolved; monks protest and are instead regifted their land in honour of their previous service.

845

Shaolin Temple ordered destroyed in anti-foreign purges of Tang emperor Wuzong.

954

Shaolin Temple abandoned.

1002

The Transmission of the Lamp sets down stories of the death of Bodhidharma and sightings of his spirit returning to India.

1220

Shaolin Pharmacy Bureau set up.

1260

Shaolin monk Fuyu becomes abbot of Wanshou Temple in Khubilai Khan's capital (Beijing). Establishment of five Shaolin sub-temples.

1351

Red Turban rebels lay siege to the Shaolin Temple.

1361

Shaolin Temple population purportedly reduced to only twenty monks.

1393

The 'Thirty-Six Families' migrate from China to Naha, Okinawa.

1477

King Shō Shin of the Ryūkyū Islands bans the use of weapons.

1552

Shaolin monk Yuekong leads forty fighting monks against Japanese pirates, dying in battle in 1554.

1603

Japan: The Shōgun, Tokugawa Ieyasu, appoints a Minister of Go. The four competing Houses of Go are soon established, with members ranked in a *dan* system based on the nine court ranks of ancient China.

1609

Samurai from the Satsuma domain conquer the Ryūkyū Islands.

1638

Japan: Chen Yuanbin, a ceramics master from China, reputedly instructs several masterless samurai in the art of 'seizing a man without the use of weapons'.

1641

Destruction of the Shaolin Temple by rebel forces led by Li Zicheng. Substantial loss of archives.

1669

China: The *Epitaph for Wang Zhengnan* first introduces the concept of a split between internal-Daoist-'Wudang' and external-Buddhist-Shaolin martial arts.

1727

China: The Yongzheng Emperor forbids the teaching of 'boxing and staff'.

1786

Lin Shuangwen's uprising on Taiwan is the first documented instance of the term *Tiandihui* ('Heaven and Earth Gathering'), i.e. Triads.

1789

Two sumo wrestlers perform a ring-entering ceremony not seen before in the sport.

1794

China: White Lotus Rebellion rages for eight years, put down with the aid of local militia.

1813

China: Buddhist 'Eight Trigram' rebels rise up against the Manchus. Fang Keshan, one of the leaders, is a teacher of 'Plum Blossom Fist'.

1850

China: Taiping Rebellion flourishes for fourteen years. Again put down with militia.

1861

Cantonese opera troupes are banned for ten years in the wake of the Red Turban Uprising. Up to a million southern Chinese die in post-revolt purges.

1867

Establishment in [British] boxing of the 'Marquess of Queensbury Rules'.

1868

Japan: The Meiji Restoration spells the end of the samurai and the mass unemployment of hundreds of martial arts instructors.

1873

Japan: Introduction of universal military conscription creates the need to have a national standard in martial arts instead of hundreds of variant schools.

1874

The Ryūkyū Islands terminate their tributary relationship with China.

1875

The Ryūkyū Islands are brought under the purview of the Japanese Home Ministry, rather than the Foreign Ministry.

1876

Japan: Samurai are banned from carrying swords in public. End of the practical relevance of weapons-based martial arts in Japanese public life.

1879

Japan: A young Kanō Jigorō is among the martial artists who demonstrate sword-fighting and grappling techniques for the former US President, Ulysses S. Grant. Abdication of the last king of the Ryūkyū Islands sees the islands officially re-established as part of Japanese territory.

1880

Oskar Korschelt publishes an article in German on 'the Sino-Japanese game Go, a rival to chess'.

1882

Japan: Kanō Jigorō founds the school later known as the Institute for the Transmission of Japanese Judo (*Nihon Den Kōdōkan Jūdō*) in Tokyo.

US: Chinese Exclusion Act prevents immigration of Chinese labourers.

1883

Japan: Kanō Jigorō confers the title of *shōdan* (first grade) on two of his students, importing the ranking system from the Houses of Go.

1886

Japan: Kanō Jigorō suggests that his *shōdan* students are distinguished from beginners by wearing black belts.

Canada: Construction of the Canadian Pacific Railroad brings in 15,000 Chinese labourers – likely arrival of kung fu in Canadian Chinatowns, although whites are excluded.

1895

Foundation of the Dai Nippon Butoku Kai (Greater Japan Martial Virtue Society), a government body designed to standardise and rationalise the Japanese martial arts.

1898

Edward Barton-Wright returns to England from Japan, and introduces the fighting art of 'bartitsu'.

1901

Arthur Conan Doyle's Sherlock Holmes attributes his survival to *baritsu* [sic], 'the Japanese system of wrestling'.

Japan: Itosu Ankō introduces karate into Okinawan public schools.

Australia: Immigration Restriction Act – not repealed until 1958.

1903

First judo demonstration in the US, by Yamashita Yoshitsugu.

In Indonesia, police sergeant Ki Ngabei Soerodiwirjo begins teaching the traditional fighting art of *pentjak* (Pencak Silat) under the cover of 'the fraternity of initiates'.

1904

US publication of *The Complete Kano Jiu-jitsu* by H. Irving Hancock and Higashi Katsumi – disowned by Kanō Jigorō as an outmoded rip-off.

China: *The Travels of Lao Can*, a potboiler kung fu novel, introduces the notion that Bodhidharma was the inventor of Shaolin kung fu.

1906

Japan: A Kyoto conference standardises the judo forms to be taught at Japanese public schools.

Australia: First official Australian demonstration of jujutsu, by Cecil Elliott.

1907

Japan: Kanō Jigorō introduces the modern *jūdōgi* or judo uniform. It is white, as a symbol of purity and simplicity.

1908

Japan: Judo or kendo are now compulsory for all middle-school students (law repealed in 1996). From Okinawa, Itosu Ankō instead recommends Kara-te to the ministries of education and war.

1909

Founding of the Pure Martial (*Jingwu*) Callisthenics School in Shanghai; beginning of the Chinese martial arts as a 'cultural recreation.'

Japan: Sumo wrestling referees start to dress like Shinto priests. Sumo wrestlers are now expected to arrive at matches wearing *haori* and *hakama* – Tokugawa-era formal dress.

c.1910

The Japanese term literary term *bukyō* (martial arts heroic fiction) slips into Chinese as *wuxia*.

c.1911

China: Shaolin Temple establishes its own security regiment.

Bill Underwood, a student of Tani Yukiō, emigrates from the UK to Canada.

1915

China: Publication of *Secrets of Shaolin Boxing* by an anonymous author.

Japan: Funakoshi Gichin gives the first Kara-te demonstration in Tokyo.

1916

First kendo dojo in Vancouver brings Japanese martial arts to Canada.

1919

Wong Fei-hung gives a demonstration at the opening ceremony of the Jingwu school's Guangzhou branch.

1922

Funakoshi Gichin publishes *Ryūkyū Kenpō: Kara-te* (*The Fist Law of the Ryūkyūs: China-hand*), introducing Kara-te to a wide readership on the Japanese mainland.

1924

First Kara-te club established in mainland Japan, at Keiō University, Tokyo. Funakoshi Gichin confers the first *shōdan* ranks for Kara-te, and introduces a grading system based on that of judo. Kara-te students must wear a facsimile of the *jūdōgi*.

Tagaki Shinzo opens the first judo school in Canada.

1925

An editorial in the *Japan Times* complains that staged matches between 'American' boxers and Japanese martial artists only incite 'useless racial prejudices'.

1926

Sumo wrestling rules changed to make it easier to declare one clear winner.

1927

Coloured belts for judo competitors below black belt are introduced in England.

1928

Shaolin Temple burns down again – substantial loss of archives. The term *Guoshu*, or 'national arts', briefly flourishes as the Chinese term for martial arts.

1931

Japan: The Kokugikan (national sports hall) where sumo-wrestling matches are held is redesigned to incorporate a new roof over the wrestling ring in the style of a Shintō shrine.

1932

The Republic of China bans stories of the martial arts, although they continue to flourish overseas – the clampdown takes greater effect with the 1934 Film Censorship Law.

1933

First Caucasians admitted to a judo club in Honolulu, Hawaii.

1935

France: Kawaishi Mikonosuke encourages his lower-ranking judo students in Paris by introducing a system of coloured belts for the *kyū* ranks below the first-grade black belt.

Japan: The Kōdōkan judo association posthumously confers the first 10th-*dan* rank, an honorary position, on Yamashita Yoshitsugu.

1936

In an era of rising nationalism, the characters used to write Kara-te in Japanese are officially changed from 'China-hand' to *karate* – 'empty-hand.'

Sō Dōshin visits the Shaolin Temple.

1937

The Royal Canadian Mounted Police send a judo team to the 10th Canadian Judo Championship.

1940

British-born Canadian Bill Underwood develops his martial arts system Combato.

1942

Ueshiba Morihei begins describing his fighting style as aikido. Japanese occupation of Indonesia; Pencak Silat, once associated with anti-Dutch movements, is encouraged as a means of preparing for an Allied counter-attack.

1943

Japan: Akira Kurosawa's directorial debut, *Sugata Sanshirō*, valorises judo.

US: Chinese Exclusion Act repealed – immigration to the US now possible.

1945

Japan: *Zoku Sugata Sanshirō* (a.k.a. *Judo Story II*) features the judo hero defeating an American boxer.

The US Occupation authorities in Japan censor all martial and feudal content from media.

Canada: Bill Underwood renames his martial arts system Defendo, later known as British jiu-jitsu.

1946

First karate dojo in the continental US, established by Robert Trias in Phoenix, Arizona.

1947

Sō Dōshin founds Shorinji Kempo ('Fist Way of the Shaolin Temple') in Japan. In order to evade occupation scrutineers and qualify for tax breaks, he categorises it as a *religion* with a 'dance' component.

Canada: Repeal of the Chinese Exclusion Act – immigration to Canada now possible.

1948

Organisers of the London Olympics refuse to invite Japan.

American Occupation authorities permit the resumption of the all-Japan Kōdōkan judo tournament.

British immigrant George Grundy establishes the first judo club in New Zealand.

Foundation of the United States Karate Association.

Eugen Herrigel publishes *Zen in the Art of Archery* in German.

The newly independent Indonesian government promotes '*pentjak* and *silat*' (Pencak Silat) as a symbol of nationalist unity. The term is officially adopted, combining common words for 'martial art' in Java and Sumatra/Borneo.

1949

Proclamation of the People's Republic of China.

In Hebei, Party cadre Huang Yueting announces the clinically-approved exercise regime of *qigong*.

Hong Kong: Wu Peng attempts to revitalise Cantonese cinema by making a film about the martial arts master Wong Fei-hung. It is the first of many.

1952

End of US Occupation of Japan.

Resurgence of martial arts, often rebranded as 'democratic sports'.

Foundation of the Judo Federation of Australia.

1953

China: The Traditional Physical Culture and Sports Commission is founded to review and recreate the ancient sporting practices of the Han Chinese. A decade follows in which many forms are nationally standardised.

Japan: The Dai Nippon Butoku Kai is refounded with similar aims – to preserve the purity and history of Japan's martial arts.

Japan: Death of Miyagi Chōjun leads to multiple splits in Gōjū-ryū karate.

Foundation of the US Judo Black Belt Federation.

Ten leading Japanese martial artists, in judo, karate and aikido, tour US Air Force bases.

Zen in the Art of Archery is translated into English.

US: Ace Comics releases *Judo Joe*, the first American martial arts comic.

1954

US: Ed Parker starts teaching his American Kenpo Karate (sic) in Utah.

1955

Disparate Korean martial arts schools united under the name *taekwondo* (kick-punch way), under the influence of former karate practitioner Choi Hong-hil.

Hong Kong: Jin Yong's serial novel *The Book and the Sword* depicts 'the Red Flower Society', an underground organisation dedicated to overthrowing the Manchus.

1956

Jhoon Rhee begins teaching taekwondo in San Marcos, Texas.

Eugen Herrigel's *Zen in the Art of Archery* is translated into Japanese, heavily influencing local ideas on the martial arts, despite being filtered through the perception of a foreigner.

Funakoshi Gichin's *Karate-dō: My Way of Life* suggests that karate combines two rival forms from China: Shaolin and Wudang.

Choi Yeong-eui, a.k.a. Ōyama Masutatsu, a Japanese national of Korean ancestry, begins teaching karate in his own dojo. Later regarded as the beginning of the Kyokushin (Ultimate Truth) off-shoot of karate.

Formation of the Australian Society of Jujitsuans.

Karate and aikido reach Montreal through France.

1957

Disagreements escalate over the funeral arrangements for Funakoshi Gichin, causing his Shōtōkan karate organisation to split into two factions, the Shōtōkai and the Japan Karate Association.

1958

China: the establishment of the All-China Wushu Association attempts to regulate martial arts in sporting competitions.

1959

Japan: Yamada Fūtarō's novel *Kōga Ninpōchō* (*The Kōga Nina Scrolls*) portrays rival clans of superhuman assassins duelling at the beginning of the Tokugawa era. It spawns two-dozen sequels over the next decade. First ninja manga published by Sanpei Shirato.

US: Disguised as a man, Rena 'Rusty' Glickman is part of a winning judo team at the New York YMCA. She is forced to return her medal when the deception is discovered.

Bruce Lee arrives in Seattle and begins teaching Wing Chun in a car park.

1960

US TV: *The Detectives* features a karate demonstration.

Elvis Presley acquires a black belt in karate.

1961

US film: *Karate: Hand of Death* introduces karate to American cinemas.

US TV: Ricky Nelson, black belt in karate, shows off his skills in an episode of *The Adventures of Ozzie and Harriet*.

First issue of *Black Belt Magazine*. Ten-year ban on women in US judo competition.

Hong Kong novel: *Heaven Sword and Dragon Sabre*, by Jin Yong (Louis Cha) popularises the idea of a fictional 'Wudang' sect, contending with Shaolin.

1962

UK TV: Honor Blackman introduces judo to audiences of *The Avengers*.

1963

US TV: Lucille Ball tries her hand at karate on *The Lucy Show*.

France: Founding of the European Karate Union.

1964

Japan: The animated series *Fujimaru the Wind Ninja*, based on the manga *Ninja Clan* by Sanpei Shirato, features live-action documentary inserts presented by martial artist Hatsumi Masaaki.

Construction completed on Tokyo's giant Olympic martial arts hall, the Budōkan.

Judo introduced as a sport at the Tokyo Olympics.

Establishment of the Iga-ryū Ninja Museum.

Several rival karate organisations, including the JKA, Gōjū-ryū, Shitō-ryū and Wado-ryū, agree to recognise each other's ranks, paving the way for a unified karate presence in sport.

1965

Japan: National (re)building programme creates modern appearance of most 'old' castles. The publication of Yamaguchi Masayuki's *Ninja no Seikatsu* (*Life of the Ninja*) apocryphally suggests that ninja have played an unmentioned role in every major Japanese historical event of the samurai era.

International Judo Federation introduces weight classes.

US: The superhero Judomaster first appears in *Special War Series #4*.

US: Immigration and Nationality Act removes many barriers to Asians.

US: First televised karate matches.

1966

US TV: *The Green Hornet* features Bruce Lee as Kato.

US comics: Judomaster gets his own title from DC Comics.

France: First European Karate Championships, with competitors from ten countries.

Yamamori Hirokazu introduces Shorinji Kempo to the United States.

1967

Bruce Lee founds Jeet Kune Do ('Way of the Intercepting Fist'), a 'non-classical' martial art with elements of Wing Chun. The James Bond film *You Only Live Twice* introduces ninja to a global audience.

1969

Hong Kong: Jin Yong's serial novel *The Deer and the Cauldron* publicises the notion that the Heaven and Earth Gathering was an offshoot of an underground organisation formed by Ming loyalists.

US: In New York's Chinatown, the newly formed *I Wor Kuen* left-wing pressure group derives its name from the Boxer Uprising.

Foundation of the American Taekwondo Association.

Foundation of the US Judo Association.

1970

Formation of the Australian Karate Federation.

On a visit to Japan, Canadian Prime Minister Pierre Trudeau is upgraded from brown to black belt in judo at the Kōdōkan.

1971

US TV: Bruce Lee appears in four episodes of the crime drama *Longstreet*, demonstrating Jeet Kune Do.

1972

The Gates of Jingwu (Jingwu Men) features Bruce Lee as a hero of the Jingwu School, fighting the Japanese in 1909 Shanghai. Released internationally as *Fist of Fury*, and as *The Chinese Connection* in the US.

Napoleon Fernandez, a former jujutsu and Jeet Kune Do practitioner, begins teaching his own Yaw Yan ('Dance of Death') martial art in the Philippines.

US TV: *Kung Fu* is first aired, starring David Carradine in a role originally intended for Bruce Lee.

1973

US/HK film: *Enter the Dragon*, starring Bruce Lee takes kung fu into the mainstream.

'Kung Fu Fighting' by Carl Douglas goes to number one in a dozen countries, and becomes the cheesy anthem of many future martial arts events.

Establishment of the French Shorinji Kempo Federation.

1974

After Choi Hong-hi moves to Toronto, it becomes the headquarters of the International Taekwondo Federation.

1975

C. W. Nicol's *Moving Zen: Karate as a Way to Gentleness* is the first of dozens of memoirs to be published by foreigners studying the unarmed martial arts in Japan.

c.1978

Steven Seagal takes over his Japanese father-in-law's Tenshin Aikidō dojo in Osaka, presumably becoming the first white American to run a martial arts school in Japan.

1978

Hatsumi Masaaki founds the Bujinkan, an organisation of martial arts skills that favours his own specialty, *ninjutsu*.

1979

China: State Commission for Physical Culture and Sports is tasked with standardising most forms of martial arts. First scientific conference on *qigong*.

China: The cartoon *Nezha vs the Dragon King* features *wushu*-influenced gymnastics routines.

China: Monks at the Shaolin Temple are permitted to wear their robes for the first time since the Cultural Revolution, in order to welcome Sō Dōshin from Japan.

Japan: Foundation of the Nihon Kobudō Association, a federation of schools teaching classical samurai martial arts.

1980

Death of Sō Dōshin. His daughter Yūki becomes the leader of Shorinji Kempo.

Establishment of British Shorinji Kempo Federation.

An Australian government initiative establishes the National Judo Coaching Scheme.

China: launch of *Qigong* magazine.

US book: *Ninja: Spirit of the Shadow Warrior*, by Stephen Hayes.

1981

US film: *Enter the Ninja* integrates ninjutsu into the modern spy thriller.

1982

Chinese film: *Shaolin Temple*, the first martial arts film made in Communist China, and a watershed event in the modern popularisation of kung fu.

1983

Hong Kong film: *Shaolin and Wu Tang* presents a fictional rivalry between Shaolin and 'Wudang' schools.

Japan: In defiance of the Shorinji Kempo authorities, Sugihara Masayasu enters and wins a karate competition under the pseudonymous brand of 'the White Lotus Association' (*Byakuren Kaikan*).

1984

Japan: Sugihara Masayasu splits from Shorinji Kempo to form Byakuren karate.

US film: *The Karate Kid*, featuring a 'Mr Miyagi' named after Miyagi Chōjun.

US comic: *Teenage Mutant Ninja Turtles* – cartoon in 1987, movie in 1990.

1985

US film: *American Ninja*.

1986

US film: *Big Trouble in Little China* takes martial arts movies into camp and comedy.

US film: *The Karate Kid II* outperforms the original at the box office.

Netherlands: Controversial introduction of the alternate blue judo outfit for competition, to aid judges and TV viewers in telling opponents apart.

1988

Taekwondo is an Olympic demonstration sport (official from 2000), as is women's judo (official from 1992), with Rusty Kanakogi, *née* Glickman, coaching the US team.

1989

English Shōtōkan Academy splits from the Karate Union of Great Britain over sportification.

1990

China: foundation of the International Wushu Federation marks the withdrawal of the State Commission from managing martial arts, and an increasing sportification of martial arts forms.

1992

US: First issue of the *Journal of Asian Martial Arts*.

China: *Qigong* master Li Hongzhi founds the Falun Gong sect.

1993

Japan: Chadwick Rowan from Hawaii becomes the first 'obviously foreign' *yokozuna* (champion) in sumo wrestling.

US: *Enter the Wu-Tang (36 Chambers)* by the Wu-Tang Clan co-opts martial arts samples into hip-hop culture. First broadcast of *The Mighty Morphin' Power Rangers*.

Japanese Judo Federation threatens to boycott European competitions over the use of the blue outfits.

1994

Ōyama Masutatsu dies without designating an official successor. Kyokushin Karate splits into two groups.

1995

Official 1,500th anniversary celebrations of the foundation of the Shaolin Temple.

1996

New Chinese legislation attempts to distinguish responsibility for *qigong* between medical and sports bureaucracies – any religious status is denied.

Falun Gong is banned in China.

1997

Charles Palmer is the first Briton to be awarded 10th-*dan* in judo.

Hong Kong Handover – substantial acquisition of foreign passports by Hong Kong residents.

2000

Crouching Tiger Hidden Dragon adapts a *wuxia* novel by Wang Dulu, revitalising interest in fantastical martial arts.

2002

Japan: *Naruto* TV anime begins broadcast.

US: The syncretic Marine Corps Martial Arts Program now confers a 'black belt' after 150 hours of training.

2003

After the death of Enoeda Keinosuke, the Karate Union of Great Britain splits from what is now called JKA England.

2004

Shaolin Temple moves into pharmaceuticals with the establishment of the Shaolin Yaoju (Medicine) Co. Ltd.

2008

The US cartoon *Kung Fu Panda* introduces the 'Furious Five' – a team of kung fu masters modelled on totem animals from traditional martial arts.

A *wushu* competition runs parallel to the Beijing Olympics, but is not officially regarded as a demonstration sport.

Rusty Glickman Kanokogi is awarded the Order of the Rising Sun.

2010

UNESCO confers World Heritage status on the Shaolin Temple and its Forest of Pagodas.

The British Shorinji Kempo Federation splits from the World Shorinji Kempo Association, leading to a trademark dispute with the latter.

2011

International Judo Federation introduces approval requirements for standardised materials and quality in judo outfits.

2012

Ishihara Shintarō, the governor of Tokyo, comments that 'Westerners practising judo is like beasts fighting'.

2013

Mie University begins offering lessons in Ninja Studies.

2020

Tokyo Olympics – strong pressure in Japan for the introduction of further martial arts as demonstration sports.

2022

Judo is added to the core sports at the Commonwealth Games.

Sources and
Recommended Reading

......

Never before have I come across a subject in which materials are published in such a diverse and uncollated number of places. Martial arts are an intensely personal experience, and have led to many individual memoirs, themselves often issued by small presses or self-publishing schemes, reflecting the isolated readerships of separate disciplines. Rob Jacob's *Martial Arts Biographies*, for example, lists over 140 figures whose encounter with Asian fighting styles has become the subject of a book, from the founding figures in Asia, through their overseas proponents like Bruce Lee and Chuck Norris, through to celebrity practitioners like Elvis Presley, Honor Blackman and Vladimir Putin.

Understandably, many authors usually focus on their personal journey, stopping only to pay lip service to a few things they may have heard about their particular discipline's origin in ancient times. Sometimes, one finds oneself in the middle of what feels like a boys' club where everybody knows everybody else, particularly in the 1950s and 1960s, when Donn Draeger and his Tokyo housemates seemed to turn up in each other's books, often with different perspectives on the same incident – their house in Ichigaya seems to have a place in martial arts history equivalent to that of the Tokiwa-sō in the manga world, a salon and crucible for much of the next few decades' big names. Draeger himself was a leading light of twentieth-century scholarship, penning over a dozen books, from groundbreaking histories to cash-in ephemera. Despite coining the term *hoplology* for the scholarly study of the martial arts and writing many robust works that have stood the test of time, some of Draeger's assertions seem flawed or methodologically unsound today, although nowhere near as much as those of his associate 'John Gilbey'. According to *Martial Musings*, the memoirs of Draeger's sometime co-author Robert Smith, the housemates created the persona of the larger-than-life martial arts expert Gilbey as 'a joke, an exaggeration, a fantasy' in 1961. Under this pseudonym, Smith wrote three books on the martial arts, injudiciously mixing meaningful research with outright lies and parodies, many of which were unwittingly repeated by later authors who were not in on the joke.

Others have personal axes to grind, owing to doctrinal or jurisdictional disputes that are often opaque to the outsider. John Stevens, in *The Way of Judo*, reasonably criticises several books for relying too heavily on secondary sources or Internet research, but is far more cryptic in his objection to a rival biography: 'The less said about Brian N. Watson's *The Father of Judo* . . . the better.' Sometimes, we find ourselves reading a manuscript that contends with unseen detractors, such as Shi Yongxin's *Shaolin Temple in my heart*, framed as a history of his vocation, but heavily influenced by his desire to answer critics of his often controversial management of the monastery, or Funakoshi Gichin's *Karate-dō: My Way of Life*, which delicately disregards the styles of certain fellow teachers.

For a more general overview, going into greater depth than I can here, Peter Lorge's *Chinese Martial Arts: From Antiquity to the Twenty-First Century* is a recommended first-stop for the interested reader. The works of Brian Kennedy and Elizabeth Guo, particularly their *Chinese Martial Arts Training Manuals* and *Jingwu: The School That Transformed Kung Fu*, offer much-needed critical assessment of many traditional sources. Although supposedly a book about a single martial art, Alexander Bennett's recent *Kendo: Culture of the Sword* contains a valuable run-down of the nine major modern

Japanese *budō* martial arts, and of their centrality to politics and culture in the twentieth century. In Chinese, Kang Gewu's *Zhongguo Wushu Shiyong Daquan* and Zhang Yaoting's *Zhongguo Wushu Shi* have both proved invaluable to me, not merely in their own right, but as the places to check the more far-fetched assertions of other authors with less rigorous citation policies. In Japanese, Inoue Shun's *Budō no Tanjō* builds upon his previous work on the invention of traditions, which can be found in English in Vlastos' *Mirror of Modernity.*

In terms of martial arts in the film world, there are far too many shoddily compiled filmographies in existence, but there are some hidden gems. Craig Reid's *The Ultimate Guide to Martial Arts Movies of the 1970s* offers a vigorous, highly detailed account of five hundred films' content, context and reception, along with gossip from behind the scenes. Even in terms of the terrible ones, there is the recurring sense throughout the book that he has watched them so you don't have to. Stephen Teo's *Chinese Martial Arts Cinema* grounds the rise of modern *wuxia* in the film industry and audiences of 1920s Shanghai, shortly after the financial decline of the original Jingwu school.

I have done my best to give page numbers from paper editions in my citations. However, there are a couple of occasions where I have had no option but to include location numbers from eBooks instead, such as the new edition of C. W. Nicol's *Moving Zen*, which is only available in electronic format.

[Anon.] 'History of Daito-ryu' –
http://web.archive.org/web/20070706040728/http://www.daito-ryu.
org/history1_eng.html
[Anon.] 'Introduction of Jujutsu to Australia' –
www.jujitsu.net.au/home/what-is-jujutsu

[Anon.] 'Jiu-Jitsu For Militants: Sylvia Pankhurst Also Wants Them Drilled and to Carry Sticks' in *The New York Times*, 12 August 1913.

[Anon.] 'Taizu Zhangquan' – www.china.com.cn/aboutchina/zhuanti/lddw/2007-11/22/content_9276212.htm, 22 November 2007.

Abernethy, Iain. 'The 10 Precepts of Anko Itosu' – www.iainabernethy.co.uk/article/10-precepts-anko-itosu (not dated).

Aston, W.G. *Nihongi: Chronicles of Japan from the Earliest Times to A.D. 697* (Rutland, VT: Tuttle, 1972).

Awakawa, Yasuichi. *Zen Painting* (Tokyo: Kodansha International, 1981).

Barton-Wright, Edward. 'Judo and jujitsu' in *Transactions of the Japan Society*, No. 5 (1902), p.261.

Beckwith, Christopher. *Empires of the Silk Road: A History of Central Eurasia from the Bronze Age to the Present* (Princeton: Princeton University Press, 2009).

Bennett, Alexander. *Kendo: Culture of the Sword* (Berkeley: University of California Press, 2015).

Boretz, Avron. *Gods, Ghosts, and Gangsters: Ritual Violence, Martial Arts, and Masculinity on the Margins of Chinese Society* (Honolulu: University of Hawai'i Press, 2011).

Bowen, Richard. *100 Years of British Judo: Reclaiming of its True Spirit*, in two volumes. (London: Indepenpress, 2011).

Bridges, Brian. *The Two Koreas and the Politics of Global Sport* (Leiden: Global Oriental, 2012).

Broughton, Jeffrey. *The Bodhidharma Anthology: The Earliest Records of Zen* (Berkeley: University of California Press, 1999).

Brousse, Michel and David Matsumoto. *Judo in the U.S.: A Century of Dedication* (Berkeley, CA: North Atlantic Books, 2005).

Bulag, Uradyn. *Collaborative Nationalism: The Politics of Friendship on China's Mongolian Frontier* (Lanham: Rowman and Littlefield, 2010).

Buswell, Robert and Donald S. Lopez (eds). *The Princeton Dictionary of Buddhism* (Princeton: Princeton University Press, 2014).

Canzonieri, Sal. *The Hidden History of the Chinese Internal Martial Arts* (Whippany, NJ: BGT ENT, 2013).

Chamberlain, Basil H. *Things Japanese*, fifth edition (London: John Murray, 1905).

Chen, Jack. *The Poetics of Sovereignty: On Emperor Taizong of the Tang Dynasty* (Harvard: Harvard University Press, 2010).

Chinese Health Qigong Association. *Mawangdui Daoyin Shu: Qigong from the Mawangdui Silk Paintings* (London: Jessica Kingsley Publishers, 2014).

Choy, Rita Mei-wah. *Read and Write Chinese: A Simplified Guide to the Chinese Characters* (Fourth Edition. San Francisco: Choy Hirschberg [no publisher name given], 1981).

Clark, Paul. *The Cultural Revolution: A History* (Cambridge: Cambridge University Press, 2008).

Clarke, Christopher M. *Okinawa Karate: A History of Styles and Masters* (Huntingtown, MD: Clarke's Canyon Press, 2012).

Clements, Jonathan. *Coxinga and the Fall of the Ming Dynasty* (Stroud: Sutton Publishing, 2004).

Clements, Jonathan. *A Brief History of the Samurai* (London: Robinson: 2010).

Clements, Jonathan. *The Art of War: A New Translation* (London: Constable, 2012).

Clements, Jonathan. *The First Emperor of China*, second edition (London: Albert Bridge Books, 2015).

Clouse, Robert. *The Making of Enter the Dragon* (Burbank: Unique, 1987).

Cott, Jonathan. *Wandering Ghost: The Odyssey of Lafcadio Hearn* (Tokyo: Kōdansha International, 1990).

Cuyler, P. *Sumo from Rite to Sport* (New York: Weatherhill, 1979).

Dawes, Mark. *Understanding Reasonable Force*, second edition (Hampshire: National Federation for Personal Safety, 2012).

DeMarco, Michael (ed.). *Asian Martial Arts: Constructive Thoughts and Practical Applications* (Santa Fe: Via Media Publishing, 2012).

Doyle, Arthur Conan. *The Return of Sherlock Holmes* (Reprint of book originally published in 1905. London: Headline, 2011).

Draeger, Donn. *Ninjutsu: The Art of Invisibility* (Tokyo: Lotus Press, 1971).

Draeger, Donn. *The Martial Arts and Ways of Japan* [Modern Bujutsu and Budo volume 3] (New York: Weatherhill, 1974).

Driscoll, Mark. *Absolute Erotic, Absolute Grotesque: The Living, Dead, and Undead in Japan's Imperialism, 1895–1945* (Durham: Duke University Press, 2010).

Esherick, Joseph W. *The Origins of the Boxer Uprising* (Berkeley: University of California Press, 1987).

Farkas, Emil. *An Illustrated History of Martial Arts in America – 1900 to Present* (North Hills, CA: Rising Sun Productions, 2007).

Farthing, John. 'Recreational Sportification Ruins Historical Combat Discipline', Association for Renaissance Martial Arts website, May 2012. www.thearma.org/essays/sportification-ruins-discipline.html#. Vl10-I70bw

Farrar, D.S. and John Whalen-Bridge (eds). *Martial Arts as Embodied Knowledge: Asian Traditions in a Transnational World* (Albany, NY: State University of New York Press, 2011).

Filipiak, Kai. 'From Warriors to Sportsmen: How Traditional Chinese Martial Arts Adapted to Modernity' in the *Journal of Asian Martial Arts*, Vol. 19, No. 1 (2010), pp.30–53.

Fitzpatrick, Merrilyn. 'Local administration in northern Chekiang and the response to the pirate invasions of 1553–1556', unpublished PhD dissertation, Australian National University, 1976.

Frederic, Louis. *A Dictionary of the Martial Arts* (London: Athlone Press, 1991).

Friday, Karl. *Legacies of the Sword: The Kashima-Shinryu and Samurai Martial Culture* (Honolulu: University of Hawai'i Press, 1997).

Funakoshi Gichin. *Karate-dō: My Way of Life* (Tokyo: Kōdansha International, 1975).

Gainty, Denis. *Martial Arts and the Body Politic in Meiji Japan* (London: Routledge, 2013).

Geertz, Clifford. *The Interpretation of Cultures* (New York: Basic Books, 1973).

Goodrich, Luther Carrington. *The Literary Inquisition of Ch'ien-Lung* (Baltimore: Waverly Press, 1935).

Gordon, Leonard. 'Taiwan and the Powers, 1840–1895', in Leonard Gordon (ed.) *Taiwan: Studies in Chinese Local History* (New York: Columbia University Press, 1970), pp.93–116.

Green, Thomas and Joseph R. Svinth (eds). *Martial Arts in the Modern World* (Westport: Praeger, 2003).

Green, Thomas and Joseph R. Svinth (eds). 'Sense in Nonsense: The Role of Folk History in the Martial Arts' in *Martial Arts in the Modern World* (Westport: Praeger, 2003), pp.1–36.

Guttman, Allen and Lee Thompson. *Japanese Sports: A History* (Honolulu: University of Hawai'i Press, 2001).

Gyves, Clifford. 'An English Translation of General Qi Jiguang's "Quanjing Jieyao Pian" (Chapter on the Fist Canon and the Essentials of Nimbleness) from the *Jixiao Xinshu* (New Treatise on Disciplined Service)' (Unpublished Master's thesis, Department of East Asian Studies, University of Arizona, 1993).

Haines, Bruce A. *Karate's History and Traditions*, revised edition (Rutland, VT: Tuttle, 1995).

Halpin, James. 'The Little Dragon: Bruce Lee (1940–1973)' in Thomas A. Green and Joseph R. Svinth (eds), *Martial Arts in the Modern World* (Westport: Praeger, 2003), pp.111–28.

Hamm, John Christopher. *Paper Swordsmen: Jin Yong and the Modern Chinese Martial Arts Novel* (Honolulu: Hawai'i University Press, 2005).

Han Bong-soo. *Hapkido: Korean Art of Self-Defense* (Los Angeles: Ohara Publications, 1974).

Harvey, Peter. *An Introduction to Buddhist Ethics* (Cambridge: Cambridge University Press, 2000).

Hearn, Lafcadio. *Out of the East: Reveries and Studies in New Japan* (Boston: Houghton, Mifflin and Company, 1895).

Henning, Stanley E. 'The Chinese Martial Arts in Historical Perspective' in *Military Affairs*, Vol. 45, No.4, pp.173–79.

Henning, Stanley E. 'Ignorance, Legend and Taijiquan' in the *Journal of the Chen Style Taijiquan Research Association of Hawaii*, Vol. 2, No. 3 (1994), pp.1–7.

Henning, Stanley E. 'Chinese Boxing: Internal vs External Schools in the Light of History & Theory' in the *Journal of Asian Martial Arts*, Vol.6, No.3 (1997), pp.10–19.

Henning, Stanley E. 'Southern Fists & Northern Legs: Geography of Chinese Boxing' in the *Journal of Asian Martial Arts*, Vol. 7, No. 3 (1998), pp.24–31.

Henning, Stanley E. 'The Maiden of Yue: Fount of Chinese Martial Arts Theory' in the *Journal of Asian Martial Arts*, Vol. 16, No.3 (2007), pp.26–29.

Hess, Rob. '"A Death Blow to the White Australia Policy": Australian Rules Football and Chinese Communities in Victoria, 1892–1908', in Sophie Couchman et al. (eds), *After the Rush: Regulation, Participation and Chinese Communities in Australia 1860–1940* (Kingsbury, Victoria: Otherland Literary Journal (No.9), 2004), pp. 89–106.

Ho Chooi-hon and Kee Pookong. 'The Chinese Association of Victoria: a case study of community development' in Kee et al. (eds), *Chinese in Oceania* (Melbourne: Association for the Study of the Chinese and their Descendants in Australasia and the Pacific Islands; Chinese Museum (Museum of Chinese Australian History); Centre for Asia-Pacific Studies, Victoria University of Technology, 2002), pp.135–48.

Hobsbawm, Eric and Terence Ranger (eds). *The Invention of Tradition* (Cambridge: Cambridge University Press, 1983).

Holcombe, Charles. 'The Daoist Origins of the Chinese Martial Arts' in the *Journal of Asian Martial Arts*, Vol. 2, No.1 (1993), pp.10–25.

Hu, William. 'The I-chin Ching: Fact or Fancy – An Extensive Study of the I-Chin Ching and Bodhidharma's Connection with the Oriental Martial Arts' in *Black Belt*, November 1965, pp.28–30.

Huang, Ray. *1587: A Year of No Significance* (New Haven: Yale University Press, 1981).

Huang Xinchuan. 'Yindu Yujia yu Shaolin Gongfu' [Indian Yoga and Shaolin Kung Fu], in *Wuxue*, issue 1, 2015. pp.1–10.

Huss, Ann and Liu Jianmei. *The Jin Yong Phenomenon: Chinese Martial Arts Fiction and Modern Chinese Literary History* (Amherst: Cambria Press, 2007).

Hsu, Adam. *The Sword Polisher's Record: The Way of Kung-Fu* (Rutland, VT: Tuttle, 1997).

Inoue Shun. 'The Invention of Martial Arts: Kanō Jigorō and Kōdōkan Jūdō' in Stephen Vlastos (ed.) *Mirror of Modernity: Invented Traditions of Modern Japan* (Berkeley: University of California Press, 1998), pp.163–72.

Inoue Shun. *Budō no Tanjō [The Birth of Martial Arts]* (Tokyo: Yoshikawa Hirofumi-kan, 2004).

Ip Ching and Ron Heimberger. *Ip Man: Portrait of a Kung Fu Master* (Springville, UT: King Dragon Press, 2003).

Jacob, Rob. *Martial Arts Biographies: An Annotated Bibliography* (New York: iUniverse, 2005).

Johnston, Ian. *The Book of Master Mo* (Harmondsworth: Penguin, 2013).

Jones, David. *Martial Arts Training in Japan: A Guide for Westerners* (Rutland, VT: Tuttle, 2001).

Judkins, Benjamin, and Jon Nielson. *The Creation of Wing Chun: A Social History of the Southern Chinese Martial Arts* (Albany: State University of New York Press, 2015).

Kang Gewu (ed.). *Zhongguo Wushu Shiyong Daquan [A Practical Encyclopaedia of Chinese Martial Arts]* (Beijing: Zhonghua Shusuo, 2014).

Kato Bunnō (ed.). *The Threefold Lotus Sutra* (New York: Weatherhill, 1975).

Kato, M.T. *From Kung Fu to Hip Hop: Globalization, Revolution and Popular Culture* (Albany: State University of New York Press, 2007).

Kennedy, Brian and Elizabeth Guo. *Chinese Martial Arts Training Manuals: A Historical Survey* (Berkeley, CA: Blue Snake Books, 2005).

Kennedy, Brian and Elizabeth Guo. *Jingwu: The School That Transformed Kung Fu* (Berkeley, CA: Blue Snake Books, 2010).

Kenrick, Doug. *The Book of Sumo: Sport, Spectacle and Ritual* (New York: Weatherhill, 1969).

Kim Un-yong. *Taekwondo* (Seoul: Korea Overseas Information Service, 1976).

Kim Wee-hyun. 'Muyedobo T'ongji: Illustrated Survey of the Martial Arts' in *Korea Journal* Vol. 26, No. 8 (August 1986), pp.42–54.

Kinjō Hiroshi. *Kara-te kara karate e [From China-hand to Empty-hand]* (Tokyo: Nihon Budōkan, 2011).

Klens-Bigman, Deborah. 'Fighting Women of Kabuki Theatre and the Legacy of Women's Japanese Martial Arts' in the *Journal of Asian Martial Arts*, Vol. 19, No. 3 (2010), pp. 64–77.

Knoblock, John and Jeffrey Riegel. *The Annals of Lü Buwei: A Complete Translation and Study* (Stanford: Stanford University Press, 2000).

Koizumi Gunji. 'Judo and the Olympic Games,' in *Budokwai Quarterly Bulletin* Vol. 3, No. 1 (April 1947), pp.7–8.

Kubo Tsugunari and Yuyama Akira. *The Lotus Sutra* (Taishō 9:262) (Numata: Numata Center for Buddhist Translation and Research, 2007).

Kuhn, Anthony. 'Chinese Martial-Art Form Sports Less Threatening Moves' in the *LA Times*, 16 October 1998. http://articles.latimes.com/1998/oct/16/news/mn-33160

Law, Mark. *The Pyjama Game: A Journey into Judo* (London: Aurum, 2008).

Lee, Bruce. *The Tao of Jeet Kune Do* (Santa Clarita: Ohara, 1975).

Legge, James (trans.) *The Book of Rites*. Online edition at http://ctext.org/liji accessed 31 August 2015. Digital edition of *Sacred Books of the East*, volume 28, part 4: 'The Li Kî', 1885.

Lewellen , Wendy. 'Rusty Kanokogi: Mother of Women's Judo', in the *Jewish Women's Archive* http://jwa.org/weremember/kanokogi-rusty (2005).

Li Shaohao. *Liushiliu-shi Longxing Taijiquan [The 66 Forms of Dragon Style Taiji Quan]* (Chongqing: Chongqing Daxue Chubanshe, 2010).

Liao Waysun. *T'ai Chi Classics* (Boston MA: Shambhala Classics, 1990).

Little, John (ed.). *Bruce Lee – Letters of the Dragon: Correspondence, 1958–1973* (Rutlant, VT: Tuttle, 1998).

Liu, James. *The Chinese Knight-Errant* (London: Routledge and Kegan Paul, 1965).

Liu, Petrus. *Stateless Subjects: Chinese Martial Arts Literature and Postcolonial History* (Ithaca, NY: Cornell University East Asian Program, 2011).

Lorge, Peter. *Chinese Martial Arts from Antiquity to the Twenty-first Century* (Cambridge: Cambridge University Press, 2012).

Lowry, Dave. *Autumn Lightning: The Education of an American Samurai* (Boston: Shambhala, 2013).

Luk, Charles (Lu K'uan Yu). *Taoist Yoga: Alchemy & Immortality – a translation, with introduction and notes, of The Secrets of Cultivating Essential Nature and Eternal Life (Hsin Ming Fa Chueh Ming Chih) by the Taoist master Chao Pi Ch'en, born 1860* (New York: Samuel Weiser, 1970).

Ma Lianzhen. 'Cong "Wushu" dao "Guoshu"' [From Martial Arts to National Arts], in *Wuxue*, issue 1, 2015, pp.130–49.

Ma Mingda. 'Biantun Heshang yu Shaolin Gunfa Yanjiu' [The Monk Biantun and Research into Shaolin Staff Techniques], in *Wuxue*, issue 1, 2015, pp.11–89.

Ma Mingda and Ma Lianzhen. 'Huaquan Rumen, Cuole Yisheng' [Introduction to the Flowery Fist, Initial Fallacies], in *Wuxue*, issue 1, 2015, pp.90–98.

Madis, Eric. 'The evolution of tae kwon do from Japanese karate', in Green and Svinth (eds) *Martial Arts in the Modern World* (Westport: Praeger, 2003), pp.185–208.

Manser, Martin (ed.). *Concise English-Chinese Chinese-English Dictionary*, fourth edition (Oxford: Oxford University Press, 2010).

Manzenreiter, Wolfram. *Sport and Body Politics in Japan* (New York: Routledge, 2014).

Maryono, O'Ong. 'The Origin of Pencak Silat as Told by Myths' in *Rapid Journal* Vol. 4, No. 3 (1999), pp.38–9, www.kpsnusantara.com/rapid/rapid2.htm.

Maruyama, Paul. *Escape from Manchuria* (Bloomington: iUniverse, 2010).

McCarthy, Patrick. *Bubishi: The Classic Manual of Combat* (Rutland, VT: Tuttle, 2008).

McCullough, Helen Craig. *Yoshitsune: A Fifteenth-Century Japanese Chronicle* (Stanford: Stanford University Press, 1971).

McCullough, Helen Craig. *The Tale of the Heike* (Stanford: Stanford University Press, 1988).

Megill, Allan. *Historical Knowledge, Historical Error: A Contemporary Guide to Practice* (Chicago: University of Chicago Press, 2007).

Miller, Rory. *Meditations on Violence: A Comparison of Martial Arts Training and Real World Violence* (Boston MA: YMAA Publication Center, 2008).

Miyake Taro and Tani Yukio. *The Game of Jujitsu for the Use of Schools and Colleges* (London: Hazell, Watson and Viney, 1906).

Morrell, Robert. *Sand & Pebbles (Shasekishū) The Tales of Mujū Ichien, A Voice for Pluralism in Kamakura Buddhism* (Albany: State University of New York Press, 1985).

Nash, John. 'The Martial Chronicles: Jiujitsu Conquers Australia' – www.cagesideseats.com/2012/11/4/3599474/the-martial-chronicles-jiu-jitsu-conquers-australia

Nash, John. 'The Martial Chronicles: All-In Down Under With Sam McVea' at www.bloodyelbow.com/2013/2/18/3993346/martial-chronicles-sam-mcvea-MMA-Australia-Ju-Jitsu-Boxing?_ga=1.15623 0652.618224801.1451472231

Nash, John. 'The Martial Chronicles: L'Idole de Paris Versus the Fraud of London' at www.bloodyelbow.com/2013/2/7/3957558/martial-chronicles-sam-mcvea-lidole-de-paris-fraud-london?_ga=1.1562 30652.618224801.1451472231

Nelson, Andrew. *The Modern Reader's Japanese-English Character Dictionary*, second revised edition (Rutland, VT: Tuttle, 1962).

Nicol, C. W. *Moving Zen: Karate as a Way to Gentleness* (eBook reprint of 1975 original: C. W. Nicol, 2013).

Ohlenkamp, Neil. 'The Judo Rank System – Belts' at http://judoinfo.com/obi.htm (2007).

Olson, Stuart. *Steal My Art: The Life and Times of T'ai Chi Master T.T. Liang* (Berkeley: North Atlantic Books, 2002).

Order of Shaolin Ch'an. *The Shaolin Grandmasters' Text – History, Philosophy, and Gung Fu of Shaolin Ch'an*, revised edition (Beaverton, OR: Order of Shaolin Ch'an, 2006).

[Organisationskomitee für die XI. Olympiade Berlin].*The XIth Olympic Games – Berlin, 1936 Official Report* (Berlin: Wilhelm Limpert, 1936). http://library.la84.org/6oic/OfficialReports/1936/1936spart6.pdf

Page, Tony (ed.). *The Mahayana Mahaparinirvana Sutra*, translated into English by Kosho Yamamoto, 1973, from Dharmakshema's Chinese version (Taisho Tripitaka Vol. 12, No. 374, 2007). www.shabkar.org/download/pdf/Mahaparinirvana_Sutra_Yamamoto_Page_2007.pdf

Palmer, David. *Qigong Fever: Body, Science and Utopia in China* (London: Hurst & Company, 2007).

Perry, Susan (ed.). *Remembering O-Sensei: Living and Training with Morihei Ueshiba, Founder of Aikido* (Boston: Shambhala, 2002).

Preston, Diana. *A Brief History of the Boxer Rebellion: China's War on Foreigners, 1900* (London: Robinson, 2002).

Red Pine. *The Zen Teachings of Bodhidharma* (New York: North Point Press, 1987).

Reid, Craig D. *The Ultimate Guide to Martial Arts Movies of the 1970s* (Valencia, CA: Black Belt Books, 2010).

Robinson, Joshua. 'Judo Icon, a Fighter for her Sport, is Facing a New Battle,' in *The New York Times*, 17 February 2009. www.nytimes.com /2009/02/17/sports/othersports/17judo.html?_r=0

Rossabi, Morris. *Khubilai Khan: His Life and Times* (Berkeley: University of California Press, 1988).

Rousseau, Robert. 'Biography and Profile of Jigoro Kano', at http:// martialarts.about.com/od/martialartsbasics/p/Biography-And-Profile-Of-Jigoro-Kano.htm

Saba, Paul (ed.). 'History of I Wor Kuen' in *Encyclopedia of Anti-Revisionism Online*. Originally published 1978, https://www. marxists.org/history/erol/ncm-1a/iwk-history.htm

Sakamaki Shunzō. 'Ch'ên Yüan-pin' in Arthur Hummel (ed.), *Eminent Chinese of the Ch'ing Period* (Washington: Government Printing Office, 1943), pp.106–7.

Sawyer, Ralph with Mei-chün Sawyer. *The Seven Military Classics of Ancient China* (New York: Basic Books, 1993).

Schafer, Edward. *The Golden Peaches of Samarkand: A Study of T'ang Exotics* (Berkeley: University of California Press, 1963).

Schmieg, Anthony L. *Watching Your Back: Chinese Martial Arts and Traditional Medicine* (Honolulu: University of Hawai'i Press, 2005).

Schuessler, Axel. *ABC Etymological Dictionary of Old Chinese* (Honolulu: University of Hawai'i Press, 2007).

Sekida Katsuaki. *Two Zen Classics: The Gateless Gate/The Blue Cliff Records* (Boston: Shambhala, 2005).

Shahar, Meir. *The Shaolin Monastery: History, Religion and the Chinese Martial Arts* (Honolulu: University of Hawai'i Press, 2008).

Shi Yongxin (ed.). *Shaolin-si: Handbook for Shaolin Temple Tour* (Beijing: Contemporary China Publishing House, 2006).

Shi Yongxin. *Shaolin Temple in my heart* (Beijing: China Intercontinental Press, 2013).

Shine, Jerry. 'Sōhei: The Warrior Monks of Old Japan' in the *Journal of Asian Martial Arts*, Vol. 2, No. 1 (1993), pp.84–91.

Sō Dōshin. *Shorinji Kempo: Philosophy and Techniques* (Tokyo: Japan Publications, 1970).

Sō Dōshin. *This is Shorinji Kempo* (Cambridge: Perfect Publishers, 2014).

Smith, Robert. *Martial Musings: A Portrayal of Martial Arts in the 20th Century*, ebook edition of book originally published in 1999 (Santa Fe: Via Media, 2013).

Spiessbach, Michael. 'Bodhidharma: Meditating Monk, Martial Arts Master or Make-Believe?' in the *Journal of Asian Martial Arts*, Vol.1, No.4 (1992), pp.10–27.

Stevens, John. *The Way of Judo: A Portrait of Jigoro Kano and His Students* (Boston, MA: Shambhala, 2013).

Stroud, David. *Force Laws: A Practical Guide to Using Reasonable Force in Self-Defense* (2014).

Sugie Masatoshi. 'The Problems of the Modernisation of the Martial Arts of Japan' in *Nihon Budōgaku Kenkyū [Research in the Study of Japanese Martial Arts]* (Tokyo: Shimazu Shobō, 1988).

Svinth, Joseph. 'The Spirit of Manliness: Boxing in Imperial Japan 1868–1945', in Thomas A. Green and Joseph R. Svinth (eds) *Martial Arts in the Modern World* (Westport: Praeger, 2003), pp.37–46.

Teo, Stephen. *Chinese Martial Arts Cinema: The Wuxia Tradition* (Edinburgh: Edinburgh University Press, 2009).

ter Haar, Barend. *The White Lotus Teachings in Chinese Religious History* (Honolulu: University of Hawai'i Press, 1999).

ter Haar, Barend. *The Ritual and Mythology of the Chinese Triads: Creating an Identity* (Leiden: Brill, 2000).

ter Haar, Barend. *Telling Stories: Witchcraft and Scapegoating in Chinese History* (Leiden: Brill, 2006).

Thanissaro Bhikkhu [Geoffrey DeGraff]. *Anapanasati Sutta: Mindfulness of Breathing* at www.accesstoinsight.org/tipitaka/mn/mn.118.than. html, 2006.

Thompson, Eldon. 'Evaluating Customer Motivations and Expectations in American Martial Arts Businesses'. PhD thesis, Northcentral University, 2011.

Thompson, Lee. 'The Invention of the Yokozuna and the Championship System, Or, Futahagoro's Revenge', in Stephen Vlastos (ed.). *Mirror of Modernity: Invented Traditions in Modern Japan* (Berkeley: University of California Press, 1998), pp.174–90.

Tonami Mamoru. *The Shaolin Monastery Stele on Mount Song* (Kyoto: Italian School of East Asian Studies, 1990).

Tuhy, John. *Sam Hill: The Prince of Castle Nowhere* (Portland: Timber Press, 1983).

Turnbull, Stephen. *Ninja: The True Story of Japan's Secret Warrior Cult* (Poole: Firebird Books, 1991).

Turnbull, Stephen. 'The Ninja: An Invented Tradition?' in the *Journal of Global Initiatives*, Vol. 9, No.1, 2014, pp.9–26.

Twigger, Robert. *Angry White Pyjamas: An Oxford Poet Trains with the Tokyo Riot Police* (London: Weidenfeld & Nicolson, 2010).

Ueshiba Morihei. *The Art of Peace* (Boston: Shambhala, 2011).

Vlastos, Stephen (ed.). *Mirror of Modernity: Invented Traditions in Modern Japan* (Berkeley: University of California Press, 1998).

Wakeman, Frederic. *Strangers at the Gates: Social Disorder in Southern China, 1839–1861* (Berkeley: University of California Press, 1997).

Wang Guangxi. *Chinese Kungfu: Masters, Schools and Combats* (Beijing: China Intercontinental Press, 2010).

Wang Zheng-ting. 'Chinese music during the Goldrush period in Victoria, 1851–1870' in in Kee et al. (eds) *Chinese in Oceania* (Melbourne: Association for the Study of the Chinese and their Descendants in Australasia and the Pacific Islands; Chinese Museum (Museum of Chinese Australian History); Centre for Asia-Pacific Studies, Victoria University of Technology, 2002). pp.52–64.

Wang Zhuoran. *Wushuxue [The Study of the Martial Arts]* (Taiyuan: Shanxi Chuban, 2011).

Watson, Brian N. *Judo Memories of Jigoro Kano*, revised edition (Bloomington, IN: Trafford Publishing, 2014).

Wen Yucheng. *Tuwen Ben: Shaolin Shihua [Illustrated History of Shaolin]* (Beijing: Jincheng Shuban, 2009).

Werner, E.T.C. *A Dictionary of Chinese Mythology* (New York: Julian Press, 1961).

Wieger, Léon. *Wisdom of the Daoist Masters: Lao Zi (Lao Tzu), Lie Zi (Lieh Tzu), Zhuang Zi (Chuang Tzu)*, translated by Derek Bryce (Llanerch: Llanerch Enterprises, 1984).

Wile, Douglas. *T'ai Chi's Ancestors: The Making of an Internal Martial Art* (New York: Sweet Ch'i Press, 1999).

Wilson, Lee. *Martial Arts and the Body Politic in Indonesia* (Leiden: Brill, 2015).

Wong Kiew Kit. *The Complete Book of Shaolin* (Kedah: Cosmos, 2002).

Woodside, Andrew. 'The Ch'ien-ling Reign' in Willard J. Petersen (ed.), *The Cambridge History of China: Volume 9, Part 1, The Ch'ing Dynasty to 1800* (Cambridge: Cambridge University Press, 2002). pp.230–309.

World Taekwondo Federation. *Taekwondo (Poomse)* (Seoul: Shin Jin Gak, 1975).

Wu Cheng'en. *Journey to the West*. Translated by W. J. F. Jenner, in three volumes (Beijing: Foreign Languages Press, 1986).

Wu Cheng'en. *Xiyouji [Journey to the West]*, in two volumes (Hong Kong: Zhonghua Shuju, 1996).

Xuan, Danny and John Little. *The Tao of Wing Chun: The History and Principles of China's Most Explosive Martial Art* (New York: Skyhorse Publishing, 2015).

Yang Jwing-ming. *Qigong – The Secret of Youth: Da Mo's Muscle/Tendon Changing and Marrow/Brain Washing Classics* (Boston: YMAA [Yang's Martial Arts Academy] Publication Center, 2000).

Yang Xuan-zhi. *A Record of Buddhist Monasteries in Luoyang*, translated by Wang Yitong (Beijing: Zhonghua Book Company, 2007).

Yu Zhijun. *Zhongguo Taijiquan Shi [History of Chinese Tai Chi Chuan]* (Beijing: Zhongguo Renmin Daxue Chubanshe, 2012).

Zhang Yaoting. (ed.). *Zhongguo Wushu Shi: Guojia Tiwei Wushu Yanjiuyuan Bianzuan [A History of Chinese Martial Arts: Collated by the National Institute for the Research of Physical Martial Arts]* (Beijing: Renmin Tiyu Chubanshe, 1996).

Notes

....

INTRODUCTION: THE INVENTION OF TRADITION

1 Judkins and Nielsen, *The Creation of Wing Chun*, p.3.
2 Kennedy and Guo, *Jingwu: The School That Transformed Kung Fu*, pp.1–2.
3 Kennedy and Guo, *Chinese Martial Arts Training Manuals: A Historical Survey*, p.xiv.
4 Turnbull, 'The Ninja: An Invented Tradition', p.25.
5 Kang, *Zhongguo Wushu Shiyong Daquan*, p.1, similarly regards the 1560s as the dividing line between supposition and documentation.
6 Kennedy and Guo, *Chinese Martial Arts Training Manuals: A Historical Survey*, p.39. I say 'healthy' but the 1920s debate was also politicised and had agendas of its own. See Chapter Six.
7 Sugie, 'The Problems of the Modernisation of the Martial Arts of Japan', p.191.
8 Little, *Bruce Lee – Letters of the Dragon: Correspondence, 1958–1973*, pp.82, 110.
9 McCarthy, *Bubishi: The Classic Manual of Combat*, p.21.
10 Matsuda Ryūichi, quoted in Kennedy and Guo, *Chinese Martial Arts Training Manuals: A Historical Survey*, pp.61–2.
11 I use the terms here with deliberate scholarly intent, as Nescience (i.e. ignorance), Aesthesis, Tradition and Commemoration are Allan Megill's 'four ways of evading history'. Megill, *Historical Knowledge, Historical Error*, p.33.
12 Geertz, *The Interpretation of Cultures*, p.448.
13 Green, 'Sense in Nonsense: The Role of Folk History in the Martial Arts', p.1.
14 Ibid.
15 Henning, 'Ignorance, Legend and Taijiquan', p.1.

16 Judkins and Nielson, *The Creation of Wing Chun*, p.7.
17 Stevens, *The Way of Judo*, p.11; Jones, *Martial Arts Training in Japan*, l.1039 of 3028.
18 Shi, *Shaolin Temple in my heart*, p.61.

NOTE ON TRANSLATION AND SPELLING

1 Stevens, *The Way of Judo*, p.191.
2 Clements, *The Art of War: A New Translation*, p.3.
3 Nelson, *The Modern Reader's Japanese-English Character Dictionary*, pp.51, 501. For *wuxia*, see Hamm, *Paper Swordsmen: Jin Yong and the Modern Martial Arts Novel*, p.11; Teo, *Chinese Martial Arts Cinema*, p.2.
4 Kennedy and Guo, *Jingwu: The School That Transformed Kung Fu*, p.xi.
5 Funakoshi, *Karate-dō: My Way of Life*, p.35.
6 See, for example, Judson and Nielson, *The Creation of Wing Chun*, pp.11–12 for some discussion of this, and for the opening salvos of the Chinese debate, Kang, *Zhongguo Wushu Shiyong Daquan*, pp.1–6.
7 Schmieg, *Watching Your Back*, p.10.
8 Bennett, *Kendo: Culture of the Sword*, l.233 of 7908.

CHAPTER ONE: THE ARTS OF WAR

1 Zhang, *Zhongguo Wushu Shi*, p.2.
2 Lorge, *Chinese Martial Arts*, p.16. But compare this with the Mongol tradition of shooting 'ghost arrows', the 'ritualised execution of a prisoner by archery' (ibid, p.143).
3 Legge, *Book of Rites (Liji)* 46:5, 'Sheyi – The Meaning of the Ceremony of Archery'.
4 Schmieg, *Watching Your Back*, p.27.
5 Lorge, *Chinese Martial Arts*, p.40.
6 Zhang, *Zhongguo Wushu Shi*, p.29.
7 Manser, *Concise English-Chinese Chinese-English Dictionary*, p.530. See also the extensive argument on the 'martiality' of *wu* in Schmieg, *Watching Your Back*, pp.15–19.

8   Lorge, *Chinese Martial Arts*, p.26.

9   Legge, *Book of Rites (Liji)* 6:93, 'Yueling – Proceedings of Government in the Different Months'.

10 Clements, *The First Emperor of China*, p.14.

11 Manser, *Concise English-Chinese Chinese-English Dictionary*, p.245.

12 Zhang, *Zhongguo Wushu Shi*, p.151; see also Benn, *China's Golden Age: Everyday Life in the Tang Dynasty*, p.161.

13 Benn, *China's Golden Age*, p.161.

14 Aston, *Nihongi*, I:173.

15 [Anon.], 'History of Daitō-ryū.'

16 For the nature of such immortals, see Holcombe, 'The Daoist Origins of the Chinese Martial Arts', p.19, evocative of the later *wuxia* heroes so at one with the universe that they can float in combat.

17 I have discussed this performative element further in Clements, *The Art of War: A New Translation*, p.11.

18 Schuessler, *ABC Etymological Dictionary of Old Chinese*, p.207.

19 Wieger, *Wisdom of the Daoist Masters*, p.7.

20 Ibid., p.20.

21 Ibid., pp.21, 39, 35, 37.

22 Ibid., pp.39–40.

23 Schuessler, *ABC Etymological Dictionary of Old Chinese*, p.423; Wang, *Wushuxue*, pp.319–20.

24 Kennedy and Guo, *Chinese Martial Arts Training Manuals: A Historical Survey*, pp.29–30.

25 Holcombe, 'The Daoist Origins of the Chinese Martial Arts', p.12.

26 Knoblock and Riegel, *The Annals of Lü Buwei*, p.200.

27 Wang Chong, quoted in Holcombe, 'The Daoist Origins of the Chinese Martial Arts', pp.14–15. These channels and meridians, of course, might also be blocked and confounded by pressure on the right point, leading to an entire sub-section of martial arts regarding the use of acupressure points. Wang, *Wushuxue*, p.319.

28 Chinese Health Qigong Association, *Mawangdui Daoyin Exercises*.

29 Luk, *Taoist Yoga*. Luk's book was a translation of a Chinese Daoist text that was itself less than a century old when he acquired it. The 'Five Animal Forms' today are widely regarded as Monkey, Crane,

Mantis, Tiger and Snake, but this is due to the selection of those particular animals in the cartoon *Kung Fu Panda* (2008), overriding other candidates in favour of just one tradition.

30 Clements, *The Art of War: A New Translation*, pp.66–7. McCarthy, *Bubishi*, p.27 notes that Sun Tzu forms part of the manual for karate (and possibly all the Chinese forms from which it derives), with Funakoshi Gichin publishing notes on the subject in one of his earliest introductions to the martial art. For an example of how practical martial artists might try, a little bit desperately, to integrate Sun Tzu into unarmed combat, see Xuan and Little, *The Tao of Wing Chun*, pp.51–68.

31 Henning, 'The Maiden of Yue: Fount of Chinese Martial Arts Theory', pp.27–8.

32 Clements, *The Art of War: A New Translation*, p.135. See also my extensive note (7n) on the translation of 'coy like a woman', and its implications in terms of contemporary language and Sun Tzu's openness to female students.

33 Johnston, *The Book of Master Mo*, 39.12.

34 Clements, *The Art of War: A New Translation*, p.91. And in response, Mozi would probably cite his own comments on readiness: Johnston, *The Book of Master Mo*, 52.1. No wonder Chinese civil service exams took three days.

35 Lorge, *Chinese Martial Arts*, p.6.

CHAPTER TWO: THE SHAOLIN TEMPLE

1 From the Pei Cui inscription, 728 AD, quoted in Tonami, 'The Shaolin Monastery Stele on Mount Song', p.33.

2 Shi, *Handbook for Shaolin Temple Tour*, p.4. The fact that a Manchu Emperor would send gifts of calligraphy to the Shaolin Temple makes a complete mockery of the later assertion that a Manchu Emperor would order the Temple destroyed. See Chapter Four.

3 Buswell and Lowell, *The Princeton Dictionary of Buddhism*, p.799. Actually, I have still had to shuffle the order of the documents a little bit to keep them coherent. But the story I tell here of the

Shaolin Temple avoids most of the later interpolations that have made it so historically confusing in other works. Zhang's *Zhongguo Wushi Shi*, a general and critical history of the martial arts, does not discuss Shaolin as a specifically *martial* institution until the 1500s, p.261ff.

4 Zhang, *Zhongguo Wushu Shi*, p.125.
5 Order of Shaolin Ch'an, *The Shaolin Grandmasters' Text*, p.25. This, at least, is one explanation, although the slope and subsidiary peak of Mount Song where the temple was founded is called Shaoshi. So another translation might be 'the groves of Shao'. Still another possibility would be that Shaoshi derived its own name from the buildings on it 'the new cabins', and that the slope's name hence post-dated the siting of the Shaolin Temple there. Meanwhile, Wong's *Complete Book of Shaolin*, p.2, has a different story, relating (linguistically unconvincingly) to the slopes of the mountain being divided between two wives of an ancient emperor.
6 Yang, *A Record of Buddhist Monasteries in Luoyang*, pp. 24–5.
7 Sekida, *Two Zen Classics: The Gateless Gate / The Blue Cliff Records*, pp.147–8.
8 Shahar, *The Shaolin Monastery*, p.13.
9 Spiessbach, 'Bodhidharma: Meditating Monk, Martial Arts Master or Make-Believe?', p.12.
10 Red Pine, *The Zen Teachings of Bodhidharma*, p.13.
11 Shi, *Handbook for Shaolin Temple Tour*, p.96–7.
12 Red Pine, *The Zen Teachings of Bodhidharma*, p.ix.
13 Broughton, *The Bodhidharma Anthology: The Earliest Records of Zen*, p.62.
14 Spiessbach, 'Bodhidharma: Meditating Monk, Martial Arts Master or Make-Believe?', p.20.
15 Kato, *The Threefold Lotus Sutra*, p.141.
16 Kubo and Yuyama, *The Lotus Sutra*, p.193.
17 Reid and Croucher. *The Way of the Warrior: The Paradox of the Martial Arts*, p.32.
18 Thanissaro, *Anapanasati Sutra: Mindfulness of Breathing*; for An Shigao, see Holcombe, 'The Daoist Origins of the Chinese Martial Arts', p.15.

19 Chen, *The Poetics of Sovereignty: On Emperor Taizong of the Tang Dynasty*, p.18.
20 Tonami, 'The Shaolin Monastery Stele on Mount Song', pp.11–12.
21 Ibid., p.35.
22 Zhang, *Zhongguo Wushu Shi*, p.138.
23 Buswell and Lopez, *The Princeton Dictionary of Buddhism*, pp.502–4.
24 Harvey, *An Introduction to Buddhist Ethics*, p.163.
25 Ibid., pp.137–8.
26 Page, *The Mahayana Mahaparinirvana Sutra*, p.37.
27 Tonami, 'The Shaolin Monastery Stele on Mount Song', p.34.
28 Ibid., p.35.
29 Ibid., pp.24–5.
30 Lorge, *Chinese Martial Arts*, p.108.
31 Morrell, *Sand & Pebbles*, p.180.
32 Hu, 'The I-Chin Ching: Fact or Fancy?', p.30.
33 Huang 'Yindu Yujia yu Shaolin Gongfu', p.6.
34 Shahar, *The Shaolin Monastery*, pp.163–70, includes translations of both the doubtful prefaces.
35 Yang, *Qigong – The Secret of Youth* refers to Bodhidharma by his shortened Chinese name, Da Mo.
36 Werner, *Dictionary of Chinese Mythology*, p.268. At the time of Bodhidharma, it seems, the concept of the *luohan* was known to Chinese Buddhists, but there were only sixteen of them.
37 Order of Shaolin Ch'an, *The Shaolin Grandmasters' Text*, p.28.
38 Henning, 'The Chinese Martial Arts in Historical Perspective', p.174.
39 Zhang, *Zhongguo Wushu Shi*, p.180.
40 McCullough, *Tale of the Heike*, p.30.
41 Schafer, *The Golden Peaches of Samarkand*, p.51.

CHAPTER THREE: THE FIST CANON

1 Zhang, *Zhongguo Wushu Shi*, p.189. For the books themselves, see Sawyer, *The Seven Military Classics of Ancient China*.

2 Kang, *Zhongguo Wushu Shiyong Daquan*, p.195.

3 [Anon], 'Taizu Zhangquan'.

4 Lorge, *Chinese Martial Arts*, p.130.

5 Ibid., p.130.

6 Ibid., p.132.

7 Zhang, *Zhongguo Wushi Shi*, pp.251–3.

8 Beckwith, *Empires of the Silk Road*, p.xxiii.

9 *Yuan-shi [The History of the Yuan]*, quoted in Lorge, *Chinese Martial Arts*, p.150.

10 Zhang, *Zhongguo Wushu Shi*, p.225.

11 Rossabi, *Khubilai Khan: His Life and Times*, p.41.

12 Shi, *Shaolin Temple in My Heart*, p.227.

13 See, for example the History section of the Ottawa Chinese Martial Arts Association; www.ottawakungfu.org/shaolin/shaolin-history

14 Lorge, *Chinese Martial Arts*, p.174.

15 ter Haar, *The White Lotus Teachings in Chinese Religious History*, pp.115–6.

16 ter Haar, *Telling Stories*, p.13.

17 Fitzpatrick, 'Local administration in northern Chekiang and the response to the pirate invasions of 1553–1556', p.77.

18 Shine, 'Sōhei: The Warrior Monks of Old Japan', pp.86–7.

19 Ibid., pp.87–8.

20 Lorge, *Chinese Martial Arts*, p.164.

21 Shahar, *The Shaolin Monastery*, p.69. The Ming dynastic chronicle also mentions that about forty of the monks fighting, roughly 30 per cent of the fighting force, hailed from Shaolin. See Ma and Ma, 'Huaquan Rumen Cuole Yisheng', p.91. In a rare error, Peter Lorge's *Chinese Martial Arts* misreads Zheng Ruoceng's surname as Zhang.

22 Shahar, *The Shaolin Monastery*, p.70.

23 Gyves, 'An English Translation of General Qi Jiguang's "Quanjing Jieyao Pian"', p.14.

24 Huang, *1587: A Year of No Significance*, p.159. Ray Huang has a whole chapter on Qi and observes (p.188) that Qi's shameful dismissal on trumped-up charges probably deprived the Ming dynasty of the last military man whose influence could have saved it from the Manchus.

25 Gyves, 'An English Translation of General Qi Jiguang's "Quanjing Jieyao Pian"', pp.11–12.
26 Shahar, *The Shaolin Monastery*, p.63.
27 Gyves, 'An English Translation of General Qi Jiguang's "Quanjing Jieyao Pian"', p.34.
28 Ibid., pp.34–5.
29 Ibid., p.41.
30 Lorge, *Chinese Martial Arts*, p.176.
31 Gyves, 'An English Translation of General Qi Jiguang's "Quanjing Jieyao Pian"', p.46.
32 Hemming, 'The Chinese Martial Arts in Historical Perspective', p.176. Controversially and rather gloriously, the 1930s martial arts historian Tang Hao dared to suggest that Shaolin kung fu and taiji really weren't that different, and that the latter had probably evolved from the former in the seventeenth century. See Shahar, *The Shaolin Monastery*, p.133.
33 Lorge, *Chinese Martial Arts*, p.177. As a caution to Chinese researchers investigating further, this is first-tone *huā* (flowery) not second-tone *huá* (Celestial, glorious, Chinese), which would also be used to refer to some styles, particularly in the Nationalist era of the twentieth century.
34 Xuan and Little, *The Tao of Wing Chun*, p.2; see also Nicol, *Moving Zen*, l.463 of 1953, in which he alludes to 'intricate moves of the hands to baffle opponents in free-fighting'.
35 See, for example, Ma and Ma, 'Huaquan Rumen, Cuole Yisheng', p.90, which suggests that all martial arts tend towards the 'orchestic' (i.e. dance-like or performative), and that drives against 'flowery' elements are natural and periodic correctives to restore the original martial intent. See also Kang, *Zhongguo Wushu Shiyong Daquan*, p.199.
36 Kim, 'Muyedobo T'ongji: Illustrated Survey of the Martial Arts', pp.42–54. Unsurprisingly, there is no mention of any of this on the relevant pages of the World Taekwondo Federation's own history of taekwondo, which claims it was invented by cavemen and has formed an integral but overlooked facet of Korean life ever since, nor in Kim Un-yong's *Taekwondo*, which claims it began in 2333 BC.

Kim sets up something of a straw man (pp.19–20) by acknowledg-
ing claims that taekwondo originated in kung fu, but then pointing
out that there are Korean illustrations that predate Bodhidharma's
arrival at Shaolin.

37 Zhang, *Zhongguo Wushu Shi*, p.276.
38 This, at least, is the suggestion of Meir Shahar, *The Shaolin
Monastery*, p.131. But the truth is that nobody knows why Qi dropped
unarmed combat from the later edition.
39 Shahar, *The Shaolin Monastery*, p.132.
40 Wu, *Journey to the West*, 2: 356. I've used the Jenner translation
here, but you can compare the original Chinese in Wu, *Xiyouji*
2:628–9.
41 Lorge, *Chinese Martial Arts*, p.174.
42 Ibid., p.143. But see Harvey, *An Introduction to Buddhist Ethics*,
pp.159–65, for discussion of the history of vegetarianism within
Buddhist thought.
43 Judkins and Nielson, *The Creation of Wing Chun*, p.89.
44 Lorge, *Chinese Martial Arts*, p.197.
45 Judkins and Nielson, *The Creation of Wing Chun*, p.75.

CHAPTER FOUR: SECRETS AND SHADOWS

1 Li Shaohao, *Liushiliu-shi Longxing Taijiquan [The 66 Forms of Dragon
Style Taiji Quan]*.
2 The first chronological incident I have found of a shaven head
obscuring hairstyle-related intrigues is 1650 and actually goes the
other way, when the Ming admiral Shi Lang is alleged to have
adopted the Manchu style, and then changed his mind and hastily
shaved his whole head, claiming instead that he was planning on
becoming a monk. See Clements, *Coxinga and the Fall of the Ming
Dynasty*, p.288, n.19.
3 See for example, Goodrich, *The Literary Inquisition of Ch'ien-Lung*,
for such tales as that of Dai Mingshi, executed for using the reign
names of Ming pretenders in a history book (p.77), or He Zhongzao,
who unwisely writes a line of poetry that refers to 'the light of the

sun and moon have left the earth', when the characters for sun + moon make the character *Ming* (p.94).

4 Goodrich, *The Literary Inquisition of Ch'ien-Lung*, p.261.

5 Woodside, 'The Ch'ien-lung Reign', pp.289–92. Woodside observes, and it bears repeating here, that although Qianlong's acts sound awful and despotic, they were little different from many similar purges of unwelcome publications enacted in Christian Europe around the same time.

6 Henning, 'Chinese Boxing: Internal vs External Martial Arts in the Light of History and Theory', p.16.

7 Wile, *T'ai Chi's Ancestors*, p.53.

8 Ibid., p.58.

9 Henning, 'Ignorance, Legend and Taijiquan', p.1.

10 Liao, *T'ai Chi Classics*, pp.88–9.

11 Wile, *T'ai Chi's Ancestors*, p.1.

12 Henning, 'Ignorance, Legend and Taijiquan', p.3.

13 Yu, *Taijiquan Shi*, p.3.

14 Bingham, quoted in Judkins and Nielson, *The Creation of Wing Chun*, p.94.

15 Order of Shaolin Ch'an, *The Shaolin Grandmasters' Text*, p. 35–6.

16 ter Haar, *Ritual and Mythology of the Chinese Triads*, pp.18–19.

17 These have met with varying degrees of support. In Hong Kong, the society is illegal, associated as it is with many 'Triad' criminal organisations. In Taiwan, it has a somewhat Masonic cachet, with many famous members including the Chinese leaders Sun Yat-sen and Chiang Kai-shek. In Mainland China, it transformed into a political party in 1925, the Zhi Gong, which remains part of the Chinese People's Political Consultative Conference.

18 Both, for example, are pronounced *siu lahm* in Cantonese. See Choy, *Read and Write Chinese*, pp.112, 172.

19 ter Haar, *Telling Stories: Witchcraft and Scapegoating in Chinese History*, p.197.

20 Order of Shaolin Ch'an, *The Shaolin Grandmasters' Text*, p.29.

21 McCarthy, *Bubishi*, p.66.

22 Ibid., p.98.

23 See, for example, Maryono, 'The Origin of Pencak Silat as Told by

Myths'. In another version, she learns by watching monkeys and uses it to fight off her 'furious husband' who then asks to be taught the skill.

24 Judkins and Neilson, *The Creation of Wing Chun*, p.60.
25 Lin Yu, quoted in Judkins and Neilson, *The Creation of Wing Chun*, p.60.
26 Judkins and Nielson, *The Creation of Wing Chun*, p.62.
27 Xuan and Little, *The Tao of Wing Chun*, p.39.
28 Wakeman, *Strangers at the Gates*, pp.149–50.
29 Xuan and Little, *The Tao of Wing Chun*, p.34.
30 Hamm, *Paper Swordsmen*, pp.34–8, 56.
31 Xuan and Little, *The Tao of Wing Chun*, p.38.
32 Esherick, *The Origins of the Boxer Uprising*, p.46. Esherick deliberately leaves 'Yi-he Boxers' untranslated, as he does not regard them as direct ancestors of the *Yihe quan* sectarians of a century later.
33 Notably, observers immediately assumed that the sects were targeting troubled young men to recruit them into violent activities. This is the precise opposite of many martial arts later in the twentieth century, which were regarded by their founders as efforts to *save* such youths from lives of crime. Several oral traditions of modern martial arts feature the founders deliberately selecting the roughest of towns for their dojo.
34 Esherick, *The Origins of the Boxer Uprising*, pp.54–7.
35 Preston, *A Brief History of the Boxer Rebellion*, p.23.
36 Esherick, *The Origins of the Boxer Uprising*, p.150.
37 Kang, *Zhongguo Wushu Shiyong Daquan*, pp.199–201.
38 Esherick, *The Origins of the Boxer Uprising*, p.xiv.
39 Ibid., p.334–5.
40 ter Haar, *The White Lotus Teachings in Chinese Religious History*, p.284.
41 Esherick, *The Origins of the Boxer Uprising*, p.336. Zhang, *Zhongguo Wushu Shi*, p.303 does not state outright that there is no such martial art as *Yihe quan*, but does seem to discuss it as an organisation rather than a technique.
42 Esherick, *The Origins of the Boxer Uprising*, p.340.

43 Sō, *This is Shorinji Kempo*, p.33. Draeger, *Modern Budo and Bujutsu*, p.165, expresses his doubts about the claims of Sō Dōshin, founder of Shorinji Kempo, to have truly inherited a Chinese grandmaster's role in what he called *Giwamon-ken*, the Japanese pronunciation of *Yihemen quan*, but see my Chapter Six.

CHAPTER FIVE: THE WAY OF THE WARRIOR

1 McCullough, *Yoshitsune: A Fifteenth-Century Japanese Chronicle*, p.97. The comments that follow about the legendary powers of the book are also from McCullough, as is the observation about the fifteenth-century author's 'lack of accurate information' about the book's content.

2 Thompson, 'The Invention of the Yokozuna and the Championship System, Or, Futahagoro's Revenge,' p.175.

3 Clements, *A Brief History of the Samurai*, pp.40, 105.

4 Sakamaki, 'Ch'ên Yüan-pin', pp.106–7. Sakamaki claims it is impossible to date the *Secret Manual* with any greater precision than 'before 1683,' but since Chen's second and longer sojourn in Japan did not begin before 1638, I think 'mid-seventeenth century' is reasonable here.

5 Bennett, *Kendo: Culture of the Sword*, l.152 of 7908, observes that even the name kendo was rare before the twentieth century, and that fencing with *shinai* and armour was previously more likely to be called *gekken*.

6 As noted in Clements, *A Brief History of the Samurai*, p.300, much of the modern Japanese sense of the meaning of *bushidō* derives from a book on the subject first written in English in 1900. Bennett, *Kendo: Culture of the Sword*, l.991 of 7908, regards this interpretation of a transition from *jutsu* to *dō* as overly simplistic, relying too much on the work of Donn Draeger in the 1970s. I think it is still relevant enough to bear repeating in a generalist book such as this.

7 Lowry, *Autumn Lightning*, l.180 of 2805.

8 Bennett, *Kendo: Culture of the Sword*, l.514 of 7908.

9 Inoue, *Budō no Tanjō*, p.59.

10 Chamberlain, *Things Japanese*, p.514.

11 Sugie, 'The Problems of the Modernisation of the Martial Arts of Japan', p.194.

12 Watson, *Judo Memoirs of Jigoro Kano*, p.7.

13 Kanō's *Secrets of Judo*, quoted in Rousseau, 'Biography and Profile of Jigoro Kano'.

14 Kanō's article 'The Contribution of Judo to Health and Education', quoted at http://pacificjudo.com/philosophy

15 Stevens, *The Way of Judo*, p.80.

16 Inoue, 'The Invention of Martial Arts: Kanō Jigorō and Kōdōkan Jūdō', p.167.

17 Ohlenkamp, Neil, 'The Judo Rank System – Belts'.

18 Karate outfits, for example, are lighter, to afford swifter movement, and in anticipation of fewer grapples. See Nicol, *Moving Zen*, 1.179 of 1953.

19 Hearn, *Out of the East*, pp.186–8.

20 Ibid., p.193.

21 Ibid., p.242. His predictions even applied to himself. In 1903, having taken Japanese citizenship, he was forced out of his position at Tokyo University since he no longer qualified for a foreigner's salary. He was conveniently replaced by the author Natsume Sōseki, newly returned from London. The university also refused him his contracted year of sabbatical, leading him to comment that the Japanese had 'no souls'. See Cott, *Wandering Ghost*, p.394.

22 Watson, *Judo Memoirs of Jigoro Kano*, pp.79–80; Stevens, *The Way of Judo*, p.46.

23 Stevens, *The Way of Judo*, p.48.

24 Brousse and Matsumoto, *Judo in the U.S.*, p.110. Kanō changed his mind by 1936, suggesting in a letter that he would not necessarily mind if others chose to make judo an Olympic sport. See Koizumi, 'Judo and the Olympic Games', p.7.

25 Stevens, *The Way of Judo*, p.50.

26 McCarthy, *Bubishi, The Classic Manual of Combat*, p.38. Kim, *Taekwondo* (p.20) suggests that the martial art practised in Okinawa was actually learned by the locals on trips to Korea, and that hence

karate is really a divergent form of taekwondo. I repeat this theory here because it is frankly no more shaky than the official version. Kinjō Hiroshi in his recent *Karate kara Karate e*, pp.113–4, does not quite agree that Korea is the home of karate, but concedes that cross-pollination between the Ryūkyūs and Korea is entirely feasible.

27 Haines, *Karate's History and Traditions*, p.86.
28 Ibid., p.87.
29 Funakoshi, *Karate-dō: My Way of Life*, p.37. The uncredited translator of Funakoshi's memoirs faithfully translates his original prose as 'Wutang and Shōrinji Kempō', but see my Chapter Six for details of why this is a misnomer.
30 Funakoshi, *Karate-dō: my Way of Life*, p.38.
31 Abernethy, 'The 10 Precepts of Anko Itosu'. I have altered Abernethy's 'karate' to 'Kara-te' to reflect the semantic distinction I describe above in my Note on Translation and Spelling.
32 Clarke, *Okinawan Karate*, pp.11–12.
33 Haines, *Karate's History and Traditions*, p.100. Many sources erroneously claim that the first demonstration was in 1922, confusing the date of the book's publication and Funakoshi's first arrival in Tokyo with the first time that he was on the mainland.
34 Funakoshi, *Karate-dō: My Way of Life*, p.9.
35 Stevens, *The Way of Judo*, p.50.
36 Clarke, *Okinawan Karate*, p.159.

CHAPTER SIX: NATIONALISM AND MODERNISM

1 Clarke, *Okinawan Karate*, pp.79–81. A similar incident had occurred in 1842, when sailors aboard a British ship were similarly massacred upon landfall in Taiwan. See Gordon, 'Taiwan and the Powers, 1840–1895', p.96.
2 Kennedy and Guo, *Jingwu: The School That Transformed Kung Fu*, p.10.
3 Svinth, 'The Spirit of Manliness: Boxing in Imperial Japan 1868–1945', pp.38–9.

4 Kennedy and Guo, *Jingwu: The School That Transformed Kung Fu*, p.77.

5 Filipiak, 'From Warriors to Sportsmen', p.37.

6 Chiang Kai-shek, quoted in Kennedy and Guo, *Jingwu: The School That Transformed Kung Fu*, p.20.

7 Kennedy and Guo, *Jingwu: The School That Transformed Kung Fu*, pp.86–90.

8 Judkins and Nielson, *The Creation of Wing Chun*, p.133.

9 Henning, 'Southern Fists and Northern Legs', p.28.

10 Judkins and Nielson, *The Creation of Wing Chun*, p.141. I choose to quote Judkins and Nielson here, rather than their main source Ip and Heimberger, in order to repeat their criticism and correction of certain factual issues in the latter book. See Judkins and Nielson, ibid, p.303, 46n.

11 Ma, 'Cong Wushu dao Guoshu', pp.143–4.

12 Judkins and Nielson, *The Creation of Wing Chun*, p.150.

13 Morris, *Marrow of the Nation*, p.234. 'Trophy-ism': *jinbao-zhuyi*.

14 Ibid., p.205.

15 [Organisationskomitee für die XI. Olympiade Berlin].*The XIth Olympic Games – Berlin, 1936 Official Report*, p.1097.

16 Morris, *Marrow of the Nation*, p.224.

17 Liu, *The Chinese Knight-Errant*, p.136. *Jiang Hu Qixia Zhuan* – Liu chooses to translate it as *Extraordinary Knights Roaming Over Rivers and Lakes*, but I don't see any 'roaming' in the original Chinese. I also choose to translate *xia* as 'hero', reflecting several decades of Chinese movie titling that post-dates the publication of Liu's book in 1967.

18 Teo, *Chinese Martial Arts Cinema*, p.24. *Lady Knight Feifei* (*Nüxia Li Feifei*) is now lost. Shaw Renje's name in Pinyin is Shao Renjie – my text uses the romanisation that he usually employed, which reflects his Shanghai accent and the name of the later Shaw Brothers studio.

19 Robert Kung, quoted in Teo, *Chinese Martial Arts Cinema*, p.33.

20 Mao Dun, quoted in Teo, *Chinese Martial Arts Cinema*, p.39.

21 Teo, *Chinese Martial Arts Cinema*, p.43. Teo adds that some martial arts films *were* produced during the 'orphan island' period when Shanghai was divided into zones of interest ruled by different powers.

22 Sugie, 'The Problems of the Modernisation of the Martial Arts of Japan', p.199, makes a similar claim for the development of kendo: that its modern heartland was also the dumping ground for much of the surviving Shogunal loyalists.

23 Bulag, *Collaborative Nationalism: The Politics of Friendship on China's Mongolian Frontier*, p.41

24 Stevens, *The Way of Judo*, p.51.

25 Bridges, *The Two Koreas and the Politics of Global Sport*, pp.27–8.

26 Madis, 'The Evolution of tae kwon do from Japanese Karate', pp.204–5, as his title implies, goes considerably further, arguing that the evolution of taekwondo was a blatant, government-sponsored purge of overt Japanese links from what was basically karate in Korea.

27 World Taekwondo Federation, *Taekwondo (Poomse)*, p.18.

28 Han, *Hapkido: Korean Art of Self-Defense*, p.9.

29 Kim, *Taekwondo*, p.20.

30 Clements, *A Brief History of the Samurai*, p.241.

31 Driscoll, *Absolute Erotic, Absolute Grotesque*, p.102.

32 Maruyama, *Escape from Manchuria*, p.vii notes that some 1.7 million Japanese survivors made it home to Japan in the 1940s – an incredible movement of population in both directions.

33 Sō, *This is Shōrinji Kempō*, p.31.

34 Kennedy and Guo, *Jingwu: The School That Transformed Kung Fu*, p.68.

35 Sō, *This is Shōrinji Kempō*, p.32. His account of his education implies that White Lotus teachings and Boxer teachings were part of the same continuum, whereas the historical record suggests that they were mutually opposed – see ter Haar, *The White Lotus Teachings in Chinese Religious History*, p.284.

36 Sō, *This is Shōrinji Kempō*, p.33. I should also note that 'Taizong' seems to me to be an odd name for a Chinese person, since it is usually employed as an ancestral title for emperors.

37 Sō, *This is Shōrinji Kempō*, p.33.

38 Sō, *Shorinji Kempo: Philosophy and Techniques*, p.15.

CHAPTER SEVEN: JOURNEY TO THE WEST

1 Barton-Wright, 'Jujitsu and judo', p.261.
2 Doyle, *The Return of Sherlock Holmes*, p.3.
3 *New York Times*, 'Jiu-Jitsu For Militants: Sylvia Pankhurst Also Wants Them Drilled and to Carry Sticks', 12 August 1913.
4 Nicol, *Moving Zen*, l.269 of 1953, claims that in the 1950s 'there had been perhaps one Karate teacher, only one, in the entire UK'.
5 Ho and Kee, 'The Chinese Association of Victoria', p.137; Wang, 'Chinese music during the Goldrush period', p.53.
6 Hess, 'A Death Blow to the White Australia Policy', p.95.
7 Anon. 'Introduction of Jujutsu to Australia'.
8 The name is variously romanised as Fukishima in contemporary accounts, Fukushima in some articles, and Fushishima in the records of some Australian judo clubs. I have selected the most likely. See Nash, 'The Martial Chronicles'.
9 Nash, 'The Martial Chronicles: Jiu-Jitsu Conquers Australia'.
10 Fukushima's letter to the Sydney Morning Herald, signed 'R. Shima' as per his habit, quoted in Nash, 'The Martial Chronicles: Jiu-Jitsu Conquers Australia'.
11 Tuhy, *Sam Hill: The Prince of Castle Nowhere*, p.57. There is some suggestion in Japanese books that Hill was the excuse rather than the impetus, and that Yamashita had been 'sent' to America by Kanō specifically to promote judo.
12 Tuhy, *Sam Hill: The Prince of Castle Nowhere*, p.160.
13 Farkas, *An Illustrated History of Martial Arts in America*, p.7.
14 ōkubo Kōichi, quoted in Victoria, *Zen at War*, p. 103. Ibid.
15 Guttman and Thompson, *Japanese Sports*, p.176.
16 Farkas, *An Illustrated History of Martial Arts in America*, pp.37–8.
17 Ibid., p.21.
18 Stevens, *The Way of Judo*, p.190.
19 Lewellen, 'Rusty Kanakogi'.
20 Teo, *Chinese Martial Arts Cinema*, pp.59–60. Fong Sai-yuk, in Mandarin, is Fang Shiyu.
21 Teo, *Chinese Martial Arts Cinema*, p.70.

22 Teo, *Chinese Martial Arts Cinema*, pp.61–4

23 Clouse, *The Making of Enter the Dragon*, p.17.

24 Reid, *The Ultimate Guide to Martial Arts Movies of the 1970s*, p.98. 'Beating the crap out of the Japanese', of course, is still a recurring theme in Chinese cinema.

25 Halpin, 'The Little Dragon: Bruce Lee (1940–1973)', p.112.

26 Reid, *The Ultimate Guide to Martial Arts Movies of the 1970s*, p.98.

27 Kato, *From Kung Fu to Hip Hop*, p.45.

28 Smith, *Martial Musings*, l.1825 of 6334.

29 Reid, *The Ultimate Guide to Martial Arts Movies of the 1970s*, p.97. In 1969, inspired by the racial politics of the Black Panthers and the Young Lords a left-wing Asian-American pressure group assembled in New York. They had somewhat muddled aims, proclaiming a revolution was about to start, but seemingly limiting much of its activism and focus to the few streets of Chinatown. Determined to improve the lot of the people of Chinatown, the group adopted a name derived from the 'revolutionary fervour' of the Boxer Uprising, calling themselves the Yi Wor Kuen – the Cantonese pronunciation of *Yihe quan*, the Righteous and Harmonious Fist. Earnest but seemingly misguided, the IWK started with noble intentions, including protesting against the Vietnam War and organising a healthcare programme for the Chinatown poor. But they soon got into spats with other community associations, many of which had affiliation to Taiwan or the Chinese diaspora, and did not take kindly to rants from self-styled urban guerrillas following a Maoist party line. Their most prominent action was a protest aimed at tour buses bringing non-Chinese tourists into Chinatown, much to the annoyances of many local shops who counted on the business they brought. Sadly, I have never seen a copy of *Getting Together*, the IWK's magazine – I would love to know whether they thought *Fist of Fury*, and indeed, the teaching of martial arts in general, was a beacon of affirmation or crypto-imperialist propaganda. Wei, *The Asian American Movement*, p.251. See also Saba, 'History of I Wor Kuen'.

30 Shi, *Shaolin Temple in my heart*, p.57. Craig Reid (p.19) decided to count the number of occurrences of certain words in the title of martial arts movies of the 1970s. He reported that of the 354 Chinese movies surveyed, 'kung fu' was the most popular term, occurring in

eighty-three original titles (131 foreign retitlings). 'Shaolin' was the second most common term, appearing in sixty original titles (108 foreign retitlings). The next rankings in his list comprised the most commonly-occurring animal styles: Dragon, Tiger, Monkey, Mantis, Crane, Snake and Eagle. However, it should be noted that many of these titles are in fact retitlings thought up by Western distributors, and do not necessarily reflect the actual martial arts depicted.

31 Morris, *Marrow of the Nation*, p.237.
32 Ibid., p.239.
33 Xuan and Little, *The Tao of Wing Chun*, p.24.
34 Ibid., p.23.
35 Palmer, *Qigong Fever*, p.29.
36 Clark, *The Cultural Revolution: A History*, p.165.
37 Schmieg, *Watching Your Back*, p.10.
38 Palmer, *Qigong Fever*, pp.47, 93.
39 Xuan and Little, *The Tao of Wing Chun*, p.25.
40 Kuhn, 'Chinese Martial-Art Form Sports Less Threatening Moves'.
41 Ibid.

Chapter Eight: Ball of Kungfusion

1 Funakoshi, *Karate-dō: My Way of Life*, p.127.
2 The term seems to have its origin in German: *Versportlichung*. See Guttman and Thompson, *Japanese Sports*, p.176.
3 Ibid., p.178.
4 Ibid., p.179.
5 Ibid., p.178. Popular (internet) opinion credits this innovation to the French eight years later.
6 Xuan and Little, *The Tao of Wing Chun*, p.x. C. W. Nicol observes in *Moving Zen*, l.959 of 1953, a practice common in 1960s karate of fighters who have been away from the dojo for a while attending in white belts until they and/or their teachers believe them to have justified the black belt they once had. One wonders if there has been any talk of such 'decaying' attributes in the generation since the adoption of belts as a loyalty scheme.

7   Nicol, *Moving Zen*, l.741 of 1953.

8   Xuan and Little, *The Tao of Wing Chun*, p.xi.

9   Ibid., p.xi.

10 Guttman and Thompson, *Japanese Sports*, p.180.

11 Stevens, *The Way of Judo*, p.79.

12 Jones, *Martial Arts Training in Japan*, l.1851 of 3028.

13 *Newsweek*, 3rd August 1964, quoted in Turnbull, *Ninja: The True Story of Japan's Secret Warrior Cult*, p.144.

14 See for example www.ninjutsu.com/soke-hatsumi.shtml

15 Clarke, *Okinawan Karate*, pp.292–94.

16 Dawes, *Understanding Reasonable Force*, l.249 of 2014.

17 Jones, *Martial Arts Training in Japan*, l.2092 of 3028. There's also an element of common sense of course. One of the stories told about the founder of aikido mentions his fury with his pupils whenever they 'hurt' a tree by punching it. Perry, *Remembering O-sensei*, l.542 of 1945.

18 Bennett, *Kendo: Culture of the Sword*, l.325 of 7908.

19 Nicol, *Moving Zen*, l.774 of 1953.

20 Nicol, *Moving Zen*, l.1251 of 1953.

21 Stroud, *Force Laws: A Practical Guide to Using Reasonable Force in Self-Defence*, p.107.

22 Schmieg, *Watching Your Back*, p.92.

23 Lowry, *Autumn Lightning*, l.447 of 2805.

24 Miller, *Meditations on Violence*, p.8.

25 Bennett, *Kendo: Culture of the Sword*, l.540 of 7908.

26 Ibid., l.557 of 7908.

27 Ibid., l.588 of 7908.

28 *Daily Yomiuri*, 3 August 2012, quoted in Bennett, *Kendo: Culture of the Sword*, l.596 of 7908.

29 Guttman and Thompson, *Japanese Sports*, pp.186–7. Jesse Kuhaulua was unkindly referred to as 'the Black Ship', implying that he was an agent of foreign infiltration like Commodore Perry's fateful vessels of the 1850s.

30 Nonaka Takashi, quoted in Perry, *Remembering O-Sensei*, l.248 of 1945.

31 Bennett, *Kendo: Culture of the Sword*, l.456 of 7908.

32 Lee, *The Tao of Jeet Kune Do*, p.23.

Index